DARE
TO
DREAM

DARE TO DREAM

LAFARRIS L. RISBY, CFLE

Copyright © 2019, LaFarris, Inc.

All rights reserved. No part of this publication may be reproduced, distributed, or transmitted in any form or by any means, including photocopying, recording, or other electronic or mechanical methods, without the prior written permission of the publisher, except in the case of brief quotations embodied in critical reviews and certain other non-commercial uses permitted by copyright law. For permission requests, write to the publisher, addressed "Attention: Permissions Coordinator," at the address below.

1531 St. Mary's Road, Junction City, KS 66441

ISBN: 978-1-7332272-2-3

Cover Artwork by Morgan Burks | www.morganburks.com
Interior Format by Veronica Lee | www.yourImMEDIAteSolutions.com

Printed in the United States of America.
First printing edition, 2019.

www.lafarrisrisby.com

CONTENTS

Dedication vii

Chapter 1   Motherless Child...1
Chapter 2   Growing Up Fast..17
Chapter 3   Mommy to Be...43
Chapter 4   Big Girl Britches..75
Chapter 5   Rocky Road...95
Chapter 6   Next Level Crazy..113
Chapter 7   Germany..133
Chapter 8   Same Old, Same Old..149
Chapter 9   New Beginnings..173
Chapter 10 Breaking the Cycle...183
Chapter 11 Daring to Dream...213
Chapter 12 Faith to Go Further..229
Chapter 13 Life's New Season..243
Chapter 14 Lessons from Loss...257
Chapter 15 Cutting Your Losses..277
Chapter 16 Coming Full Circle..291
Chapter 17 Reflections to the Reader 299

About the Author 309

DEDICATION

This memoir is dedicated to the loving memory of my mother, Edna Louise Garrett. You died so that I could live, and I'm forever grateful. To my father Woodrow Garrett, whose infamous words, "The decisions you make today will ultimately affect your tomorrow, right or wrong, good or bad," will forever echo in my mind.
Also,
To my family: My husband, Kevin; my daughter, Tyronica; my son, Tyrone Jr. and his wife Morgan; my grandchildren, Tavon and Alani, And my friends and business partners who supported the development of this work.

CHAPTER 1

Motherless Child

The early memories of most six-year-old girls are carefree and fun. The most conflicting decisions probably being centered around which Barbie doll to dress or which make-believe game to play. My early recollections, however, are not laced with such whimsical beginnings. The beginnings of my memories consist of witnessing my mother's lifeless body being covered up with a white sheet. Going back and forth in my mind over the years, pieces of other occurrences pop up here and there—but nothing stands out quite like the memory of my mother's death.

My mother's name was Edna Louise Garrett, and she had been sick for some time after giving birth to me. I was the baby of her five children, and she was strongly warned by her doctor that the birth of an additional child could possibly enlarge her heart in such a way that it would be fatal. My father, Woodrow Garrett, even warned her. She didn't care, though—she wanted me to be here. When presented with the option to terminate the pregnancy, she dismissed it immediately.

My father even admitted to initially being ok with terminating their pregnancy with me to salvage my mother's life. As an adult, he would tell me rather bluntly that, "If I woulda had a choice between you and her, I woulda chose her. But it was her body and her choice."

Divulging his statement runs the risk of painting him in a negative light, but I know that's not how he intended for it to come across. I can't say that I blame his way of thinking. Losing his wife and ultimately becoming a single father over a pregnancy, having had four children already, seemed like volunteering for unnecessary sorrow. My mother, however, chose to embrace such a risk, and the rest, as they say, is history. In essence, my mother died so I could live. For that reason alone, she is my greatest hero. Her life to me, in so many ways, reminds me of Jesus. In the same way that He gave His life so that I could live eternally in heaven, my mother gave hers, so that I could live on earth. I was born January 13th, 1968, and my parents officially deemed their family complete.

Though the doctors warned my mother about the risk of dying due to giving birth to me, I suppose for a moment, at least, she thought she had beat their prognosis. She was alive for six of my birthdays before their prediction set in. We lived in a four-bedroom house that sat on a corner lot on Rock Street, in a small Arkansas town by the name of Warren. I remember the week or so before my mother died, sitting in the middle of the floor, playing in the bedroom of my sixteen-year-old sister, Sue, who we called Sue-Baby. Her bedroom was next to my mother's bedroom. I can't explain the factuality of what I'm about to disclose other than to just describe it as it vividly occurred.

Sue-Baby was reading to me from a storybook like she frequently did. Looking back, I can't remember what story it was. All I honestly remember was being stunned at what happened next. Suddenly, a transparent-like figure came through Sue-Baby's bedroom window, wisped past our feet, and then proceeded underneath the bedroom door of where our mother was laying sick. We both saw the presence and jumped, asking one another what it was. At that time, we honestly didn't think anything of it past that and carried on with the story.

Days later after this occurred, I can recall my mother having long conversations with everyone; it seemed, except me. I was the baby of the family, and as such, was selectively left out of conversations of heavy substance. The conversations took place one-by-one in my mother's bedroom behind closed doors with my older siblings and father. At the time, I didn't know what was being said. As an adult, I came to decipher my own understanding of those conversations—in later years, my family affirmed the same. My mother was preparing our family for her impending death.

My mother died in our home. I remember Reverend Easter, our family's pastor, and my mother's physician, Dr. Wynn, arriving at our house and the fear that I felt. Dr. Wynn, Reverend Easter, and my father were in the room with her body, conversing with one another and covering her up. I wasn't supposed to see it but did while hiding in the small passageway on the side of my mother's bedroom that I used to sneak into. After witnessing that, I remember leaving out the front door of our house by myself and running over to our neighbors—Rachel and Paul's—house. Rachel was the best friend of my oldest sister, Carla, and I frequently tagged along with her when she would go over to visit. They lived diagonally across the street from us in a trailer-style home. I remember a feeling of terror creeping across my body as I snuck into their home in the middle of the night, crawled under their kitchen sink, and sat there for what seemed like days. With my six-year-old mind, I remember thinking, *"If they cannot find me, then that means this isn't real."* But it was real—my mother was gone.

My mother was buried 15 miles away from where her services were held, but it seemed like it took an eternity to reach the cemetery. I can't remember much about what others were doing around me but do remember my great aunts arguing about who was going to ride in the family car. It's funny; I was only six years old, but I could sense that the irrelevance of their exchange was really a manifestation of their grief. I remember sitting front row on Reverend Easter's wife's lap at the gravesite. Like any six-year-old who doesn't want to be somewhere, I was extremely fidgety, uncomfortable, and doing a lot of excessive moving around.

Arguably my most vivid memory of the funeral, was the moment I bounced around so much that I fell over onto my mother's body during the last viewing. I distinctly remember how hard her body felt. It was like it wasn't even her. *"Where is she? What is happening?"* I thought. Mrs. Easter picked me up, and shortly after, I remember them closing the casket. *"What are they doing?"* I recall thinking. I felt confused. I still didn't comprehend that I wasn't going to see my mother anymore. I remember my father crying and someone holding him up. I'm not even sure I had ever seen my father cry before then. It was all so strange. I couldn't see my other siblings around me and felt a tangible sense of loneliness.

For years after that, whenever I attended funerals, viewed and touched the bodies, my mind would immediately go back to touching my mother and even seeing her face. It didn't matter who was in the casket; I saw my mother. Truth be told, for quite some time, I had a strong fear associated with attending funerals altogether.

As life went on, my immediate family didn't talk much about my mom. My father would tell us how much he loved her, but he never discussed her in an in-depth way beyond that. I didn't even have any pictures of her to cling to, besides one that he kept on the mantle at our house on Rock Street, and I didn't understand why. All the memories that I had of her were the ones I had to stitch together on my own. To deal with the void of my mother's death, I conjured up an illusory image of her. This image was comparable to most children's imaginary friend phase, except my illusion looked like my mom, talked like my mom, and did everything just like her.

I would sit in the middle of my bed, eating orange slice candies—which were my mother's favorite—portioning out some for myself, and then some for her. I wasn't battling severe mental issues or anything like that—just self-soothing in a way. I knew in all actuality that no one was there with me in the room, but it was my right to remember her in whatever capacity I wanted and needed to. There would be a pile of orange slices in my bed until I felt led to rock myself to sleep. My mother rocking me to sleep was etched in my being so vividly. She would sit in a wooden rocking chair in our den in front of a window, rocking me or just resting. Most times, she would sit there and write out her dues to give to the church.

"You always pay your dues." She'd say to me adamantly. I remember that instruction clearly and make sure that I do the same – for my own personal beliefs and in a small part, I'd like to think because of her words. Sometimes, she'd hum as she rocked in her chair. "When The Saints Go Marching In" was a favorite of hers. I can see her now, just rocking back and forth. As a child, I'd literally be lying in bed, rocking back and forth until I fell asleep. I did that well into my teen years and to this day, finding myself subtly rocking back and forth on occasion; sometimes, it's not even a sleep aid but simply a subconscious association. I rock at my desk, I rock at home in my living room, and I even find myself rocking at church.

Of course, rocking is more so on the smaller and insignificant scale of valuable things I gleaned from my mother. More notably, I believe that I got the gift of business from her. Before she died, our family owned a restaurant and pool hall. I can remember being in the restaurant as my mother walked about, giving instructions to workers and working on the cash register. People all over Warren would stop by for a good meal, though my mother wasn't doing the cooking whatsoever. She wasn't exactly domesticated, but she was smart. She also was passionate about civic matters like politics and being active in her community. She actually spearheaded the project for the road where our family house was, being paved.

She left in each one of her children natural knacks and qualities of her own. My brother, Mitchell, has her gift of being good with his hands; my sister, Carla, has her gift of being skilled with musical instruments; my sister, Patricia Diane, took on her gift of writing, and my sister, Sue-Baby, walked directly in her career path of medical service. In fact, my mother was one of the first nurses to integrate the all-white Bradley County Memorial Hospital, the only hospital in Warren, Arkansas.

When my mother died, my father and others didn't think I would get past it. The lack of details surrounding her death was so much to process in my younger years. At times, I was even borderline angry and resentful towards her for dying on me. It was a bit of a love-hate association that I had for her, in all honesty. I loved, cherished, and respected her memory from the grave and would never do anything that I thought would dishonor her—yet still, I held on to a feeling of resentment towards her for leaving me. I can recall thinking, *"What was so wrong with me that she didn't love me enough to stay and raise me?"* I was the baby, so I even felt slighted by the fact that some of my older siblings had more time with her. I felt abandoned.

I remember back in elementary school, around the month of May to celebrate Mother's Day, it was customary for teachers to give the students roses to go home and give to their mothers. Everyone else who had a mother to go home to, received a red rose, and children like me without a mother received a white rose, in memoriam, I suppose. It was always a big celebration at school, and all that stood out to me was the fact that I got this white rose and other children got red ones. I always felt separated.

As a child, I was fully aware that my mother was dead—it wasn't news to me. Things like the rose incident just seemed to magnify the difficulty of it even further. Perhaps, the root of handling the difficulty was that I never really had any closure. While my age complicated the concept of closure, either way, not having it at all was something that majorly affected how I dealt with her death. No matter how difficult, it's key to deal with death when it interrupts our lives. It's even more key to help children deal with it. If only I were sat down and talked to or even walked through a final goodbye, perhaps I could have healed in a healthier way.

After my mother died, my dad tried to supplement the time I spent around other female influences. When I was about seven or eight, he started dating a lady by the name of Janie Mae. I would tag along with him to her house as she had three daughters—a set of twins who were closer to my age, and another daughter. Other weekends, I would stay with my oldest sister, Carla, for a while. I honestly preferred this over being toted to some other woman's house who wasn't our mother. Carla had her own place near our family's home, where she lived with three of her four children, Robin, Darion, and Tory who were close to my age. Her oldest daughter, Tammy, had lived in Michigan since she was a baby with our maternal grandmother, who we called Big Momma. Carla had her as a teenager, and for whatever reason, whether to spare my parents social shame or simply to lend a hand to our already-at-capacity household, Tammy was taken to live there for the first part of her life. I stayed with Carla here and there as she was my oldest sister and treated me a lot like her child. Though three out of five of my father's children had moved out, he naturally felt overwhelmed at times having children as he still had two daughters to raise by himself, who were under the age of eighteen.

I attended Eastside Elementary, an integrated primary school in Warren. In fact, my siblings were among the first black students to be a part of school-wide integration when it first took place. By the time I was in school, in the seventies, the concept was the only norm that I had known. I wasn't even aware of racism, in fact, until I was in the third grade. I had a teacher by the name of Mrs. Francis, who was an old white woman with grayish white hair. She was very stern and rigid. I can remember there being a general sense of fear and intimidation in her class, as my fellow students and I were always hesitant to ask questions because of her cold receptivity.

One day, I was doing something typical of the average 3rd grader—what exactly I can't remember—when she blatantly and without hesitation told me that she didn't like me because my skin was too dark. I didn't even understand what she said. However, I somehow recall sensing that what she said to me was inappropriate for an adult to be saying to a child.

Nevertheless, at the time, it went right over my head. I'm so glad that I didn't go home and tell my father. He and my mother did not play about education or justice by any means, and God only knows what he would have done if he had known. I didn't realize until years later, when I thought back on the incident that she indeed was the first time that I had encountered racism. She was also my first dose of reality that all teachers were not created equal. I started elementary school right after my mother had passed away, and my first-grade teacher, Ms. Gibbs, set my expectations for teachers high. She was a petite white woman with brown hair, who was probably in her early thirties. She was so loving and warm. She constantly hugged us and affirmed us. My second-grade year with Ms. Colon as my teacher only solidified my premature assumptions that all teachers were kind and caring. She was African-American with a caramel complexion, middle-aged, and had short curly hair.

I recall being in her class and bumping up against my desk and hitting a knot in my breast one day. What I had somehow forgotten was that the origin of the knot came from carelessly running around in my house and falling, days prior. Bumping it at school, however, brought the pain back in full effect. I began to cry from panic and exaggerated worry, as children sometimes tend to do. Ms. Colon, who was the stark opposite of Ms. Francis, comforted me and asked me what was wrong. I told her about the knot, and her next question was, "Well, have you told your dad?" I told her that I hadn't. Not having my mother made personal and private matters awkward for me, but I imagine even more so for my dad. Knowing my family well, Ms. Colon took it upon herself to call my dad and inform him of what was going on. Upon picking me up from school that day, my father let me know that my teacher had called him. He then questioned me concernedly, asking how come I hadn't come to him. I was only seven and in the second grade, mind you, so I didn't exactly know *how* to tell him. My father foresaw other future instances playing out the same way.

In his mind, it was only a matter of time before he'd be forced to face the notion of bras and periods—but this time, as a single parent. Although I had older sisters, by the time I was to begin the fourth grade, my older sister, Sue-Baby, was off to college, and it was just my father and I living in the house together. Often times feeling ill-equipped to give me the feminine guidance that I needed as a little girl, my father made the decision to send me to Cleveland to live with my Aunt, Athalean.

Aunt Athalean, age 46, was my mother's baby sister, who lived in Cleveland, Ohio. It was 1979, and she had just lost her husband, Uncle Bill, that winter prior. She had no children of her own, but Uncle Bill did have children from a previous marriage, who were adults. Her only companionship was their dog, Max. With my mother and Uncle Bill being gone, my father figured that my moving with her would do us both some good. From her, I could glean care from a woman's influence, and she could glean companionship from me. However, if my father or I knew just how much companionship she needed, I think his decision to send me to live with her for as long as he did might have been altogether different. Aunt Athalean was one of those women who had the luxury of being a domestic housewife while her husband was the breadwinner. Uncle Bill left her in a really good place, but she never knew how to manage anything on her own. There's a big difference between not having to do mundane things and not knowing how to.

Besides decorum, cooking, and other typical duties of a housewife, Uncle Bill took care of everything else. So much so that when he died, she was practically lost—that and/or maybe she was functionally depressed. She and Uncle Bill had a car, but she never drove it after he died. Everywhere she needed to go, she either got rides to or asked someone else to drive her car. When it came to shopping, she ordered everything from department store catalogs like Roman, Spiegel, and Montgomery Ward. As far as everything else, *I* was her delivery. I was eleven at the time going on twelve, and I would have to walk to get groceries, walk to pay her bills, and walk wherever else she needed. Because of this, I became introduced to grown woman responsibilities at a very young age. She just didn't seem able to get past Uncle Bill's death.

Though she was as loving as she knew how to be, mothering instincts weren't that natural for her, as she had never been a mother before. Don't get me wrong; I wore the best clothes with her, I ate good meals, and I even went to Sunday school, but I don't recall "enjoying" living with her. She was stern and didn't really allow me to have friends at the house. Maybe it's just how she was, or maybe she was being overprotective. I had one friend in the neighborhood named Glinda whom she would allow to come over sporadically, but none other than her. All of the other friends I had were from school, and I didn't get to hang with them much outside of that. I started calling home and talking to my dad, telling him about my living in Cleveland. Since I was twelve, however, my dad and siblings thought I had the tendency to be exaggerating. But I wasn't. My dad would regularly mail money orders to Aunt Athalean for me. In addition to earnings from work, I think the money he sent was mainly from the social security checks that Sue-Baby and I still received from my mother's death.

The saving grace for my humdrum life in Cleveland came along when one of Uncle Bill's children, Beverly, came to live with us around the time I was in the 7th grade. Beverly was married and had fled Phoenix, Arizona with her four-year-old daughter, Shaquila, or "Qui" as we called her, to escape her abusive and controlling husband, Victor. They moved in and occupied the downstairs of Aunt Athalean's house. Aunt Athalean's home was a whopping four-stories with an attic, two floors for full living, and a basement with a laundry room. It was like two apartments under one roof. Aunt Athalean and I lived on the second living level, and Beverly and her daughter stayed on the main living level. Beverly was able to enter the main living level from an outside back door without having to come in if she didn't want to. At the same time, we could move upstairs and downstairs between the levels from the inside. On both levels, there were two bedrooms, a living room, a kitchen, and a bathroom. Beverly was an adult woman, so she knew how to drive, knew how to pay bills, and instead of depending on me, Aunt Athalean, therefore, became dependent on Beverly. Beverly was kind, warm, loving, but wasn't a pushover. I spent a lot of time tagging along with her and Qui to places as she significantly enriched my quality of life while living in Cleveland.

After about a year of being in Cleveland, one day, Qui was outside playing in the front yard as she usually did. Beverly and I were on the inside when we suddenly heard Qui call, "Momma, Momma" from the outside. Not thinking anything of it at first, Beverly went to the door to see what Qui wanted, when all of a sudden, she noticed Vic's car out front. She ran outside the door, and by the time she got out there, he had sped off down the street. I went outside to where Beverly was as she had knelt down to her knees in the front lawn crying hysterically.

"Oh my God, Vic took Qui again!" She wailed as I stood there, not knowing what to say, although I felt sadness for her.

Aunt Athalean even came to the porch to see what the commotion was about.

"You need to call the police," Aunt Athalean advised her.

But Beverly didn't want to do that. She knew the ins and outs of what the police were going to say. They'd tell her that a custody agreement would need to be drawn up going forward, and that meant going through a divorce and a custody battle—both of which would only put their daughter through more unnecessary heartache. Apparently, this wasn't the first time that Vic had popped up to come and take Qui. Before coming to Ohio, Beverly had fled to Flint, Michigan where her other siblings and family were, and Vic popped up there as well. Each time this occurred, the only way she was able to get Qui back was to lay low for a while, catch his guard down and take Qui back. That day at Aunt Athalean's was the last time I ever saw Qui. Looking back as an adult, I think it was at that moment when Beverly had to decide whether she was going to be a victim or a survivor.

I remember her conversing and saying that she couldn't keep taking her daughter through this. This last time, Beverly didn't fight to go and get her back. Even then as a child, I observed a unique strength in Beverly that she didn't even realize she had. I'm sure the situation was extremely difficult to walk away from. She, of course, was able to talk to her daughter regularly on the phone, but Vic didn't let Beverly visit. At that time, even during the early eighties, women had yet to come into the full realization of the power within themselves. They didn't always have the money, resources, or support to combat a lot of situations that they encountered. They learned to play the hand they were dealt and made the best of it. Instead of staying a victim, Beverly chose to be a survivor. Her husband was very emotionally and physically abusive to her but was a good father to their daughter. She made a very difficult peace with the fact that her daughter was safe and taken care of. Although not at all ideal, Beverly in a way took her power back.

Aunt Athalean was naturally very controlling. I thought, at first, it was just with me since I was a kid, but she was the same with Beverly. She didn't want Beverly to go anywhere, she didn't want her to have company over, and Beverly eventually grew tired of that. Beverly was a young woman in her prime and eventually decided to move out. When she did, I was heartbroken. Now, things would go back to how they were before she came—humdrum, with Aunt Athalean depending on me again. Aunt Athalean was bitter after Beverly left.

"She just up and left me high and dry." Said Aunt Athalean.

She felt that Beverly had abandoned her while she was still grieving the loss of Uncle Bill. She didn't want me to call or talk to her, so I had to find ways to sneak and do so. Beverly was the only person who I felt understood my life in Cleveland, and I wasn't going to let Aunt Athalean interfere with our connection. My dad and siblings thought I was exaggerating because the Aunt Athalean that they knew was different than the one I had come to know after Uncle Bill's death. Unbeknownst to me, Beverly called and confirmed to my father and siblings that I wasn't exaggerating about the strict living environment at Aunt Athalean's. She told them about Aunt Athalean's insecure ways since Uncle Bill had died. Prior to actually living with her, during the summers when I would be with Big Momma in Michigan,

Tammy and I would visit Aunt Athalean and Uncle Bill. That's why at first, I was thrilled with the idea of going to live with her. But she wasn't the same as a widow. As an adult, I can empathize with her situation, but as a kid, I couldn't. She was uneducated and had been dependent on her husband all of her life.

Upon first arriving at Cleveland, Aunt Athalean enrolled me into a public school. There I attended from fourth through sixth grade and would have remained for the seventh, but a scandalous police raid took place due to suspicious student activity of some sort and Aunt Athalean wasn't going for it. She transferred me to a Catholic School, which was way across town. It was so far that I would have to leave my house at 6:30 in the morning, just to be at school by 8:00. It was easily 35 to 45 minutes away, and with Beverly now gone, I was back to catching the bus and walking everywhere I needed to go.

Moving from a small town like Warren, where you knew everyone you encountered, to a big city like Cleveland, meant that I experienced a bit of culture shock. Cleveland was fast-paced, and I found myself being fast right along with it. Maybe it was because Beverly was gone, or maybe I was just feeling myself as a pre-teen, but I was conducting myself in a manner that was way too mature for the age that I was. I started hanging out with girls from school who were much older than me, and as such, blended into many of the places that they went. They had fake IDs, so I had one. I was twelve years old, getting into the club with them, and no one batted an eye. I would leave the house in my uniform for school and then wait until I got to a girlfriend's house and change into something more mature. We'd skip school and hang at their houses since their parents were at work, walk around downtown or even frequent a club in the daytime. Whatever I did, I made sure to do before Aunt Athalean expected me home.

Though I had grown accustomed to Aunt Athalean's ways, the final straw for me was when she tried to burn me with an iron. I don't remember exactly what I did to set her over the edge—I probably said something smart as she was trying to iron. All I knew was she reached for it and then tried to burn me. She would have succeeded, had her dog, Max, not snapped at her. I ran down the stairs and out of the door to the nearest corner store at the intersection of Buckeye and Lardet Avenue. I used the payphone and made a collect call to Beverly and told her what had happened. She and my brother Mitchell had started dating one another. She told me that as soon as my brother got off from work, they would come and get me. First, they called my dad and told him what happened. I guess he gave them permission to come because the next thing I knew, they were there to pack me up and we went to Flint, Michigan where they lived. Shortly after that, we were heading back home to Arkansas.

CHAPTER 2

Growing Up Fast

The summer before I was to begin the eighth grade, I moved back home to Arkansas from Cleveland. I was so happy to be back home. The inside of our family house seemed different, and the presence of my mother was no longer there. From the way she kept house, the way things were so meticulous and clean, even to the layout of the furniture. My second to oldest sister, Patricia Diane, or Trish Ann as we called her, now lived in the house and she didn't care much about housekeeping, which quite frankly made me mad. She and her long time and often abusive boyfriend, Otis, had broken up yet again, and she was back at home, living with my Dad. By now, my dad had made up his mind between dating Ms. Janie Mae and a lady named Ms. Dorothy. He and Ms. Dorothy were dating exclusively now, and that's whose house he spent most of his nights at. I was never really super excited about the idea of my father dating any woman as I felt he would be forgetting my mom, and then eventually, me as well.

Fred Barnett and Tyrone Burks were high schoolers in my neighborhood who were among the who's who of popularity in Warren High School. Fred Barnett was the son of Ms. Alma, who was one of my mother's best friends when she was alive, as well as her hairdresser. They lived three houses down from me. As for Tyrone, I had always known him. His brother and I were in the same grade, and before I moved away, they lived directly across the street from my house for years. I had memories of playing with Tyrone and other neighborhood kids from when I was younger before my mother died. My niece, Robin and I would yard hop between my house and the houses of other neighborhood friends directly as we played tag, hide and go seek, mother may I, Simon says, and a host of other "back in the day" kid favorites. I can remember my mother warning us not to throw rocks and sticks carelessly as we could run the risk of busting someone's windows out or harm one another in the process. Now that I was back home in Arkansas, the house that Tyrone's family lived in was torn down.

One summer day, I was outside talking to my neighbor, Douglas Anthony Moore, who we called Mo. He lived diagonally across the street from my house and was Tyrone's best friend. I seemed to have a lot in common with Mo. Mo's mother, Ms. Rosie Ann, had died while I was in Cleveland, and he lived at home with just his father, Mr. "Bud" Moore. I never knew his real name, but that's what everyone called him. Actually, Ms. Rosie Ann and Mr. Bud weren't Mo's real parents. I'm not sure who his real parents were, but I don't remember him being adopted or anything—just more so, dropped off to live with Ms. Rosie Ann and Mr. Bud who were more than likely his extended blood family. I'm not sure if it was a small-town thing or a black community thing, but it was common for kids to be dropped off to live with relatives for various reasons. Whatever the background story was, Mo knew they weren't his birth parents. After Ms. Rosie Ann died, he spent quite a bit of time at Tyrone's house. Tyrone had a big family with lots of brothers and sisters that was like a surrogate family for Mo.

"Hey, you remember the family who used to live right across from y'all?" Mo asked me one day, referring to Tyrone's family.

Growing Up Fast

"Yes, I remember," I said.

"They moved down the street now, and I'm about to go down there. Wanna come hang out?"

I told him sure and walked with him down to their new home, which I had never been to. As Mo and I walked into the house, Tyrone and his siblings were surprised to see me, as they knew I had moved to Cleveland for a while.

"Hey, when did you get back?" One of his sisters asked.

I told them that I had just moved back home a couple of weeks ago. They asked me if I was home visiting for the summer, and I told them that I was finally home for good.

"That's good," Tyrone said. "Maybe we all should hang out sometime."

I thought nothing of it and agreed. I started going down to their house regularly whenever Mo went, and we all would hang out. Tyrone's family house had three bedrooms, one bathroom, and was always full of people, whether it was family or friends. For the duration of the summer, I spent most of my time there, playing cards and board games, listening to music, and just talking, laughing, and hanging out. Most days, I would be there until it was about to become dark outside and then Mo and/or Tyrone would walk me home. My dad knew Tyrone's parents, of course, so he was fine with all of the time I had been spending at their house that summer. Also, Tyrone's first cousin, Alice, who was my childhood best friend, lived down the street from Tyrone's house and would always be among the group of us hanging. On the occasions where just Tyrone would walk me home, we'd shoot the breeze, talking about random things—him being in football camp and lifting weights, my being in Cleveland and what it was like, me asking him what high school was like, and so on. I enjoyed the mature conversation with him, as at this point in my life, I felt I was practically grown, anyway.

One evening, Mo was walking me home, and as we were talking, he told me that Tyrone wanted to go out with me. I really didn't think anything of it at first as I never had looked at Tyrone in that way before. After Mo told me that Tyrone liked me, I remember feeling sort of awkward. A few days later, when just Mo and I were walking back home from Tyrone's house, he reached into his pocket and pulled out a folded-up piece of paper and handed it to me.

"This is from Tyrone." He said.

I grabbed it and put it in my own pocket.

"Oh, ok," I said.

When I finally got home, I placed the letter on the dresser and did my nightly routine. I got a bath, put on my nightclothes, and grabbed the letter as I got into my bed. I unfolded it, and Tyrone had written how he had enjoyed spending time with me that summer, that he was glad that I was back home, and that he liked me. At the end of the letter, there was a question asking if I would go out with him, followed by three checkboxes for "yes, no, or maybe." I checked "yes," folded the letter back up and went to sleep. It was so funny to think that he was older than me and acting so shyly. I guess he was more so laid back most of the times, but there were others when he seemed so tough. For instance, Tyrone would never shy away from a fight. He wasn't the type to start fights, but he definitely was the one to finish them. If someone were starting trouble with one of his siblings, they would later regret it once Tyrone was at the scene. Under the surface, he had a temper, and on his bad side was not a good place to be. I fell asleep, and the next day, I gave the letter back to Mo, who gave it back to Tyrone. After that, Tyrone and I were officially a "couple."

The school year started, and I was so excited to be dating an 11th grader, since I, myself, was still in junior high school. Tyrone and I spent a lot of time together. We were practically inseparable after his football practices and on the weekends. Mo had his dad's car that he would use all the time. He would pick me up in the morning time and then drive down the street and pick up Tyrone. They would drop me off at the junior high school and then drive over to the high school.

They had open campus for lunch, and sometimes they'd drive over and pick me up from school, and we'd go to somewhere like Sonic, but most of the time, we went to one of our houses as all of our parents were at work. We couldn't go to Sonic a lot because it was extremely busy during lunch hour and I couldn't be late going back to school; mainly because I wasn't supposed to be leaving in the first place. If my dad had known that I was leaving campus with my "boyfriend," I would have been in a world of trouble. Tyrone tried to be attentive to me as a boyfriend, but more often than not, he wasn't a big talker. He was actually quite shy. I never had a boyfriend before him, though, so I didn't have a whole lot to compare him to. We held hands a lot and kissed often. I had my first kiss—a small peck—while I was in Cleveland. Tyrone, however, was my first "real kiss." Tyrone and I were each other's "person." I didn't realize it then, but my heart still had this unchecked void from not having my mother. I was searching for love to offset the love I missed from her, and that position of vulnerability left me wide open for unhealthy attachment.

When my sister Carla found out that her daughter Robin was pregnant, she took preventive measures and made Tammy, who had now moved home to live with her after Big Momma died, get on birth control and insisted that I do the same. Tammy actually wasn't even sexually active, and in my case, my period had barely even started. I say barely because it started while I was in Cleveland but had always been extremely sporadic. It would come on time for a few months and then stop altogether for another slew of months. Upon learning this, Carla was just as insistent that I go get a check-up. Once the doctor realized that I was fifteen and having inconsistent periods, he prescribed me a low dosage of birth control that would induce a more regular occurrence of my cycles. I began taking the birth control as directed, and about three weeks later, I got my first period since being back home in Warren.

Around this same time, the topic of sex had begun to come up more frequently between Tyrone and I. I had a little too much freedom to be fifteen years old. Tyrone and I knew our parents' schedules like the backs of our hands. Tyrone's mother worked in the day, so when she got off, she shut her door and went to sleep. His stepdad worked in the evenings, so he was never home at night. As the baby of my parent's children, all of my siblings had moved out or away and had their own lives. My dad worked, and when he was off, he spent most of his time at Dorothy's house. I would never want to go to her house as she only had one daughter who was much younger than me, or rather, not as fast or as mature as I was. Her other kids were around my age, but they were boys. There was really no difference in hanging out with them than hanging out with Mo—but hanging with them would mean I couldn't see Tyrone. So, whenever my dad would try to make me go to Dorothy's house, I would dish out reasons not to go. I'd say I had homework to finish, ask to go down to Alice's house instead, or ask to go to Sue-Baby's house, which was on our family lot, right next to our own house. She had gotten married to her husband, Ira Joe, and the two bought a house that was so close that we could literally talk to one another from our porches.

My father was comfortable with the reasons that I came up with, so he would go on to Dorothy's without me, not thinking anything of it. Not to mention that sometimes, my sister Trish Ann was back home from another on-again, off-again spat between her boyfriend, and I could just stay with her. At any rate, as long as I would be home when my father got home that evening, he was none the wiser. Because his pattern was consistent and I had it down to a science, I got away with spending massive amounts of unsupervised time with

Tyrone. I always kept my grades up, so my father never had any signs that all the while, his fourteen-year-old daughter was in a hot and heavy relationship with a high schooler right under his nose.

My father decided to marry Dorothy, and I wasn't too happy about it at all. He wanted to move her into our family's house, and I told him quite frankly that it wasn't about to happen. He could live over there with her all he wanted, but he wasn't about to move her into my mother's house and erase my mother's memory altogether. As a teenager, more than ever, I had come to master the art of manipulating my father with guilt. I'd say things like, "If my momma were alive, then I wouldn't have to worry about you being gone all the time" and other phrases that I came up with to pain him. When it came to the possibility of Dorothy and her kids moving in with us, I was not having it. I wasn't about to share a bedroom, clean up behind anyone, wash endless sinks of dishes, have someone trying to play my mother, or any of that. Though my dad was strong, when it came to issues about my mother, he kind of backed down. Growing up, I had been told by him and my siblings that I was headstrong and determined, much like my mother. And as such, when I made up my mind about something, there was no turning back; I think this reminded him of my mother even more. My dad was also pushing sixty at the time, and for the sake of his own peace and sanity, obliged most of my craziness and conceded that he would just go and stay with Dorothy at her house. This meant my dad was taking care of two households.

Our house was paid for but he, of course, still had utilities to look after. The majority of his clothes still remained at our house, and he would come home daily to change, check on me, make sure that I had what I needed, and go back to Dorothy's for the evening. Looking back, I'm sure that was a lot of stress and pressure on him. On one hand, I was guilting him, and on the other, he had a new bride to appease. As far as I was concerned, that was his problem. My selfishness and immaturity demanded that I got my way, and I did.

In May of 1983, I was preparing to wrap up my freshman year of high school. Tyrone had just graduated, and was getting ready to turn 18. Early one weekend evening, Tyrone popped up at my house with one of my favorite treats: some soft-serve vanilla ice-cream and a bag of plain potato chips on the side for me to crush up and mix inside. I was pleasantly surprised to see him and invited him in. At my house in particular, Tyrone and I could really be in our own little world. I didn't have siblings around to bother us, so we usually had a house to ourselves with my dad being at work or at Dorothy's.

We would watch TV, cook dinner and eat, lounge around—basically "play house." We were home alone and went into my family den and sat down on the couch to watch television as I ate my ice-cream and chips. I had my legs outstretched across his, and before long, Tyrone and I started to engage in a heavy kissing session. As the kissing intensified and our hormones got the best of us, Tyrone stood up from the couch and took my hand as I sat there, looking up at him. He had a beckoning look in his eye to move things to my bedroom. I felt a slight sense of fear deep down on the inside as I wasn't sure if I was ready to go all the way. I had always been a thinker, and because of that, couldn't help but think that having sex would change our relationship forever afterward. At the same time, however, part of me wanted to go all the way with him. If I did go through with it, at least I had the insurance of being on birth control to ease my nerves about becoming pregnant—which Tyrone knew nothing about.

I stood up and followed him to my bedroom. It was the first time that we had taken one of our kissing sessions to a bedroom at my house. We usually would just stay on one of the couches in the den or living room. This session, however, would turn into more than kissing. I knew that Tyrone had sex before and trusted him to know what he was doing—which he seemed to know quite well. I, on the other hand, definitely had no clue. I officially lost my virginity to Tyrone that night. He was gentle and sweet, and afterwards, I felt a closer bond to him. We laid there together for a few moments before getting dressed. We went back into the den and continued watching television again. We were both more quiet than usual. We had been cuddled up on the couch for a while with no words when he finally broke the silence.

"Are you ok?" He asked.

"Yes, I'm ok," I replied.

"Do you feel like we made a mistake?" He quizzed.

"No…I don't." I replied.

"Then, what is it?" He asked.

"I just need to know if we're in a committed relationship," I said, unsure. "I probably should have asked that before we did…it."

"Why would you think that we're not in a committed relationship if we're only seeing each other?" He asked sort of confusedly. "When I'm not at football practice or weightlifting, when I'm not at work or home, I'm here with you." He said.

I told him that it wasn't really the now of our relationship that had me worried, but what was coming. There was a strong possibility of Tyrone going to college for football when the fall came, and I would only be starting my sophomore year of high school. His life was going to change drastically from how it was in high school, and there was the potential for college girls to be around, whom he found more mature. He reassured me that he was committed to our relationship.

"I love you, Leigh." He said.

His words gave me comfort as I told him I loved him too. I decided to let my mind rest and trust him. We continued to cuddle and watch TV as he rubbed my feet and we enjoyed the remainder of an evening that had become very special for both of us.

After our special night, Tyrone and I were even more inseparable than before. School had officially let out, so all that stood in the way of our time together was Tyrone working during the day. As soon as he got off around four in the afternoon, we were back together to spend our evenings. Our sexual escapades became more frequent, and I felt closer to him. I felt safe and protected when I was with him. I had this confidence that he wouldn't let anything happen to me or let anyone hurt me. I would never have to worry about protection or anything like that as long as he was around, and it was a magnetizing emotion. I can recall once when my sister Trish Ann and her boyfriend Otis got into a fight while she was wearing my favorite pink polo shirt that Tyrone had bought me. At some point, Otis literally ripped my shirt off of my sister's body in anger. Shortly thereafter, I wanted to wear my pink shirt and began looking for it. When I asked my sister if she had seen my shirt, she broke the news of what happened, and I was livid. We began to argue about the shirt, and Tyrone walked into my house, fresh off of work, to hear us. I immediately started telling him what had happened to my shirt and that Otis was the one who had ripped it up. I demanded that someone—whether Trish Ann or Otis, it didn't matter—buy me a new shirt and Tyrone could perceive how worked up I was about it. Otis got off of work around the same time as Tyrone did and stopped by the house too. He was stopping by to try and make up with Trish Ann as they had been fighting all weekend long. Seeing how upset I was, when Tyrone saw Otis, he got straight to the point and confronted him.

"Look man, you can't be going around and tearing up my girl's things." He said calmly.

Both men were nonchalant about the occurrence, and Otis apologized. I felt like a kid whose parent had handled a situation for her—even though no major results came about from it. Another time I can recall, Tyrone and I were lying in my bed when in the middle of the night, his older brother, Don, came knocking at my bedroom window for him. He told him that he had got into a fight and needed his help. Tyrone got up, got dressed, told me he'd be back, and left to basically go fight. I knew he could handle his own and never worried. He came back as he said, and that was that. Even though these were small things, it was instances like these that made me crazy about how Tyrone would address any situation that may have come up. For a fifteen-year-old girl, my nose was wide open, as they say, and I was undoubtedly in love for the very first time. I didn't ever want to lose the feeling I got from being with Tyrone.

One evening in the summertime after hanging out at Tyrone's house with him and Mo, I wasn't feeling well and told them that I was going to head home early. Tyrone's stepdad would sometimes drive home for his lunch break and let Tyrone keep the car for the evening. All Tyrone had to do was to drop him back off to his job, and the car would be at his disposal. Eddie Dean would have to clock back in by 9 o'clock, so he and Tyrone would leave the house by 8:45. It was about 8:30 or so, and after learning of my plans to leave early, Tyrone asked me to wait a while until it was time to drop his step-dad back to work. That way, I could hop in the car with the two of them, and on the way back, he would take me home and stay and take care of me. Though that didn't seem unreasonable, I was feeling sick to my stomach—almost like the early onset of the flu—and didn't feel like having to wait to go home when I could just go straight there and be done with it.

I told him no and asked Mo to take me straight home instead since it wasn't unusual for me to go with Mo any other time. Mo wasn't quite ready to go yet, but he was always agreeable with whatever I asked. Mo and I headed back down the street towards our houses. He parked his car in his driveway and then walked me across the street to my house. He came in, per his usual, and I excused myself to change into my nightclothes as I hoped that would help me feel a bit more comfortable, given the way my stomach felt. We started to chitchat for a while like we normally did, and the next thing I knew, over two hours had passed, and it was about 11:30. Mo was sitting on the couch that was near one of our front room windows. It had sheer whitish/cream colored drapes, and from where I was sitting in a chair, I saw Tyrone's shadow jump up on the porch, skipping several steps. My door flung open, and I caught a glimpse of rage in his face that I had never seen before. Mo and I stood up startled as Tyrone came in and B-lined to where Mo was and punched him square in the face as Mo fell back onto the couch.

"You're trying to get with my girl. I knew it!" Tyrone yelled among other phrases of rage that he uttered.

As Tyrone was preparing to hit Mo for a second time, I jumped in between them as he swung and punched me in my right eye. He hit me with such force that I fell down to the floor on my knees and began to cry. I had never been hit before by a man's strength—my father had never even whooped me. It happened so fast that I barely realized I had been hit until I began to feel my face swell instantly. I grabbed my face, which was in unbelievable pain.

"Are you f***ing crazy?" I screamed through tears.

"I thought you said you was sick; you ain't too sick since you sitting down here with my best friend in your night clothes! I came down here to take care of you, and I find y'all together!" Said Tyrone, still seething.

I made my way over towards the couch where Mo was to see if he was okay. I glanced back at Tyrone and saw a scary mix of hurt, anger, and rage. It was almost as if he was another person in that moment. After a few minutes of standing there engulfed in his anger, Tyrone seemed to begin to come to himself. It was almost like he hadn't realized what he had done. Mo sat up on the edge of the couch to see if I was okay—still on the floor. I remember the look on Mo's face as he looked at mine, and that's when I knew the pain I felt must have been visible somehow. By this time, I could barely see as my right eye was swelling shut. As Mo helped me up off the floor, Tyrone seemed ready to flare up again.

"Get your hands off of her," Tyrone said. "Don't touch her!"

Tyrone began to move towards me to try and comfort and console me.

"Let me see, let me see!" He insisted as he came towards me and I shrunk back.

"Are you f**king scared of me now?" He asked, audaciously.

He was absolutely right. I had never seen this side of him before, and I was terrified.

"What's wrong with you, ma—?" Mo yelled as Tyrone cut him off.

"Don't talk to me!" Tyrone told him. "As a matter of fact, leave, don't talk to her either!" Tyrone said.

"Are you okay?" Mo asked me.

"What do you mean is she okay?" Tyrone asked angrily. "Of course, she's okay. I'm her boyfriend—not you."

Mo just looked at him as the two of them exchanged grimaces.

"You need to leave," Tyrone said.

Mo glanced at me to make sure I was okay with him leaving. I wanted Mo to stay but was too scared to ask him to. I knew if I had asked him to, it would seem like I was validating everything that Tyrone had suspected.

"Go ahead, and go…I'll be okay," I said out loud.

Everything in the back of my mind, however, was screaming, *"Please don't leave me with him!"* Mo left, and Tyrone and I were alone. Tyrone tried to console me and began to apologize profusely.

"I'm sorry, you just made me crazy!" He said as he deflected what had happened onto me.

Dare to Dream

In my mind, I was scared on so many different levels. I was terrified to tell anyone in my family what had happened. I was crying and didn't know what to do. I immediately began to worry about what would happen once my dad got home, which could have been at any moment. As usual, he was having dinner and visiting over at Dorothy's house. My face began to get bigger and bigger, and I began to panic.

"What am I going to do? I can't stay here because if my dad sees my eye, you're going to be dead." I told him, still a nervous and emotional wreck.

We couldn't go to his house because we couldn't explain it to his Mom. I definitely couldn't go to any of my sisters' houses as the first thing they would probably do is to call Daddy. I didn't have to worry too much about Carla, as she was at work. Trish Ann had her own problems with her boyfriend to deal with. When things turned physical with him, the first thing she did was tell my father. In retrospect, I could have probably told Sue-Baby, but having not been back home in Warren that long, I was somewhat unsure of where my trust lied with my sisters now that they were adults and I was a teenager. I was rattled and couldn't think clearly of what my next move was going to be.

"Let's go to Rita's house," Tyrone said.

Short for Cherita, Rita was Tyrone's older twenty-year-old sister who lived nearby. He didn't know what to do himself but figured that his older sister might. We got into his stepdad's car and drove over to Rita's house about a mile or so away. We got to her house, and she opened the door and immediately noticed my face.

"What the f**k happened to you, Leigh?" She asked.

I glanced over at Tyrone, and she told us to come inside. She made Tyrone wait in the living room and took me into her bedroom, which also had a bathroom attached.

"What happened to your face?" She asked again. This time, more intently.

I told her everything that happened at my house.

"So *your* house is where he's been hanging out at?" She asked as if she were putting a riddle together. "So you and Tyrone are dating?" She asked.

"Um, I guess we are," I replied.

"So, were you and Mo messing around?" She inquired.

"No, we weren't," I told her.

She grabbed some witch hazel, which I had never heard of before that night, left her bedroom and came back with a cold steak. She started doctoring my face. She placed witch-hazel on my swelling and then made me hold the cold steak against the area where my eye had swollen shut. I'm not sure if she knew what to do because she was older than us or if she too had her own experiences with relieving black eyes.

"Once they start hitting you, they don't stop." She said.

Again, I'm not sure if that tidbit had come from experience or she just was aware of Tyrone's temper as her brother.

"You need to leave him alone." She said.

I got in Rita's bed, and all I could think about was how I was going to keep this from my dad. The night had escalated to something I didn't understand and didn't even know how to deal with.

The next day when I woke up, Tyrone was gone. I didn't ask about his whereabouts, and Rita didn't bring it up. Rita had always been like a big sister to me. She wasn't the type to take Tyrone's side just because he was her brother. I told Rita that I couldn't go home with my face looking like it did.

"You're right." She agreed. "There's no way you can tell Mr. Woody about this." She added.

She told me that I could stay with her as long as I needed to until my face got back to normal. I called my dad and made up a lie that Rita was going out of town and needed Alice and I to stay over and babysit for a few days. I doubted that my father or Rita would run into each other anywhere, but I briefed Rita on what I was telling him, just in case. My father bought my story because he knew that my babysitting or hanging out with Alice was nothing unusual. He knew my friends and their parents, so he felt pretty secure in my whereabouts and safety when I wasn't home. For days, I had to wear sunglasses to try and conceal the swelling of my eye. As the swelling went down, I continued to wear shades but also put on heavier makeup than usual, in hopes that it would be less noticeable to people I may have encountered. I'd come home and get clothes or other items I needed when my dad wasn't home and wouldn't see me.

Tyrone popped up at Rita's house every day that I was over there, but I refused to talk to him. It was his sister's house, so he'd come in, get a snack from her kitchen, and sit down and watch TV in hopes that I would interact with him. Each time, I would go to Rita's room and close the door. After about 30 or 45 minutes of my not coming out, he would eventually go home. This went on for three or four days until one day he came over and told me that at some point, we were going to have to talk. I agreed, although, in the back of my mind, I was still frightened of him; especially to be alone with him.

On top of that, I was still feeling queasy. I now attributed my slightly sick feeling to everything that had transpired over the last few days. I was sad, upset, hurt, and confused. Here I was, in a relationship with a man who I loved and had given my virginity to, only to discover that he wasn't the person who I thought he was. I also felt conflicted because even though everything had unfolded the other night, I still wanted to be with him. Tyrone apologized to regain my favor; of course, and I forgave him. I just wanted to put the whole messy ordeal behind me.

Mo and me talking after leaving Tyrone's house was a norm. I guess Tyrone just didn't know that. He was under the assumption that once Mo walked me to my house, he would go home, and that would be that. On the contrary, however, Mo would always come in and chat for a long time before he finally went home. We'd talk about a lot of things that I probably should have been talking to Tyrone about. Granted, Tyrone and I did talk, but he just wasn't a conversationalist like Mo was. That violent night at my house changed the dynamic of our friendships. We continued to hang out as a group sometimes, but never like we had before. For most of the time after that, Alice would be around to even things out. And though Tyrone and Mo made up, the trust that remained between them was always strained, going forward.

My face finally went down, and I was able to go home. The queasy flu-like symptoms that I was experiencing were not going away. I would be lightheaded but never would faint and would feel nauseous but would never throw up. I also had a headache. I told my dad that I wasn't feeling well and felt like I was coming down with some sort of flu or cold. Being under 18, I was still on his insurance, so I told him that I was planning to make a doctor's appointment. There was nothing more annoying than having a summer cold. I finally couldn't take it anymore, and my dad agreed to take me to my appointment with my normal physician, Dr. David Chambers.

My dad and I walked inside the building of the doctor's office. I checked in, and my dad approached the counter with me so that I could update the necessary insurance information that he had. After that, I sat down and read a magazine as I waited for my name to be called. My dad told me that he was going to go outside and come back. That was his way of excusing himself for a smoke break, which

I was used to. When the nurse finally called me back, she took my vital signs and then placed me in a room to wait for Dr. Chambers. Dr. Chambers entered and asked me more about the symptoms surrounding my visit, as well as an update on how my period was occurring. I told him everything that I was experiencing and also updated him that the birth control he had placed me was making my periods come normally. After hearing my symptoms, however, he brought up the suggestion of taking a pregnancy test.

"A pregnancy test?" I asked. "No sir, I'm not pregnant; I'm having my cycle normally."

He then asked me if I had begun to engage in sexual activity. I told him that I had.

"Well, I think we should take a pregnancy test, just to be on the safe side." He said.

I shrugged my shoulders and agreed. I knew my symptoms weren't due to pregnancy, so whatever he thought was necessary for this checkup, I was fine with. He gave me a cup to go pee in that I handed off to a nurse. I went and sat back for about ten minutes when he returned and shut the door behind him.

"LaFarris, it looks like you're going to have a baby."

My eyes widened in disbelief.

"What?" I asked. "But I'm taking birth control!" I contested.

"Yes, but at the time we placed you on birth control, the dosage was only enough to induce a normal occurrence of your period—not prevent pregnancy. You told me that you were not sexually active." He said calmly.

I sat there in silence, but my mind was a traffic jam. He went on to say that no birth control is 100 percent effective in the first place—the only birth control is *not* having sex. I sat there stuck. Trying to be helpful, he went on to discuss the next steps, what my options were, prenatal vitamins, and the whole nine, and that a nurse would be in to talk with me further. All I could think about was how in the world I was going to tell my father. It was like it was an alternate universe. I could feel tears well up in my eyes.

His reaction was, "It's going to be okay."

And in my mind, all I could think was, *"no, it's not!"* Just as he stated, the nurse came in and talked with me about a number of things that were all too much for me to process. She told me about adoption options and appointments that I could set up, but that I would need a parent with me. My mind was whirling. I was still crying as she tried to be understanding. I could sense her empathy and gentleness in dealing with me. She tried to give me a sense of calmness, but I couldn't absorb any of it. All I could think about was, what was I going to tell my dad. I remember being dazed and numb. This was something I didn't have a lie for. I had no choice but to tell him because for once, I didn't have an out. I had hidden my black eye and dating Tyrone altogether, but this was going to make everything come out like a dam bursting. This was something that directly was going to affect him. I got dressed and headed back to the car where my dad was waiting for me in the doctor's office parking lot. I opened the door and got inside and said nothing. I had a ghastly look on my face that made him curious.

"Well, what did the doctor say?" My dad asked concernedly.

Hesitantly and almost terrified, I uttered, "I'm pregnant."

My dad paused for a brief moment and then finally responded. "…In…In the family way??" He asked as his voice inflected significantly.

In retrospect now, it's a bit comical, but then it was far from. I sat there with quiet affirmation.

"I…I….I…I'll just be damned!" He managed to get out. "Well, who's the baby's father?" He asked.

I told him it was Tyrone.

Dare to Dream

"Tyrone? Eva Jean's boy? The boy who's with Doug Anthony all the time?" He asked in shock.

"Yes..." I replied, somewhat ashamed.

It was complete silence. I just looked at him. When he looked at me, it was as if he was seeing straight to my soul. Everything in my body at that moment felt numb. I could see the disappointment and hurt on his face as if he had somehow not done his due diligence as a father.

"We're going down to that boy's house to talk to him!" He said.

"No, we're not!" I said emphatically, hoping to avoid any further embarrassment.

Adamantly and authoritatively, my dad told me, "Yea, we are! If you love him enough to lay up with him, you love him enough to marry him."

"Marry him?!" I thought.

I was fifteen and having sex—I wasn't ready to be a wife!

"I don't love him." I anxiously retorted.

Now granted, I *did* love Tyrone, but again, "fifteen-year-old love," not "spend my life with you" type of love.

"Why buy the cow when you can get all the milk you want for free?" My father hastily snapped back.

My forehead and eyebrows furrowed a bit as all I could confusedly respond with was, "What?"

His choice of analogy was over my head at the time. He looked at me and replied, "The decisions you make today will ultimately affect your tomorrow—right or wrong, good or bad—every decision you make will affect someone else—this is not just about you."

He didn't know it then, but his words in that moment stuck with me. That was one piece of advice that always stayed with me, and he was so right.

"Edna Mae, Edna Mae, Edna Mae," my father lamented, saying my mother's name as if she was present. "What am I going to do with these girls?"

The car ride was unbearably silent, and I could feel my father's hurt and dismay. He hadn't yelled, but I could clearly sense his heartbreak. It was literally the worst feeling that I had ever felt. I was more devastated than I had been in losing my mother. I had never seen this look of disappointment on his face before. Out of all of the stunts and manipulations I had ever pulled in my life up until that point, I had never witnessed visible hurt that I caused him like telling him I was pregnant. It rocked my world.

On top of that, his words warning me about the consequences of my decisions haunted me. Up until that point, every decision I had made was all about me and my world. I was young and selfish. I felt that I had that right. I always felt that I had been rendered an injustice with my mother leaving me in death. This time, however, I wasn't the victim that I preferred to identify as. It seemed like time had stopped. There I was for the first time, faced with the reality of my actions. I got silent and didn't say anything else for the remainder of the ride.

We drove up to Tyrone's house, got out of the car and knocked on the door. One of his siblings opened the door and told us to come in. My father and I went inside. Tyrone was in his family's kitchen and only saw me at first. Then, he laid eyes on my father. Tyrone's eyes grew big. He looked at me and then at my dad.

"Is everything okay?" He asked, looking back and forth at both of us and then to me.

"Yea," I replied quickly, even though I knew in the back of my mind that this moment was about to be a complete disaster.

"Is your mom home?" My father asked.

"Yes," Tyrone said with an unsure look.

"I need to speak to you and your mother." My father said in a stern voice.

"Okay," Tyrone said as he turned to head towards the door of his mom's room.

As he was approaching her door, she was already coming out as she had heard our voices followed by the knock at her front door.

"Mr. Woody wants to talk to us," Tyrone told her.

Our families knew one another, so having a conversation wasn't anything out of the ordinary.

"Okay." His mother said lightly.

My dad and I were seated on the couch, Tyrone was sitting in a chair, and his mother sat on a loveseat. My dad looked at me.

"Would you like to tell them, or you want me to tell them?" He asked in a slightly chastising tone.

"I will," I said.

I fought back another round of tears as I told them about my doctor's appointment.

"I went to see Dr. Chambers today because I had been feeling sick and thought I was fighting a summer cold. But…Dr. Chambers said I was pregnant." I stumbled to get the words out at first, but as soon as I got them out, my tears broke.

Tyrone sat there and looked as if a Mach truck had hit him in his gut. His eyes were wide, and his face looked chalky. If it had to be put into words, it would have translated into, *"What the f**k?"* The look on his face wasn't disappointment—it was more like fear and like a million things were running through his mind as he processed it. My father, on the other hand, still maintained this visible sense of disappointment. Here I was, sitting in a room with two of the most important men in my life, and my world was crumbling down around me. I sobbed harder as Tyrone's mom got up to come and sit beside me. I was crying hysterically.

"It's going to be okay." She said, trying to console me.

"Eva Jean, this is *not* going to be okay." My dad said as he looked at Tyrone's mom outraged.

It was among the few times in my entire life that I had ever seen my dad be so stern and direct. She hugged me and looked at my father matter-of-factly.

"Well, Woodrow, what did you think they were doing with all the time they were spending together? Holding hands?" Tyrone's mother asked as she suspected how close Tyrone and I were ever since the summer prior.

As she said that, I could see his mind processing her words. My father was the only one who was late to the party.

"How long have you and this boy been seeing one another?" He asked demandingly.

I mumbled and stumbled out that we had been seeing one another for a year or so. He sat there dumbfounded.

"Well, I think y'all have been going together looong enough to know if y'all want to be together. Evidently, you do. So, my decision is, I think y'all should get married." My father said most seriously.

He was from the old school and didn't believe in the modern leniency of things like "shacking up" or having children outside of wedlock.

"Wait a minute." Tyrone's mother said, interjecting. "This is not a decision that needs to be made today, and we're not the ones to make it. Regardless of how you feel or how I feel, they need to make this decision."

My father objected. "Yes, it does. She's not old enough to make this decision; she's a kid!" He said.

"When the doctor told her that she's going to be a mother, she left that space of being a child, Woodrow." Tyrone's mother said, contesting what he said rationally.

Dare to Dream

My father looked over at Tyrone, who up until now was utterly silent.

"Well, what do you have to say, Tyrone? You're the oldest and should have known better!" My dad quizzed. Tyrone's mother interjected again.

"No, now you're not going to blame all of this on Tyrone. Leigh had just as much to do with this as he did." His mother said.

She defended her son as any mother would, yet still maintained neutrality that didn't vilify me. Tyrone spoke up.

"I just want to talk to Leigh," Tyrone said.

He said it in such a way that I was unsure of how our conversation was going to go. I didn't know if it would turn to yelling or if he was just going to plead a case of denial. He looked as if he wanted to bolt out the door, and I remember feeling insecure about it. My dad looked at him as if to oblige the talk taking place right that instant.

"Mom, Mr. Woody, I'd like to talk to her alone."

My dad glared at him. If looks could kill, Tyrone would have at least been strangled.

"Okay, y'all probably do need some time to talk." His mother said.

My dad looked at me.

"Are you going to be okay?" My dad asked, as I could sense he had no real intentions of having to leave me there.

I assured him that I would.

"I'll make sure she gets home safe," Tyrone said.

My dad looked at him for a few moments longer. I can only imagine what his thoughts towards Tyrone were in that moment. But he finally agreed and turned to walk out of the door. Tyrone's mother went back to her room.

"Come on, let's go back here and talk." He said as I followed him to his bedroom.

He shut the door behind us, and I was terrified of how the conversation was going to go. His quietness during the whole ordeal in the living room left me to wonder what exactly was going through his mind. We both sat down on his bed and started to talk.

"I thought you had started taking birth control?" Tyrone asked.

When our sex had become regular, I went ahead and told him that the doctor had placed me on it. I guess that further gave him assurance that we were in the clear to continue having unprotected sex. I told him what the doctor had said about my dosage and began to cry again. He put his arms around me.

"Stop crying," he said. "I can't stand to see you cry like that. We're going to figure it out."

I still felt scared.

"Do you want to get married?" He asked.

"No!" I said adamantly. "I think we're both too young for that. I have to finish school, I don't want to live here for the rest of my life, and I have to graduate." I defended.

"So, you don't want to have the baby?" He asked. "You have to help me out here—I don't know what you want to do."

We both fell silent. My mind raced. I thought about my future, his future, and the possibility of being stuck in this little town for the rest of my life. I also couldn't help but think that just a few weeks ago, Tyrone had just popped me in the face and gave me a black eye. We weren't even fully back together as a couple yet. I was still scared of him. Sometimes when he would touch me, I'd cringe; especially when he'd been drinking. I had learned to get nervous whenever his payday came around on Thursdays, as he and Mo would spend the first of their paycheck getting drunk. And when he was drunk, he was another person. Thinking about being pregnant against the backdrop of all these facts made me incredibly scared and uneasy. It was a lot of pressure for a fifteen-year-old girl to bear.

"We're going to figure this out." He repeated. "I'm not going to leave you—I'm going to be here."

I believed that he loved me, and I believed that he would be there, but in the back of my mind, I also knew that I was scared. I felt comfortable in his words for that moment, but all the while, I somehow knew my life was about to change forever.

CHAPTER 3

Mommy to Be

I was fifteen, pregnant and unmarried, in high school. In the midst of being preoccupied with experiencing my pregnancy, all I could think about was, *"I gotta graduate high school."* In my family, that was a given. You got out of school and went straight to college. That was understood straight from the beginning.

My parents were big on education. My mother was the only child of twelve who went to college and got her degree. She went to the historically black college of Philander Smith. This only furthered the advocacy for school in my mother's eyes, and my father shared the same view. They viewed education as the equalizer—the one thing that could actually get you through the door when the odds were set up to keep you from the door altogether. Needless to say, me not finishing high school on time was not an option for my father, let alone dropping out.

I started thinking about all the things I should have thought about before becoming pregnant. I remember wishing I had stuck to my guns when it came to not having sex with Tyrone. I considered how much this might affect my future—graduating on time and navigating my plans for my life post-high school—much of which I hadn't even really thought about, up until this point. I even remember wondering, *"How would I have been able to tell my mother this?"* Whenever I had a quiet moment to think, usually when I was home alone or up at night restless, I would often think to myself, *"Oh my God, what do I do now?"*

It seemed like as soon as I found out I was pregnant, my symptoms kicked into overdrive. I was throwing up all times of the day and night. In order to get out of bed, I had to have crackers or toast by my bedside and was always exhausted. Tyrone experienced morning sickness too. I started making regular doctor appointments with Dr. Chambers, and Tyrone would accompany me to every one. When it came to responsibility and financing, he could be counted upon. He insisted on paying for my appointments out-of-pocket so that I wouldn't be on my dad's insurance. He promised that he would do everything that I needed to do when it was time.

As heavy-hearted as my father was that I was having a baby, he would have been even more heavy-hearted if I had made the decision to have an abortion. Though the thought crossed my mind, I didn't have enough background information on the procedure to know where to begin. In fact, when the nurse came to talk to me the day the doctor told me that I was pregnant, abortion wasn't even presented to me as one of the options. Maybe because it was the eighties and the topic was still taboo. Maybe it was because I lived in a small town. Whatever the reason, I didn't know who to talk to or where to go to even proceed in that manner. So, with all of the alternative options off of the table, it was settled that Tyrone and I were going to be parents.

Tyrone was working constantly, so he was tired all of the time. When he wasn't working, he wanted to hang out. I, on the other hand, started to gain weight fairly quickly. When Tyrone and I made the decision to keep our baby, our levels of responsibility ramped up drastically. I no longer had the luxury of receiving parts of my father's paycheck on Thursdays.

"Since you've made the decision to be grown, I'm going to let you be grown," he said. "That includes paying your own bills, buying your own clothes, buying your own groceries—if you want to be grown, I'm going to let you."

When my dad initially told me this, I believe he wanted it to be a scare tactic. He wanted me to come to my senses and realize that depending on an 18-year old to take care of me and our soon-to-come baby was not a surefire foundation for security. In actuality, he wanted me to stay on his insurance and proposed to me the idea of he and Dorothy adopting my baby once it was born.

"No, Daddy, that won't work," I told him somewhat frustrated.

He was angered at my response. Though I was fifteen and didn't have all the answers, I knew that wasn't the best decision. First off, Dorothy wasn't my mother and was not about to adopt my baby—and she had six kids of her own—she probably didn't want to. Secondly, my father was in his sixties. Suppose something happened to him down the line and I'd have to jump through legal hoops to get my own kid back. Third, that plan totally disregarded Tyrone and his say-so. My father felt like I was making a mistake relying on Tyrone, but it wasn't his decision to make. I told Tyrone what my father said.

"I'm going to take care of it." Tyrone would say.

He was the kind of person who didn't want to be indebted to anyone and also didn't want to come across as a deadbeat in my father's eyes. He began to stay more frequently at my house, and my dad maintained his routine of staying at Dorothy's. Whenever my father was around, I reassured him that I was fine when all the while I was actually sick physically and overwhelmed emotionally.

As the summer went along, I became increasingly unhappy in my relationship with Tyrone. Tyrone worked a lot, and when he was off work, he wanted to hang out with Mo or his other friends, drink, and even started to gamble. His responsibilities preceded his age. He was

18 with a pregnant girlfriend and maintaining bills in a household. He wanted to live the life of the average non-committed eighteen-year-old, even though his life bore great responsibility. Needless to say, my experimenting with sex and ending up pregnant left a bad taste in my mouth about sex altogether. After becoming pregnant, I lost immediate interest in having sex.

I didn't lose interest in Tyrone, but I had discovered that sex in and of itself—at least under my circumstances at the time— was over glorified. All of my nerves and hesitation about having sex had been justified in an instant, it seemed. I didn't understand it. I knew lots of people my age who were having sex, and lots of it, without becoming pregnant, and here I was "knocked up" after my first few experiences. Another reason I didn't care to have it was because I was sick all the time and wasn't in the mood, anyway. I slept a lot and was barely able to get up. On top of my physical ailments, I was constantly tormented in my mind about what I was going to do when school started, how I had hurt my father, how I had embarrassed my family by becoming pregnant so young, and how I was going to be as a mother. I started to feel my feelings towards Tyrone change. The feelings of being head over heels and wanting to be up under him all the time in playful and devout intimacy were slowly but surely waning. I became withdrawn and distant. On his end, similar thoughts must have been taking place as he too became distant and changed. He was going to all of my appointments, paying for the bills in my house, and embracing this instant responsibility that he had got himself into.

I was fifteen, so I couldn't even go out and get a job; this meant the financial responsibility was solely on him. Here he was, eighteen and having to pause his own dreams and potential aspirations for being a family man before he was ready. It boiled down to the fact that we both were in a relationship that we felt obligated to be in. We both came from these broken worlds that we didn't want repeated for our child. Tyrone's biological mom and dad had gotten a divorce, and the effects of not having his birth father around always weighed on his heart. He loved his stepfather, but growing up, a part of him always longed for the affirmation and presence of his real father. On my end, my mother was dead, so I, of course, wanted a traditional family setting for the child I was about to bring into the world.

Of course, my not wanting to have sex with Tyrone started to take a toll on things also. One summer later, and our relationship was unrecognizable. The things we enjoyed doing together, we no longer did. Things like going to the carnival, riding around on Friday nights, hanging out with him if he went to play cards, us running together after he would get through working out, going to our town's annual Tomato Festival, taking walks—all the things that we did while young in love—came to a subtle halt. Half the time, I wasn't feeling good anyway, so he stopped asking me to come along to places and spent more of his time out and about. This was about the time that things changed between us. He would stay out later and later, was less affectionate, and would frequently tell me stories that wouldn't add up with the truth. For instance, he would say that he was out with Mo, and I'd see Mo later without him. He would come in late, make excuses, and I felt like I was nagging him when all the while I really didn't trust him.

On one particular Friday night in the summer, Tyrone left and said that he was going to hang out with Mo. Around ten that night, I heard Mo's car pull up across the street in his driveway. I waited for about thirty minutes to an hour, anticipating Tyrone to walk through the door. At first, I assumed they were just drinking or talking, but the more time pressed on, I grew curious as to what was taking him so long to come into the house. I got up, got dressed and went over to Mo's house and knocked on the door. All the lights were off, which

I thought strange if he and Tyrone were inside, hanging out. Mo opened the door.

"Hey, what's up, come on in." He said per his usual routine of my stopping by.

I walked into the house and looked around.

"Hey. Where's Tyrone?" I asked.

His face furrowed in thought like he was confused.

"I don't know," Mo said. "The last time I saw him, he was with you."

Tyrone hadn't taken the time to cover his bases, and Mo wasn't prepared to lie for him. I could tell because when I asked where he was, the look of confusion on Mo's face was genuine. Realizing too late the lie that he was thrown into, he attempted to cover for him.

"I don't know where he is." Mo supplemented.

Even if he didn't know exactly where he was, *I knew he knew where he probably was.* I knew he was lying and kept pressing for the truth.

"Stop lying. You're his best friend. I know you know where he is, so where is he?!" I demanded.

Mo normally looked me in the eye during conversations and was avoiding eye contact as I quizzed him. He kept maintaining that he didn't know. I began to cry and asked why he wouldn't tell me. Since Mo and I had our own friendship, my crying seemed to weigh on his conscious. I cried, begged and pleaded, but he refused.

"Don't lie. Tell me where he is!" I said.

Mo sighed and fell silent briefly. He knew my inquisition wouldn't end until he told me something.

"I know something is going on—I know he's seeing somebody, he's different," I said.

I asked him one final time if he knew where Tyrone was, and he finally confessed that he did.

"I don't think anything is going on, but he's been hanging out with this girl who's in town from California, visiting her family." Mo offered.

I began to cry again as my worst suspicion was indeed true. The man I loved was betraying me. I wasn't sure what I was going to do with the confirmed information, but I knew I was going to confront him somehow.

"Don't cry, man, it's going to be okay," Mo said, trying to console me.

I stood there as tears mixed with sadness and anger fell from my face. I was livid.

"This is something that you don't need to deal with in your cond—."

"Goodnight Mo."

I said cutting him off abruptly as I opened his front door and left to walk back to my house. I was so angry at him that I didn't want his comfort at all. I was fuming on so many different levels. I was mad that Mo had kept such a secret for so long and felt betrayed by him. Would he have told me had I not kept pressuring him? Probably not. I think it was the first time that I realized, although we were all friends, that Mo's loyalty was to Tyrone. My mind raced of nights gone by wondering had Mo known about other girls, or other instances, and whether or not the one he had just told me about had been going on for longer than what he said. I was upset with Tyrone for lying to me, especially given the circumstances of us expecting a child together. I got home and sat on the couch in our den and waited for Tyrone to come home, which had now become the norm. I turned on the TV, hoping that I could distract myself from being so emotional. As far as I was concerned, Mo was a liar, Tyrone was a liar, and I only felt more alone not having anyone I could truly trust or confide in. My weeping subsided long enough for me to finally fall asleep on the couch, still awaiting Tyrone's arrival home.

Around 7 am, Tyrone finally came home drunk. His arrival woke me up. He acted as if nothing was wrong as he came in the door and walked past my empty bedroom to the den where I was.

"What you doing on the couch?" He asked. "Why aren't you in bed?"

I stood up and stared him down.

"Waiting on you," I said sharply. "Where have you been all night?" I asked.

"What you mean where I been? I told you where I was." He said. "Mo and I went out, had a few drinks and went to play cards and gamble. We lost track of time." He said defensively.

"No, you're lying, you weren't out with Mo—I saw him last night, and he hadn't seen you since earlier in the day."

He tried to keep a straight face but was growing mad the more I began to interrogate him.

"Why you questioning me? We're not married. I don't have to answer to you." He said.

I began to act a fool.

"You're right we're not married, but we live in a house together, and I'm tired of you staying out all night." I snapped back.

I then wasted no time in telling him where I suspected he was.

"So, you mean to tell me you weren't out hanging with some girl from California all night?" I yelled in his face.

He tried to play it cool, even though I knew he was shocked I offered up such a detailed fact.

"What? What the hell you talking about?" He argued. "What were you doing at Mo's house, anyway?" He asked with an accusatory tone. "You don't need to be over there questioning my best friend about my whereabouts. You just need to stay home and wait on me!" He said, trying to throw me off from my initial question.

"Who's the girl, and why are you seeing her?" I continued.

"I don't know what you're talking about, ain't no damn girl." He said, becoming more angry and defensive. "That's some bullshit that Mo done put in your head."

Whether he knew it or not, that confirmed it for me. I had never said that Mo told me anything, so he had basically told on himself.

"I told you where I was, you either believe me or you don't." He said.

He tried to throw me off further by saying my nagging was why he stayed out gambling all night—anything to try and take the heat off of him. By this time, I'm yelling and crying hysterically, and he seemed altogether unphased by the seriousness of my being upset. Here I was, confronting him about cheating, and he couldn't seem to care less.

"I'm not about to deal with this shit. You ain't my wife." He said, turning to leave the den.

Scared that he was going to leave me, I panicked and followed behind him, trying to plead for answers. Even though he was the one who was clearly in the wrong, I didn't want to push him away—especially not into the arms of another girl. Not only that, but he was all I had to depend on. I couldn't go to my dad, my sisters had no clue about the details of what was going on between us, my brother was in Michigan, and my mother was dead. I felt hopeless.

"We need to talk about this." I pleaded as I walked behind him. "Don't leave. I'm sorry I didn't believe you about where you were last night!" I said in hopes that he would stop in his tracks and realize that he was the one that was at fault.

He should have been the one apologizing, but I was desperate for him to stay. He got to the door, opened it and walked out. I began to cry harder as I fell down to my knees in the doorway and watched him get into his car and drive off. At that moment, I realized that Tyrone had the upper hand in our situation. He had the money. He had a car to come and go as he pleased—and I didn't even have a license. I started to take stock of the situation as it was happening, and part of my tears were from realizing that I didn't want this kind of life for myself and my unborn child. Here I was, in a relationship with a man whose love for me was now questionable, when my love for him was never in doubt.

Furthermore, in the back of my mind, I was haunted by all the warnings and words that my father had said to me about my situation. He didn't have a problem with me having my baby, but he didn't agree with my depending on Tyrone to take care of me. I realized I was in over my head for my age and felt trapped like never before.

The summer was winding down, and it was time for me to get ready to start my sophomore year and my second trimester of pregnancy. As I began school, I was scared, felt alone and was ashamed. I was too big to sit behind the desks by now so had to sit at tables in most classes by myself. I kept myself up as far as my hygiene and appearance went, but my self-esteem had unraveled. My classmates seemed to shy away from me—or at least, that's how I felt. I looked around and felt that I had nothing in common with any of them—not even my own niece, Tammy, who was in the same grade. Our lives were drastically different. She was living the life of a regular high schooler like I should have been. Instead, I was an expectant mother in a relationship, enduring physical and emotional abuse. I was mentally and physically exhausted, angry, embarrassed, and frightened. I was frightened because I never knew what would trigger the next argument or fall out, nor to the extent that it would go. Maybe even more than that, I was scared of my father finding out. Our fighting was regular, but he had no knowledge of it. While in high school, I

Mommy to Be

knew for a fact that two of my older sisters, Sue-Baby, who was married to Ira Joe, and Trish Ann who still had her longtime boyfriend Otis, who was a small-town drug dealer, both dealt with abuse in their relationships.

I remember one of them living by the mantra that she'd fall asleep dressed and ready to roll. I interpreted this as her being ready for an out from her situation; to be prepared to leave her husband at a moment's notice if courage prompted her. My dad knew about my sisters' abusive situations and would come to their aid, ready to shoot their suitors! He didn't play about his daughters, and their fiascos were all the example that I needed to keep me and Tyrone's drama to myself. As I looked back on it over the years, I was bothered and almost shocked at how my sisters and I all managed to experience some form of abuse in romantic relationships. Sue-Baby, Trish Ann and myself experienced physical abuse, and Carla endured some emotional abuse.

I rekindled my friendship with Alice, Tyrone's cousin, which was good for me to have someone that I felt like I could talk to and trust. I didn't feel like I was being judged by her like I did when I was around our other peers. On top of that, she had no problem siding with me when it came to the drama between Tyrone and I.

Around my other family members, and Tyrone's as well, I pretended everything was okay whenever I was around. In reality, I felt ashamed and embarrassed. The things I had formerly identified with—dating this high school jock, being desired, and feeling more mature than my classmates, I no longer cared about. Tyrone and I were hardly out together anymore. He continued to be there financially, but not emotionally. My morning sickness wasn't as prevalent in my second trimester, but I still would have episodes from time to time. Our physical intimacy all but ceased. Because he was staying out all night, I knew that if we weren't having sex together, he was having sex with someone else. I didn't have any proof of whether or not it was the same girl from California, but I knew one way or the other, things had changed between us.

Tyrone would do just enough to appease my insecurity and make me feel like he was still into me. We would have sex sporadically when he wanted to, and part of me felt obligated to do so. He was, after all, paying all of our bills, and in spite of the things he was putting me through, I loved him deeply. In fact, I seemed to love him more than life itself and was willing to put up with just about anything, it seemed, to keep him around. I committed to focus more on school and tried not to nag him so much about his whereabouts. Since I was holding my tongue more, he seemed to try and subtly butter up to me as if nothing was ever wrong between us. It was now fall, and the annual Warren homecoming game was coming up. For a few weeks, things between us had seemed to be getting back to normal—if my life at this point even had a normal. I came home from school one day and mentioned to him that the homecoming game was that week.

"You wanna go?" He asked.

Feeling excited that my old Tyrone was back, I eagerly said yes and looked forward to the coming weekend. It was normal during homecoming week for the boyfriends or fathers of high school girls to order corsages—whether wrist ones or the pin-on kind—to be delivered that Friday of homecoming during school hours. I was in Mr. Davis's social studies class when there was a knock at the door, and Mr. Davis's teaching assistant got up to answer it. When he came back in, he walked towards me with a clear container that had a corsage in it. *"To Leigh, from Tyrone."* I beamed from ear to ear as I was shocked that Tyrone thought to order me one. I looked forward to school being out and was all the more excited to be going to the game with him later that night.

As usual, I got out of school before Tyrone got home from work. When he arrived, I greeted him with a big hug and kiss and thanked him for my surprise corsage at school.

"You're welcome." He said with a smile, followed by an "I love you."

He told me to go get dressed for the game as the kickoff was happening soon. I got dressed, and he took the corsage out of the box and pinned it to my blouse. When he kissed me, I couldn't help but notice the taste of alcohol on his breath. He had apparently stopped somewhere to have himself a drink before coming home, and by now, it was a usual happening for his weekend. Throughout the week, he would drink occasionally, but once the weekend came, it was almost a certainty that he would drink, one way or the other. He drank both beer and hard liquor, and his personality would alter, depending on how much alcohol he drank. He was like the character in Dr. Jekyll and Mr. Hyde. When he wasn't drinking, he was predominantly reserved and quiet—almost shy. When he did drink, his personality became more extroverted. Though his drinking overall was not ideal, I had to admit that there were pros and cons to when he did drink.

On one hand, when it came to me, he seemed to be more affectionate and playful if he had been drinking lightly. When we went to the game, for example, he was outwardly affectionate to me in public, and it was validating for me. I felt like the old Tyrone was back as he held my hand and was protective of me the entire night. Even so, the downside to his drinking was his aptitude for acting out on his anger more quickly. In that moment, however, I was reaping the benefits from the loving Tyrone, and I didn't want anything to disrupt the lighthearted time that we were having. After the game was over, we returned home, and I looked forward to spending the rest of the evening in for the night. As I changed into my nightclothes, I noticed that he was still dressed with no apparent intention to change.

"Are you about to go out?" I asked, thinking surely, he would want to continue the great night we were having.

"I'm just going to go out and have a few drinks—I won't be gone long." He replied.

I didn't want to nag, but I couldn't help but wonder why he wanted to go out when things seemed to be going so ideally for both of us that evening.

"Well, I'll get dressed and just come along with you—it'll be fun like old times," I suggested.

"Nah, you stay here and rest. I'll be back before long, I promise."

I felt tears well up in my eyes as I slowly realized the evening we just shared hadn't really changed our overall status quo. He looked at me and became annoyed.

"Man, don't start that nagging." He said as he started walking towards the door.

I followed behind him and began to plead.

"You don't need to go out tonight, just stay at home with me," I said.

It had been such a long time since we had gone out together and had a good time that I didn't want it to end and couldn't for the life of me understand how he did. I grabbed his arm for him to stay, and he turned, looked me in the face and jerked his arm from my grasp. When he did so, it caused me to lose my balance, and I slipped on our rug and fell.

"Look at you; you're going to mess around and hurt yourself!" He said in a way that made me feel small and desperate.

He helped me back up to my feet, and I could see on his face that he was becoming angry. For a moment, I was reminded of the feeling of fear that I had that night he had blackened my eye.

"Whatever, just go on, bye!" I said, trying to prevent him from getting angrier or the situation from escalating beyond that.

Mommy to Be

He left out of the door, and on top of my sadness, I realized my cramping sensation was coming back. Throughout my pregnancy, I had never stopped having periods in the first place. Feeling defeated and once again alone, I got in bed and went to sleep. At this point, it was no use worrying about where he was going or what he was doing. I couldn't do anything about it and felt stuck between a rock and a hard place.

The next day, I was in a lot of pain. I was alone the entire weekend and in pain. My cramps intensified, and when I went to the bathroom, I noticed that I was spotting. I expected my period to come in the next few days and climbed back in bed. The next morning, Tyrone came to the house to change his clothes so that he could go to work. He had picked up a part-time seasonal job for the weekends, which meant even more time that he would be absent from our home. All the while he was home, I pretended I was still asleep, as one, I didn't feel well, and two, I didn't want an argument or dramatic session to unfold.

After he was dressed, he left, and I stayed in bed most of the day as my cramps got worse. It wasn't really out of the norm since my cramps were always intense, even pre-pregnancy. Of course, that evening, Tyrone didn't even bother to come home. The stereotypical tales about the joys of being pregnant, I couldn't relate to. I was lonely, my symptoms were intense, and the man that should have been by my side through all of it could only be counted upon financially. Being fifteen, I couldn't adequately communicate what all I needed from him, but I knew it was more than what he was giving. Though he had work on Sunday morning, he didn't come home to change for it. I didn't see him again until Sunday evening after he got off of work. I was in so much pain and discomfort that I barely took notice to him being there at all.

"Are you feeling any better? He asked.

Dare to Dream

"No, but it will probably pass," I told him.

My period typically only lasted for three to four days, so I'd wait things out and see how I felt afterward.

When Monday came, I was still in too much pain to go to school. Tyrone had got up to begin getting dressed for work, and I was still lyings in bed.

"How do you feel today? Tyrone asked.

"The same—not good," I replied.

He asked me whether or not I was going to school, and I told him that I would just stay home in hopes that the feeling would subside.

"Are you sure you didn't hurt yourself from falling the other night?" He asked concernedly.

Knowing my body, I assured him that my pain was probably just normal period symptoms. He told me that he would be back to check on me at lunchtime, kissed me goodbye and left.

Staying in bed made me feel more depressed, so I decided to get up and be active. In the kitchen, there was a sink full of dishes that I wasn't able to get to during the weekend, so I did those, and afterwards got in some normal reading time. I liked to frequently read out loud to my belly so my baby would have an alternate soundtrack, other than Tyrone and me arguing—which we seemed to do a lot these days. It didn't really matter what I read, whether homework or magazine articles, I just wanted to be purposeful in establishing an early bond with my baby. It seemed so strange that I could separate my negative feelings about being pregnant with my excitement about having my baby.

By now, I'm feeling my baby move, and I grew excited to discover the sex when it was time to deliver. By this time, I'd begun feeling my baby move, and I grew excited to discover the sex when it was time to deliver. Back then, the technology for revealing baby gender wasn't prevalent or at least wasn't a perk that Tyrone and I could afford. So I just anticipated what I was having and had a name ready, either way. Alice, who I had asked to be my baby's godmother, helped me pick out names. If it was a boy, he was going to be Tyrone Jr., and if it was a girl, she was going to be Tyronica.

Tuesday came, and I still wasn't feeling well. Instead of bleeding lighter as if my period was ending, my bleeding had become heavier. I called Dr. Chambers' office and told his nurse what was going on. She told me to go ahead and prepare to come in that morning. I told Tyrone, and he made arrangements to call off of work for that morning and took me to the doctor. Having a high tolerance for pain, any time I opted to go to the doctor was noteworthy. I was in so much pain that I couldn't even walk. Tyrone picked me up and put me in the car and drove me to our appointment. Upon arriving and seeing Dr. Chambers, we found out that I was in premature labor. He told me that I had dilated 2 or 3 centimeters and that my mucus plug had passed. This was one of the common signs that women experienced before going into labor.

"You're going to have to go on bed rest because once you're dilated to 5, I won't be able to stop your baby from coming." Dr. Chambers said.

He gave me some medication, and Tyrone brought me back home. He put me in bed and placed things like water, juice, and crackers by my bedside. Tyrone asked me if I would be okay at home alone until he was off of work and I told him that I would. I guess he felt guilty for what had transpired days earlier as he apologized for leaving me in the house all alone that weekend.

"I'm sorry for leaving you here by yourself." He said. "I was so angry at you for not believing or trusting me."

"Well, where were you?" I asked.

He told me that he was out gambling. For some reason, my heart wanted to believe that there was truth to what he had said. Here I was, six months pregnant with his baby—I needed to believe it. Outside of the fact that he had come home smelling like booze and perfume that night, I opted to believe what he said. He kissed me and left, promising to return during his lunch break.

Wednesday, Thursday, and Friday, I still felt the same. By this point, I'd missed a week of school. Dr. Chambers provided me with a doctor's excuse that I passed on to Alice to give to the school office for me. I was grateful for her during this time. She stopped by the house daily after school with my homework assignments and to keep me company. She knew the extent of me and Tyrone's problems and even knew about my bed rest and the fall. Though he had been home during the weekday nights, once Friday night came, Tyrone wanted to go out again to drink with friends, or so he said. I stopped making a fuss about his going out altogether as I was tired of everything at this point. I was tired of being pregnant, I was tired of being lonely, and I was tired of having to wonder where we stood as far as our relationship went. All I knew was that I was about to become a mother in less than three months, and it was time for me to start shifting my focus on this life that was growing inside of me. I had to start making a mental choice about the kind of mother I was going to be.

I was either going to be the kind of mother who ran behind a man, trying to hold on to him and all the while, slighting her child, or I was going to be the kind of mother my baby deserved to have. The whole weekend passed by and Tyrone hadn't so much as called or set foot in our house. It was the longest stint of not coming home that he had ever pulled. Though the doctor ordered me on complete bed rest, I was home the entire weekend by myself and had to get up and do basic things like showering, preparing myself meals, etc. Normally, I could expect a drop by from my sister Sue-Baby on Saturdays and Sundays to check on me. Since she hadn't, I knew that meant she was working that weekend.

My father had come by during the week as normal, but this particular weekend, he hadn't stopped by the house, either. As far as my other sisters went, since Tyrone basically lived with me, our family house had now become my house. They didn't stop by unannounced like they used to, and of course, had their own drama in their own relationships.

Late that Sunday evening, Tyrone popped up at home like he hadn't been gone for days. Unbeknownst to him, I had done a lot of thinking that weekend. I made up in my mind what version of mother I was going to be and refused to be strung out over him. I heard him the entire time but laid there, continuing to pretend to be asleep. He climbed into bed, put his arms around me, and I remember feeling numb. He had obviously been lying his head elsewhere the entire weekend, and now, all of a sudden, was coming home again, acting as if nothing was wrong. At this point, I felt like I was just biding my time. I only had one more trimester to be pregnant, and once my baby was here, that's all that would matter.

The next morning, he woke up to get ready for work. I felt him get out of bed and laid there motionless so I wouldn't have to interact with him. He kissed me on my forehead and left. As far as I was concerned, it didn't matter one way or another whether we had interaction or not.

We both were just going through the motions. He had two separate lives that he was living—one at home with me and the other in streets doing who knows what with who knows who. I made it through an entire weekend without him, and as far as I was concerned, I could make it through the rest of the pregnancy the same way. Later that day, he came home during his lunch break. I heard him enter the door while I was in the den watching television. He went for the kitchen, which was near the den, and opened the refrigerator to make himself a sandwich. He glanced over at me on the couch and asked how I was feeling.

"Fine," I said, intentionally keeping my words short.

He fixed his sandwich and came in the den where I was and sat down to eat. He touched my belly lovingly and asked again how I was feeling. I gave him the same answer.

"I'm fine," I said as I continued to watch TV.

His break was only 30 minutes, so he finished his food, kissed me goodbye, and got ready to leave again.

"Oh yea, when I get off, I've got to go down to my mom's house for a little while."

I glanced at him. "Okay. I'll see you later, then," I said dryly as he exited the door and left.

Later that evening around 8 p.m. when he hadn't come home yet, I called down to his mother's house. His younger sister, Katie, answered.

"Is Tyrone there?" I asked.

"No." She said.

I told her okay and hung up the phone. In the back of my mind, from the moment he told me where he was going to be, earlier that day, I knew he was lying. My intuition somehow needed validation, though, so I called. It was becoming routine for me to go to bed alone, so I did just that. He didn't come home until later that night after I had fallen asleep.

The next morning was a repeat. He got up to get dressed, went to work, came home during break and told me he was going to his mother's house and left. During this day, my pain was creeping back on me. I had been taking the medicine that Dr. Chambers had advised, but I, of course, wasn't on complete bed rest as he ordered. By eight o'clock that evening, my pain was unbearable. I called down to Tyrone's mother's house so that I could reach him and let him know

I needed to go to the hospital. When I called, however, the line was busy. For the next two hours, I repeatedly tried to get through but had no luck. I kept getting a busy signal. I would have gone to Sue-Baby's house, but Ira Joe worked at night and had his car. I needed someone who could get me to the hospital and fast. I got up to get dressed and couldn't think of anything else to do besides walk down to Tyrone's mother's house. The house was at least a half a mile down the street.

Though the distance never bothered me before, on this particular night when I was in as much pain as I was, it seemed like it took me an hour to make it down there. When I got to the door, I knocked on it and then opened it. His sister Rita was there and came to the door. I was crying from pain and asked,

"Where's Tyrone?"

Seeing my state, she became concerned.

"Well, he's not here." She said. "Are you okay?"

I told her that I was in premature labor and needed to go to the hospital.

"Ok, let's go." She said as she realized this was an emergency.

She grabbed her keys and helped me to the car as we headed to Bradley County Memorial Hospital. When we arrived at the emergency room and told them what was going on, they admitted me immediately. Rita sat in the waiting room and told me that she wouldn't go anywhere.

"I'll try and find Tyrone, and I'll call Mr. Woody and let him know what's going on." She said.

My dad had been coming home and checking on me throughout the week, but I didn't tell him anything about my bed rest. The only people who knew were Tyrone and Alice. Rita tried to reassure me as I thanked her, and the nurses wheeled me back to an emergency room. I was scared to death. I cried the entire time, it seemed. I could scale it back to a sniffle at some points, but during others, I was full-blown boohooing. Dr. Chambers was not on duty that night, but they informed me that they would call him. The doctor who was on duty, however, was the same doctor who had delivered me fifteen years prior—Dr. Wynn. My mom had worked at the hospital as one of his nurses, so he knew me and my family well. Dr. Wynn checked my cervix, and I winced in pain.

"Stop your crying." He said to me sternly. "Something bigger than that has gone up there."

On top of being in pain, I could tell from his tone that I was now being reprimanded. All I could do was cry.

"If Edna were here, you wouldn't even be in this situation." He continued.

Realizing his words probably had some truth, I found myself sulking in self-disappointment. Here I was, fifteen, pregnant and alone. My boyfriend was nowhere to be found and I was in the delivery room with no support system—only the team of doctors and nurses. There was no time to check me into the maternity ward as I had already dilated past 5 centimeters. They had to prepare for my delivery right there in the ER.

"Call Little Rock for an Air Vac and put them on standby." Dr. Wynn said to one of his nurses. "Tell them we have a black female, 15 years in age, 26 weeks gestation delivering premature, and we'll need a unit over here immediately."

I grew scared. In Warren, they didn't have the facilities to take care of a premature infant at my baby's gestational stage. My baby wasn't due until the end of January, and it was the first part of November. There were all kinds of people in the room prepping me for delivery; one person dressed me in a gown, another shaved my private parts, and someone else checked my vitals. Dr. Wynn then ordered someone else to bring an incubator to the room. Tyrone had always made me feel safe and protected; yet now—at the moment I was about to

Mommy to Be

give birth, and needed his reassurance the most—he was nowhere to be found.. I was scared for my child's life. I didn't know much, but I knew it was too early for me to be going into labor. All I kept thinking in my mind was "God, or someone, please help me." I was having contractions but couldn't get any pain medications because the baby was too small and ingesting them would potentially kill my unborn. I had been in labor for days prior, so it didn't take long for me to have my baby.

"Send the helicopter down." The doctor told his team.

My baby was pale and translucent and looked like the alien, E.T.

"It's a girl," the doctor said. "She's 1 pound 9 ounces."

They placed her on my chest, but she wasn't breathing or crying. They immediately took her over to the side table and went to work. My tears ramped up again as I felt so hopeless and alone. Tyrone wasn't there, and only God knew where he was. I had my suspicions, of course, but so much was going on in the moment that I didn't have enough time to dwell on it.

They got my baby to breathe, though I still heard no audible cry or whimper from her. She was immediately airlifted to Children's Hospital in Little Rock, Arkansas, about an hour and a half away. I began to cry hysterically as I still didn't understand what all was going on. The doctor's team told me that they would keep me updated with my baby as they received the information. The doctor ordered that I be placed in a clean gown and in a maternity room. Once in the room, the nurses took my vitals. She told me that since my delivery, I had lost one pound in weight—which was my baby's weight. She gave me a mild sedative through my IV, which helped to calm my nerves and crying, so that I could get some rest. The nurse got me comfortable and told me that I had visitors.

"Your family is still outside, and I'll let them come in for a moment before your sedative kicks in all the way. They can come back for a longer stay later this morning during visitor hours." She said as she left the room.

The only person I knew who was there for certain was Rita. When she said she would go get "them," however, I knew someone else had to have arrived while I was in delivery. The door opened and in walked Rita, my dad, and Tyrone. The three of them entered the room, and I felt overwhelmed and started crying. I knew that I was potentially going to have to answer my father's questions that I didn't have the right answers to. Questions like, "What happened?" "Why did you end up in premature labor," and "did you know?" They walked in and posted up in various positions around my bed. My dad had a look of worry on his face.

"Are you okay?" He asked.

I nodded. "I'm okay."

"Well, they said they would let you go home tomorrow if you were able to eat something, use the bathroom, and don't have a temperature." He said, having already talked to the nursing staff.

"Okay..." I replied.

He went on to tell me more about what the doctor had said. How small my baby was, that her condition was touch and go, and they would keep me posted as they had updates.

Rita kind of hung back so that my dad could do most of the talking and Tyrone didn't say anything. The nurse came back in and stated that she needed Tyrone to come with her to fill out some additional paperwork. He followed behind her willingly and left the room. My dad stayed for a few more minutes before kissing me on my forehead and heading out. He had to be up for work in a few hours, and I understood that. In fact, I knew once everyone started to leave, I would finally get a chance to genuinely rest.

"Momma was here up until they air-vacced the baby to Little Rock, but she had to go get some rest for work in a few hours," Rita said.

"Her name is Tyronica Vonsha Burks," I said with a slight smile. "You know Alice—she came up with the name."

Rita smiled and laughed lightly.

"So, what happened?" Rita asked, getting down to the facts. "How did you end up in premature labor? Were you and Tyrone fighting again?" She asked.

"No…we hadn't been fighting," I said, feeling exhausted at the thought of getting into the details. By this time, my sedative was taking full effect, and I could feel my body trying to drift into official sleep.

"Of course, we don't have to talk about it now. You get some sleep, and I'll see you later." She said as she hugged me carefully as I was hooked up to IVs and left.

Given the night that had taken place, I was relieved to finally rest and soon drifted to sleep.

The next thing I knew, the morning had come, and I opened my eyes and remembered where I was. I looked around and saw the big hospital door and my IV hookup. Everything that had transpired the night before almost seemed like a dream — no doubt, due to the sedative I had received. As I continued to blink my eyes, I realized that I indeed had given birth just before midnight. I was now a mother to a tiny little girl. They had taken her so fast that I didn't even have a chance to hold her, let alone officially tell them her name. As I continued surveying my room and surroundings, that's when I laid eyes on him. There he was, sound asleep in a large visitor's chair that morphed into a small recliner type bed. As I looked at him as he slept, I wondered where we would go from here. Amidst all the feelings of detachment that I had that week, I was now second-guessing those thoughts and finding myself leaning more towards forgiving him. Our baby was here now, and I longed for us to be a family. The fact that he was there by my side when I woke up at least let me know that he maybe wanted the same thing. I watched him sleep for a while before the nurse came in bubbly and perky to take my vitals.

"Good morning, how are you doing today?" She said as she moved about the room.

"Good morning," I said. "I'm okay."

I tried my best to courteously match her demeanor and found myself a bit relieved. If she had walked in this cheerful, I at least assumed everything with my baby was okay. I found myself on edge every time a member of the hospital staff walked in. It was like I anxiously anticipated someone to bring me bad news about her condition. Her entry into the room awakened Tyrone, and he sat there quietly for a moment as he realized where he was. The nurse began giving me an overview of what to expect that day and that Dr. Chambers would be in to see me during his rounds. She briefed me about the breastfeeding specialist and recommended that I consider it, especially since Tyronica was premature. She went on to mention other paperwork like insurance, the birth certificate, and told me that Tyrone had filled out some, but I would need to fill in some gaps. Realizing my age, she also told me about the nurse who would stop by and discuss birth control options with me as well. It was a lot of information to take in, and I felt a bit overwhelmed as my mind was predominantly preoccupied with my baby's well-being. She made sure I was okay and told me that she would be back in a little while to give me some medication.

"How is my baby?" I asked her concernedly.

She started giving me the details of what had happened early that morning once Tyronica arrived in Little Rock. She told me that they had checked her in, and she was critical but stable. Tears started creeping back to my eyes. Upon seeing one fall, she tried to comfort me.

"I'll go check on any updates beyond that and let you know if anything's changed." She said.

Overcome by my emotion and blurry vision from the tears in my eyes, I nodded and wiped my face as she acknowledged my answer and exited the room. I glanced over at Tyrone, and he was looking in a daze. I tried to calm myself down before breaking the silence that hung in the room.

"Did you get a chance to see her?" I asked him.

He looked at me. "No. By the time I got here, they had already air-vacced her." He said somberly.

He wore an unspoken look of guilt as he had uttered part of the sentence with his head down.

"Don't you have to go to work?" I asked.

"No." He said. "I already took off."

The dead silence returned for the next five minutes or so. During that period of silence, it was like my mind was preparing itself to address all of the things that had been unspoken until now. I wanted a family with him, and I loved him, but I maintained my seriousness about putting my baby first.

"Where were you?" I asked him firmly, not quite sure if I wanted to hear the truth, but all the while, knowing that I needed to.

He had his head down still.

"I was just hanging out." He said in a monotone voice.

"No, that's not a good-enough answer anymore. You weren't where you told me you were going to be, so where were you?" I asked again, trying to remain calm.

I didn't want to make a scene in the hospital, but at this point, if I had to, I was prepared to do so. I not only needed answers but

Dare to Dream

deserved them. He paused, and he was still looking downward in his lap.

"I was out with some friends…"

"Who are these friends?" I immediately retorted.

"Just some friends…you wouldn't know them." He said.

My forehead wrinkled at the ridiculousness of his answer. We lived in Warren, Arkansas—a town where everybody knew everybody—I knew all of his "friends."

"Well, since you can't tell me who the friends are, you can just leave," I said sternly.

He slowly looked up and over at me.

"I'm not leaving." He said, calmly contesting me.

"Well, you need to tell me what's going on, then," I said, growing bolder in my demand for information.

I decided to rephrase my question.

"Are you seeing someone else?" I said.

He looked back down.

"Yes…no…I don't know." He said as he stammered with himself on the final answer.

He seemed confused. I fought back the tears again, but they started to fall down my face. I sat there for a few seconds and processed his response.

"Who is she? Do you love her? Do you want to break up?" I asked over a shaky voice.

He sighed. "Me and her are just friends…that's it."

I closed my eyes with a long, frustrated blink as I was still crying. I felt insulted by his answer.

"So, is this the girl that I asked you about a few months back?" I demanded.

"Yes, but we're just friends." He repeated. "I love you. I want to be with you and the baby." He added, trying his best to be sincere.

I could visually see a countenance of being overwhelmed upon him, but I needed these answers.

"Well, you can't continue our relationship and your 'friendship' with her," I said unrelentingly.

He looked over at me.

"I didn't ask you to end your friendship with Mo." He said, trying to take a subtle dig at me.

My face scrunched in disbelief.

"What?" I said, unable to hide my anger and offense by this comment. "You can't even compare the two. Mo and I have been friends our entire life, and you just met this girl this summer. Plus, you're the one who was always pushing me and Mo off onto each other. I've never slept with Mo—that's the difference here." I said, refusing to back down or accept his attempt to change the subject.

Realizing how fed up I was and perhaps conceding to argue in light of where we were and all that was taking place, he agreed to break off the friendship.

"What do you want to do?" I asked. "Do you want to break up?

"No!" He said as if to emphasize that it wasn't an option. "I want to be with you, and I want to be a part of Tyronica's life. We can make this work." He said, trying to sound hopeful and optimistic about our being a family.

I looked at him, wanting to believe him, but still had my doubts. A lot had transpired in the past six months of me being pregnant, and I wasn't sure if I could trust him. I knew in my heart that I loved him, however, and didn't want to raise Tyronica outside the confines of a family. I didn't want my daughter to feel abandoned by either parent like I did growing up.

I knew that wasn't the exact case with my mother dying, but growing up, I still felt that way from time to time. We came to an agreement right there in the hospital room that we were going to make our family work. We wanted to do right by each other, but more importantly, we wanted to establish a stable home and do right by Tyronica. She didn't ask to be here, but now that she was, we had to make the decision to do what was right.

The nurse re-entered the room and administered another dose of sedatives. She told Tyrone that I would be drifting off to sleep shortly due to the medication and took my vitals again. After she left the room, Tyrone got up and walked over to my bed.

"I'm going to go shower and change since you'll be asleep for a while." He said. "I'll be back before you wake up."

I told him okay.

"I'll get with Rita, and we'll pack a bag for you. I'll bring it when I come back."

I nodded. He told me he loved me, leaned down to kiss me, and left. After he left, I realized it was the first moment I had to myself after delivering Tyronica. In an instant, my whole life had changed. Though I tried to be hopeful about the conversation that Tyrone and I had just had, the emotion that seemed to dominate me most was fear of the unknown. The fear of whether or not my baby was going to be okay, the fear of whether or not Tyrone and I had made the right decision, and the overall fear of not knowing how to be a good parent. I felt so unready, even though I knew I had to be. I also felt a sense of complete love for my baby that I had never felt before. Now that I was a mother, one of my greatest fears loomed in the back of my mind: I felt so many emotions as a motherless mother—mostly wishing my mother could have been there. I had this new life that I was responsible for—and having her prematurely no less—made me extremely reflective about the circumstances that my own mother endured to have me.

During my stay at the hospital, I was on pins and needles. Every time a nurse came into my room, I cringed from the possibility of being brought bad news about Tyronica's condition. Tyrone came back as promised and stayed with me overnight again. If our baby would have been there, it would have been the perfect family moment. We talked about what we would do when Tyronica came home and our plans of going to visit her the next day after I was discharged. His loving attention was refreshing after all that he had put me through in the weeks prior. I was so scared of everything going on with Tyronica that his presence was a comfort. I felt safe in the midst of all the uncertainty.

Dr. Chambers finally came to see me in the evening and told me that if everything went as planned, he would discharge me the next morning. When the morning came, the nurses came in and discussed routine discharge details with me about breastfeeding, which they encouraged, given my baby's premature state. I knew I wanted to do whatever was best for her, so I agreed to try it. I also was bombarded with info about my follow-up appointment, and a recount of advice not to have sex for the next 6 weeks. Since I opted to breastfeed, I couldn't get on birth control right away, anyway.

I couldn't get out of the hospital fast enough as all I wanted was to be by my baby's side. She was 90 miles away, and I still had yet to truly hold her. The nurses told me that, "she made it through the night, so that's a good sign." I guess that was supposed to give me comfort, but somehow, it made me even more on edge. My baby's life seemed like it was hanging in the balance, and I was fearful of her dying before I got the chance to hold her or tell her that I loved her. I didn't want her to experience the feeling of abandonment—to die alone—to feel like I had when my mother had passed. The weight of that worry, I wouldn't have wished on my enemy, and little did I know it was only the beginning of feeling that way.

CHAPTER 4

Big Girl Britches

Observing that I was still sore from the delivery and being aware of the doctor's advice for me to bed rest for the next three or four days, Tyrone asked me if I was sure I felt up to taking the ride to Little Rock. While my body was in pain, and I felt emotionally and physically drained; I didn't have the chance to bond with her and felt the dire need to go and see her. I felt like a part of me was missing. So, we left the hospital and got straight on the highway to head to Children's Hospital. We didn't talk for much of the ride, mainly because I kept drifting in and out of sleep. When we finally arrived at Little Rock, I felt fear resurging so much that I felt sick to the stomach. I didn't know what to expect. I had never been in a neonatal unit before. When we got to the desk and told them who we were, they immediately welcomed us and told us what to expect.

Each baby in the NICU was assigned a specific nurse, and Tyronica's nurse came out to talk with us. She briefed us on what to expect and told us about the machines and treatments that were being administered to her. Though he wasn't saying anything, I could feel Tyrone's nervousness as well. I could see his eyes glisten as the nurse talked to us about Tyronica's feeding tubes and her eyes being taped shut to stifle the light. He was never the type of guy to show emotion or cry, but that was the first day I observed it. They took us to a room to prep us for entering the NICU ward where we had to scrub our hands and arms up to our elbows with soap and water and put on medical gowns, shoe covers, masks, and caps.

After we were prepared from head to toe, the nurse took us to where Tyronica's incubator was. As we approached where she was lying, I was in a quiet daze. A tarp-like plastic covered her, and there were numerous machines and tubes hooked up to her body. Tyrone looked white in the face as he stared at his daughter for the first time. Though the nurse did her best to prep us before going to see her, nothing could have prepared us for what we actually saw. We just sat by her side, not saying many words at all. It was a very solemn moment and a reality check for how serious premature birth was. We stayed for a couple of hours before deciding to head back to Warren before it got too late. Though we didn't want to leave her, it had been a draining day, and heading home seemed like a wise thing to do.

Tyronica being so far away from us was taxing on my mind. I was confident that it was the best place for her to be at the moment, but all the while, I wanted her nearer, and I wanted to know that she was out of the woods as far as surviving went; and she was not. After the bed rest that the doctors ordered me on, I went back to school almost immediately. My world was in a tailspin, and I was desperate for some type of normality and distraction from what was going on with my baby. That, and I had missed so many days here and there throughout my pregnancy that I had to get back on track. Not to mention I anticipated having to miss even more school once it was time for Tyronica to be discharged home. I had no time to waste and had to do what I had to do. Weeks passed, and Tyronica still wasn't able to come home yet. The doctors would not release her until her weight had reached four pounds. Her weight was actually dropping, and the doctors weren't certain as to why.

Traveling to Little Rock to see Tyronica during the week was nearly impossible. We had bills to take care of so Tyrone, of course, couldn't take off days in excess. My dad would also drive me some weekends, but during the week, he too had to work. I, of course, didn't have a license or a car, so the weekends were the main time that we got to drive to see her. My mother's sister Geneva lived in Little Rock and would let me stay with her on weekends I opted to stay in Little Rock. When I was back in Warren, my mind was always in Little Rock. I would call Tyronica's nurse every day before going to school and every day once I got out.

At some point when the days turned into weeks and the weeks had turned into months, my anxiety became higher than a kite. At my four- and six-week checkups, the doctor asked for a true assessment of how I was feeling, and I told him about my constant anxiety and fearfulness of Tyronica dying. I was a nervous wreck during this time. Every time the phone rang, my heart would beat fast, and my blood pressure would rise. In my mind, every call was potentially "the call" telling us that our daughter had passed in the night. At school, I could barely focus. I had been pumping milk for her and freezing it, and all the while I couldn't help but wonder if this was a waste of time. *"Would I have all this milk on hand and no baby to give it to?"* I thought. In fact, at that point, Tyrone and I never even purchased any baby clothes or items for her. In all honesty, before she was born, I thought we had a little more time. After she was born, we unspokenly were waiting for her to come home first. I couldn't imagine going on a baby-shopping spree only to have to part ways with all of the items if she ended up not being able to come home. My doctor prescribed me a low dosage of Prozac to calm my nerves, as well as aid me with sleeping. I was going on sixteen, though, and when I shared this with my oldest sister, Carla, she advised me against it for the addictive nature that the pills were known for.

One day after I got home from school, I remember checking the mail and seeing a bill addressed to me from Children's Hospital where Tyronica was receiving her care. I opened it and almost lost my breath. It was a list of all of the treatments, medicines, and routine care that Tyronica had racked up while at the hospital. It was over $100,000 and I had never seen a bill that big in my entire life. I called the hospital and told them that they must have made a mistake. Surely, they meant to send a bill with a figure like $10,000. When I asked my father's advice about it, he once again brought up the subject of adoption so that Tyronica could be placed on his insurance. While I appreciated his attempt to provide a solution, I again let him know that it was *not* an option. Thankfully for us, the hospital had plans to shoot a promotional commercial. In exchange for letting Tyronica be in the commercial, they would totally absolve our hospital debt. I couldn't believe that such a timely opportunity came around as it did. All we had to do was sign some sort of media waiver, and just like that, the six-figure debt was reduced to zero.

The first time that I was able to hold her, she was 1 month and 2 days old. Prior to that day, every time we visited, our skin-to-skin contact was non-existent, as we had to reach through a plastic gloved partition to even touch her. When January came, I turned sixteen, and that meant I was finally was able to get my license, as well as a job. This meant I was able to make my visits to see Tyronica more frequent as I was able to use Tyrone or my father's car. Tyronica was in the NICU from the day of her birth until the second week of February. Her weight finally started to pick up after plummeting for the longest time.

One day, during one of our weekend visits towards the end of January, the doctor's informed me that if Tyronica's weight improved, if she was breathing on her own, and if she was able to keep down her 30 ccs of milk every couple of hours, that she could be ready to go home within a week or two. It was the first official light at the end of our long tunnel. Tyrone and I had to undergo a number of training classes on how to properly care for her once she was home. Among them, we had to learn about CPR and how to operate the breathing machine that she had to come home on. As hoped, Tyronica's health began to improve in February, and by March, we were overjoyed yet terrified to bring her home. Tyrone beamed and was very much involved in the day-to-day routine of Tyronica's care. He worked at night and kept her during the day, so I could go to school. Given our past as a couple, I was surprised that Tyrone stepped up how he did when Tyronica was born and especially when she came home. It changed the dynamic of our relationship for the better. Once we got her home, he was extremely protective of her. If we had visitors who wanted to see her, he would be sure to emphatically add that people could see her, but not touch or pick her up. Her immune system was so sensitive.

For the first month or so, we had a nurse come to our house daily for visits. Bringing Tyronica home, of course, meant I had to start missing school again. Thank goodness for Alice and Tyrone's brother, Terrance, who made sure one way or the other, I had homework brought home to me so that I could try my best to stay on track.

One night while we slept, we were awakened by the audible alert of her breathing machine going off. We went into the bedroom where she was to find her not breathing and on the verge of changing color in the face. All the training that we had on the breathing machine went out the window for me.

"You pump, and I'll breathe," Tyrone said, springing into action. I was frozen. He looked at me still having not moved. In a panic, he slapped the shit out of me and repeated himself. "You pump, and I'll breathe. Pull it together!" I pulled it together just as he said and helped him go through the steps on the machine as we were trained.

We got her breathing and rushed to the emergency room in Warren. The doctors got her stable, and we drove her back to the hospital in Little Rock that night.

"Don't send her home until she's right." I implored the doctor. Training or not, my nerves were way too bad to play with the life of my child. Thankfully, she was able to come home shortly after. Because of her ailments, I always had a hard time getting people to watch her if I had errands to run.

I remember once asking my sister Carla to watch her briefly while I ran to the corner store. She refused. "Nuh, uhn." She said unwaveringly. "Take her with you." The store I was going to was so close to our house that you could literally yell to someone to grab an item you may have forgotten to list, and they could hear you.

"I'm just going right here," I told her. "It's cold. I don't want to have to take her out in this." I said to Carla, trying to convince her that my trip would be quick.

"No ma'am, she won't stop breathing on me—wrap her up and take her with you!" She insisted.

Tyrone came up with a unique idea to get Tyronica's breathing on par. Though we had her hooked up to the machine still, he'd let her fall asleep on his chest so that she could instinctively learn the rhythm of his breathing and match it. It seemed to work—a little too well, in fact. When she got a little older, and he insisted on placing her back into her crib after falling asleep, she'd pull her breathing cord on purpose and make the machine go off, so he'd run and pick her up. He had trained her to breathe, and she had trained him to spoil her.

When the summer came, I found a weekend job. Tyrone was off on the weekends and watched Tyronica while I worked a few hours on a local farm, collecting eggs from a henhouse. I still collected a check from my mother's social security regularly, but the extra money from my weekend job was nice for padding my pockets for gas and other odds and ends. As far as school was concerned, once we brought Tyronica home, I had to start missing out again. They were trying to keep me back from going to the eleventh grade, which ultimately would keep me from graduating with my class. Apparently, I had missed too many days between my pregnancy and Tyronica coming home. I had valid doctor's excuses, and they still insisted that my absences were in excess. I had to go to Mr. Bronson, our school superintendent, and plead my case, and my dad went to the board of education. Thankfully, they decided to let me begin the next year as a junior still with my original class.

When the school year started, Tyrone's biological father, Joe Harold, got me hired as part of a work-study program doing custodial work. I considered this my first official job and worked every day with about 15 to 20 hours a week. By now, Tyrone's schedule had changed, where he was working during the day, and I, of course, was going to school. I started to ask my dad and Dorothy to keep Tyronica when I went to work. I was working more and more towards being as independent from Tyrone as possible. I loved him and wanted to trust him, but given our past, I had to start thinking more wisely this time around, as my first and foremost concern was my baby.

It's funny that my niece Tammy and I were the same age and attended high school at the same time but had two totally different lives. I had a live-in boyfriend, had a premature infant at home, and the things most high schoolers were interested in—like narrowing down plans for a weekend sleepover with friends—I wasn't thinking about. I had a child and other obligations. I didn't go to the football or basketball games anymore as my extracurricular time centered around bottles, diapers, and trying to stay on course with my class. I did, however, manage to attend my Junior Prom. Tyrone stayed home with Tyronica, and when I returned, I had to climb through the bedroom window in my dress, because he was passed out drunk,

Dare to Dream

unable to hear my knocks at the front door. I was gorgeous that night and was upset that he was asleep.

People sometimes inquire whether or not I feel as if I missed something during that period of my life. It's kind of funny because I don't think I missed a thing. You don't miss something you never had. I got pregnant right before the typical social life of a high schooler begins to unfold. There's no sense in dwelling on what coulda been or shoulda been. My high school years were about raising my daughter, and I was just fine with that.

Before I knew it, my junior year flew by, and summer break had officially arrived. I loved it, as it gave me more time to be with Tyronica, uninterrupted. Tyrone decided that he wanted to take some summer classes at Shorter College in Little Rock, Arkansas. With Little Rock being so far away from Warren, we came up with the idea for Tyronica and I to go to Little Rock for the summer as well. I convinced my Aunt Geneva that I needed a change of scenery from Warren and asked her if Tyronica and I could visit for the summer. She agreed, and it was perfect. Tyrone solidified housing on campus, and we packed up for the summer and left.

Trish Ann was of course on another one of her on-again, off-again spells with her boyfriend, so she stayed at the house while we were gone. My Aunt Geneva had no clue that my real reason for visiting was so that Tyronica and I could be close to Tyrone during summer school. Her granddaughter, my second cousin Lisa did, however, and would drop me off to campus where Tyrone was when I wasn't driving his car around. If he made the decision to stay when the fall came, Tyrone would be eligible to live in campus housing specifically for people with families. Initially, we planned to try out the living arrangements and see if we could live in Little Rock when the fall came.

As the summer was drawing to an end, the more we discussed the possibility of staying in Little Rock for good, the cons seemed to far outweigh the pros. Though he had a scholarship to play football in Little Rock, there were so many other factors that seemed to put that to the back burner since our goal was to stay together as a family. Our household bills would increase living in a big city like Little Rock. Tyrone's scholarship only covered dormitory style living for one. With family housing, we would have to pay for rent, lights, water, gas, and so on, whereas in Warren, everything was practically paid for, or at least well within our means living at my family's house.

Even though it was my last year of high school, I was open to transferring to a high school in Little Rock. That was until we realized that Tyrone playing football on scholarship would mean that he wouldn't be eligible to work. This would mean that *I* would have to work a full-time job. That wasn't even an option as far as I was concerned, since the most important thing for me, personally, was to finish high school. I had one year left, and I was not about to disappoint my father any more than I already had. Not to mention, we hadn't even considered who would keep Tyronica if we somehow managed to make it work. Back in Warren, we had a strong support system where we could depend on my family and Tyrone's here and there. In Little Rock, I only had Geneva and Lisa, and Tyrone had no family. Running out of ways to make it work, I even suggested that Tyrone stay while Tyronica and I went back to Warren. He however refused to be that far away from his baby as he didn't want to be an absentee father. And so, after his summer classes, we moved back home, and I prepared for my senior year of high school.

I was going to graduate—on time. I had my hands full, not only with school and work, but of course, my baby. My dad and Dorothy once again agreed to help out with keeping Tyronica but were adamant about only doing so while I was at school. It wasn't that my dad was being cold; he was trying to teach me responsibility. He and Dorothy would watch Tyronica while I was at school, but as soon as school was out, I had 30 minutes to come and relieve them, and that was it. It was my last year of high school, and my main focus was trying to figure out what it was I wanted to do with my life. One thing I was certain of was that I no longer wanted to live in Warren. It had to be something better out there for me. My involvement with the Jr. ROTC had me strongly considering going into the service post-graduation.

Even with my pregnancy and missing school because Tyronica was a preemie, by the time I was a senior, I had accumulated enough credits to only have one main class during the day. I was finished with that class by noon, and so that meant more time for me to work more hours at my job. I was making a little more money, and still in the back of my mind, working on my plan to become independent from Tyrone. He and I started having candid conversations together about what was next for us. I told him that I couldn't envision raising Tyronica in Warren. He, on the other hand, seemed complacently fine with our current living situation.

"If you want to continue to live here, that's fine, but I don't," I said to him frankly.

Tyrone had a job in Warren, and maybe that was enough for him. It wasn't enough for me, however. Not only that. I still knew he was still creeping around on me, here and there. So, we sat down one day and had an honest conversation about our relationship and came to a mutual decision to take a break. That way, maybe he could get his lust out of his system, and I could focus on school and Tyronica the way that I needed to. He moved out of my family's house and back in with his mother.

Though, Tyrone and I's break was initially intended to be temporary, we were single for the time being, and I started dating someone. His name was Glenn, and he was the son of one of my neighbors. Glenn was about Tyrone's age and grew up on the southern side of

Warren. He was the total opposite of Tyrone as far as personality went. He loved to talk, hang out with me, and have a good time.

On top of that, he didn't seem bothered by the fact that I had a toddler and was good to her as well. The three of us would go out shopping, to places like the zoo, the park, and other fun outings. It was nice and refreshing; and though I enjoyed his company and kindness, somehow I couldn't see myself being with him long-term. As far as who Tyrone may have been dating, I purposely kept my mind off of it. The point of being broken up was not to be preoccupied with that info. I still loved him and didn't have time to get caught up in any feelings for him. He, on the other hand, was caught up in his feelings for me. He was trying to still be a part of my day-to-day world as if we were still an item, and we were not.

One Friday night, Glenn and I were coming back to my house after a date. He walked me to the door, and I kissed him goodnight. When I got inside the house and walked past Tyronica's bedroom, I noticed that she was in her bed, sleeping. I wrinkled my head a bit confused. It was strange because Tyrone had picked her up earlier that day and she was supposed to be staying all night with him.

"What's Tyronica doing here?" I asked my sister, Trish Ann.

"Oh, Tyrone brought her. He's here." She said nonchalantly as she was camped out in the den, watching TV. I looked around, not seeing him.

"No, he's not," I said sort of confusedly and at the same time hoping that she was joking.

"Well, he was a while ago, maybe he walked down to the corner store." She said. Unbeknownst to me, Tyrone had come to my house that night with Tyronica; I guess with the intention of all three of us hanging out.

"Why did you let him come in here? I asked her annoyed.

"He had Tyronica! What did you want me to do, leave them out in the cold?" She retorted back. I sighed. "Well, where did you say I was?" I asked her, trying to connect all of the dots.

"I told him that you were out on a date with Glenn." She said almost proudly. My eyes grew big. Seeing my face, she offered up her defense.

"What? He didn't need to think that you were sitting around here on a Friday night waiting on him." She mused.

Now granted, Tyrone knew I was dating Glenn, but in my mind, the details weren't his business. The next thing I knew, there was a demanding knock at the door. I just knew it was Tyrone. I panicked and grabbed my bathrobe and put it on over my date clothes. Tousled my hair as if I had been home relaxing for a while, mellowed my composure and opened the door. He pushed his way past me and let himself inside.

"Yea, I don't know why you're trying to act like you've been here. I saw you come in off your little date!" He said in a tone drowned with jealousy. He snatched my robe open to further bust my bubble.

"What are you doing here? You're supposed to be keeping Tyronica!" I said.

"Nah, I'm not babysitting nobody so you can go out on a date with some other dude." He said.

"You're not babysitting; you're daddysitting." I corrected him smugly.

"Oh, I'm supposed to be daddysitting so you can go out with Glenn?" He said, trying to belittle him.

"No, you're supposed to be daddysitting because you want to spend time with your daughter." He appeared to be trying to hang around for some reason, but I wasn't having it. Since Tyronica was asleep in her bed, there was no point in waking her up and taking her back to his place, and I told him such. With that, he stepped into her room and kissed her goodnight. He was still trying to pick and prod me into an argument by repeating how he wasn't a babysitter and so on and so forth. Before it could escalate there, I escorted him back towards the door and opened it so he could leave.

"Have a good night, Tyrone," I said, putting finality to the scene. He paused for a second, rolled his eyes, and left. I shut the door behind him, annoyed and in disbelief. Here we were, broken up, and he was still trying to control me.

Tyrone was finished with school already, and I was preparing to graduate. I shared with him my potential plans to take advantage of the ROTC scholarship and join the service.

"You really want to do that?" He asked.

I told him that I didn't have it all figured out yet but that I was certain that I didn't want to stay in Warren. He told me that in order to do that, I would have to give up custody of Tyronica while I went through training. He also went on to make points of how long the process of my training and school might be. I guess I hadn't got that far in my plan. Tyronica's care was way too high-maintenance for me to be away from her for an extended period of time. While Tyrone could have done it, he'd also have to work, which meant we'd have to find someone who would be willing to watch her during that time.

"How about I be the one to go into the military, so you don't have to leave her?" He offered. He went on to suggest that we might as well quit playing and get back together so that we could get married. "We can just go together wherever the military takes us." He said. It was a plan.

He took the military test, and we were married in April of 1986. We went to the courthouse, and it was a small ceremony with our families. That following month in May, I graduated high school on time and with my class, as planned, and Tyrone was off to begin basic training and AIT for his military career.

Between getting married, graduating, and my husband being shipped off to Uncle Sam, my life had changed quite a bit in a short period of time. The honeymoon period of our marriage was spent living apart from one another, and immediately, I grew accustomed to living single. I didn't allow a single mindset to lead to affairs or anything like that, but rather just came to depend and rely on myself. I learned, in essence, how to be the backbone of a family. While my husband was serving the country, I had a household to run. It gave me a sense of self-reliance. I still worked at the elementary school, and Tyrone, of course, sent money home while he was away. I started preparing to buy household necessities for us as I anticipated our moving once he returned from training. All the things we currently had were, of course, my family's, and it was time to start purchasing items of our own. There was no time to revel in my post-high school freedom or to take the leisure to "find my way" in life—my life had already begun. I was a mother and military housewife all before the age of twenty.

While Tyrone was off at basic training and AIT, it left a lot of time for my daughter and I to spend with my dad. One day, as the three of us entered my house and walked past the fireplace mantle, Tyronica took special notice of a photograph of my mother that was positioned on top. The photo was the last picture that my mom had taken when she was alive. The week that she died, she literally had everything planned out to the detail, including having that picture in particular, taken for her obituary. She had picked out a lovely dress, and her hair was beautifully styled. Tyronica walked up to the mantle while still gazing at the photo. "I saw that lady right there before," She said plainly.

I shared before that I never had significant pictures of my mom growing up, nor did I have them then, for my daughter to have ever seen. It was a tenderly bittersweet moment as I wished what my daughter was saying was even possible.

"No, you've never seen her before," I said, "She died years and years ago when I was six." My daughter looked at me and then back at the photograph.

"No, I did see her." She insisted. Her certainty was almost amusing as I thought to indulge her a little bit.

"Okay," I said, "Where did you see her at?"

She replied, "When I was a baby. She was holding me."

At that point, my attentiveness certainly piqued, if nothing else. I again tried to tell her that what she was describing wasn't possible. "Yes." She simply said again. "She had *that* around her neck." She was pointing up to the picture. My mother had a gold chain around her neck in the photo. As I listened to the persistent account of my three-year-old, I began to think back to when my daughter actually was in the hospital.

When Tyronica was in the NICU in Little Rock, she had got down to 1 pound and 5 ounces, four ounces down from her birth weight, when all the while, she should have been gaining weight. The hospital contacted us and told us early one morning that we needed to make plans to come up for her last rites. The call I had always feared receiving had finally come, and on the other end of the phone, I immediately turned to tears. Tyrone was home with me, and once he noticed my crying, he walked towards me and the phone. "What's wrong?" He said softly. I couldn't answer him though, I was an instant frantic mess. He took the phone from me and finished the conversation as I buckled to my knees in sobs. We got dressed immediately and made this surreal and devastating journey up to the hospital.

When we arrived, we checked in at the NICU as usual. The nursing staff then told me that Tyronica's grandmother had just left the hospital. I remember looking confused. *Her grandmother?* I thought

Dare to Dream

to myself and then even said aloud. The nurses looked back at me assuredly and responded, "Yes, you must have just missed her in the corridor." I thought it was very strange because we knew very few people who lived nearby, and her grandmother lived in Warren and had never been up to visit before. Reading my face, the nurse began to look around on the desk. "Here, it's on the sign-in sheet," she said. I was certainly curious, to say the least, but then the nurse's face turned puzzled as well. "It was just right here," she said, looking down but not spotting the signature. She couldn't describe the woman to me but said that after she signed in, she went to Tyronica's room and held her for a while. I was confused and concerned about who the person was who had access to my daughter's room.

At the same time, however, I didn't give thought to it for long as my mind was fried, thinking about having to hear my baby's last rites being read. We were taken to a small office waiting room to talk with our daughter's assigned nurse and her doctor, in greater detail, about what was happening with our baby. Despite the nutrition regimen that she was on, she was steadily losing weight instead of gaining. They told us that the medical staff had done all that they could do, and that at this point, she was just holding on until the inevitable occurred.

Also in the room, was the hospital chaplain, which made my tears fall harder. I tried to digest all that they were telling me about preparing for my baby's death. It was a heavy mix of emotions that seemed to literally sit on my chest. Here I was, fifteen years old, already bearing the burden of becoming an unmarried teenage mother without a mother's support, and now I was about to lose my baby.

After the doctors were done with their update, they exited the room. The chaplain then introduced himself to us and began to brief us on what exactly last rites were, asked us if we needed or wanted prayer for anything, and tried to console us for what was about to occur. I sat there in a zombie-like state from crying as Tyrone held my hand and tried to console me. He placed his arms around me and told me that we were going to get through this. While he had always made me feel safe one way or the other, this was one time where I realized his comfort couldn't cloak the pain.

This level of anguish was something different. All I could think about was how this could possibly be happening to me. I had already lost my mother, and now I was preparing to lose my own baby. What was it about me that everybody I loved seemed to die? The chaplain told us that whenever we were ready, we'd go in to see Tyronica in the NICU room and he would lead the prayer. Tyrone was clenching my hand as the chaplain talked to us. I could see the pain and concern in his face, but I also saw this attempt to mask it by being strong.

"I'll give you all a few minutes alone, and when you're ready, I'll come back." The chaplain said as he got up and exited the room.

"Ready?" I thought. How in the world would I ever be ready to prepare for my daughter's death? I hadn't even brought her home yet. Had never dressed her in her own clothes or placed her in her own bed—none of those mundane things that I should have been experiencing by now. We sat there. I cried silently and Tyrone held on to me.

"What am I supposed to do?" I said aloud.

"There's nothing we can do," Tyrone said solemnly. "We have to put it in God's hands."

Here we were, these teenage sweethearts, preparing to have to say goodbye to our baby. It didn't make sense to me—at all.

"We'll be okay—we'll get through this." He said again. But I knew in my heart that I would never be okay.

The chaplain returned and told us that we would now go together to the NICU to pray. When I stood up, I was screaming on the inside.

By the mere fact that I had agreed to have her last rites read, I felt like an accomplice to her death. On the other hand, I wanted my baby's life, though short, to be dedicated to God properly if she was to depart. It just felt wrong—it was way too soon, and my walking down the hallway to go and hear her last rites felt agonizing. We followed the chaplain into the unit, and I stood back for a second. My mind flooded with thoughts of guilt. If I hadn't been arguing with Tyrone, if I hadn't slipped and fell—maybe I wouldn't have been in premature labor and wouldn't be here now. I might have been home with my daughter resting and getting ready for our day instead of standing in a NICU, getting ready to hear her last rites. My mind even went back to my dad's infamous words telling me that the decisions I made would ultimately affect my future.

What if my decisions were the reason my baby was fighting for her life? My thoughts humbled me as I was staring in the face of what happens when you don't make good decisions. I eventually gathered enough strength to take a few steps closer to where Tyrone and the chaplain were standing as we held hands, and the chaplain began to pray. Tyronica's nurse even came over and joined hands with us as well. It wasn't a long or drawn out prayer, but the only part that I remember clearly is when he said, "If something should happen, I commend her soul to you."

Tyrone and I spent the night at the local Ronald McDonald house for families of hospitalized children. The next morning, we dejectedly returned to the hospital, and found that Tyronica's situation soon began to take a pleasantly unexpected turn. Her vitals began to revive, and her weight began increasing significantly. I was overjoyed to tears, and though I didn't understand the reason for her sudden turnaround in health, I didn't care. My baby was going to be okay, and that was all I needed to know.

Here I was now, standing at my father's house with my three-year-old looking up at my mother's picture on the mantle, as that story—which seemed so odd then—came back to me quite vividly. Had my daughter really seen my mother? Call it a phenomenon or what have you, but after Tyronica's certainty of having seen my mother before, and recounting that day at the hospital, I wholeheartedly believe that somehow, the "lady" who visited my daughter was indeed her grandmother as she identified herself. I know that when explained to someone else, that sort of thing may seem made-up or delusional, but the truth of the matter is supernatural occurrences like that happened frequently throughout my life.

CHAPTER 5

Rocky Road

When Tyrone and I first became parents, he was there every step of the way. It wasn't until after he got in the military that things changed. As a matter of fact, *we* changed. I remember being in love with him when he left for basic training and AIT in May, but by the time he came home in September, I felt like my love for him had changed somehow. Our situation and age had declared us mature enough to marry, but in reality, we weren't emotionally and mentally ready for all that we had gotten ourselves into.

I loved him, but while he was away, I realized that I didn't love him the way I once had. He was gone for five months, and during that time, I had time to grow. I missed him while he was gone, but I was unusually fine. Finer than a newlywed wife should have been, considering "the love of her life" was gone for so long. I had my daughter, and I had peace. With Tyrone gone, there were no arguments when he was drinking, no violence or aggression from his temper, no lies or worrying about what woman he was with if he wasn't with me—just clarity and contentment.

When he finally did come home in September, I was happy, but I wondered what our love would be like because I felt like I had changed. I loved him, but it just wasn't as intense. He informed me that he had received his first orders to be stationed at Fort Polk, Louisiana, and we made plans for Tyronica and I to move there with him. I was uncertain how everything would go, given my "new" feelings towards him.

At first, I tried to contest Tyronica and I moving with him. I tried to convince him that maybe he needed time to get established in his career and that perhaps we could move with him later. He said that idea was out of the question and told me that his family was his responsibility. He seemed somewhat more ready to be a husband and a father and didn't allow my excuses or fears to stop his made-up mind. He was mature and different. Since we were indeed married now, I came to my senses and realized that going with him was the right thing to do. And so, we began making arrangements to move our life from Arkansas to Louisiana.

Our first home in Louisiana was a mobile home seated in a trailer park not far from Tyrone's military base. It was quaint, but it was our first official and independent space together as a family. We agreed that at first, I would not work and focus on getting Tyronica acclimated to our new life. Just when I was mentally ready to check out on our relationship, things between Tyrone and I began to get good again. His time away had changed him quite a bit. He seemed more focused and more of a family man in a lot of ways. Then again, he also seemed different. I couldn't put my finger on it, but I did know that he had picked up his drinking again—and this time, it seemed to be more intense. We started talking about having another baby, and we both wanted a son. We talked about me starting school like I had planned to do, and we talked about finding a quality school for Tyronica.

For the first few months of our being in Louisiana, our family life was great. Two months in, Tyrone had settled into his job as a cook at one of the base's mess halls. He became buddies with his co-workers and other army personnel and found a crew to hang with in his downtime. It wasn't long before he started to hang out late nights again while drinking and coming home at odd and inconsistent hours. He'd come home sometimes at two in the morning, other times; it would be about three. Sometimes I would be asleep, other times, I would stay up and wait on him. When I did stay up to confront him, an argument always brewed.

"Where were you? What were you doing?" I'd ask.

"I was out with my friends." He'd say nonchalantly, sometimes slurring his words.

"Okay, when do I get to meet some of these friends?" I'd ask. He'd ignore me, get into our bed, and pass out. I started to feel similar feelings when he pulled these stunts when we were younger. I didn't have any proof, however, and didn't want to rock the boat of our new life in Louisiana. We'd been there for months, and not one of his so-called friends had ever stopped by, visited with their families—nothing. Being away from my family—particularly my dad—was harder on me than I thought it would be. Especially during holidays—it was around these times that I seemed to recollect and miss my mother the most. So, when December came around, we both decided that we were in need of some family time and traveled back to Arkansas for the holiday.

Once home, I still harbored feelings of resentment against Tyrone. On Christmas Eve, I planned on going out to a popular local club to have a good time of my own. I was feeling in desperate need of reigniting my social life while simultaneously giving Tyrone a taste of his own medicine by staying out late. Unbeknownst to me, he had come to the club first and saw me. He headed home and put on a show for my dad who had stopped by.

"Where's your wife?" My dad asked him as the evening got later and later.

"She's at the club," Tyrone said with feigned nonchalance.

"At the club?" My dad asked as if the notion was ridiculous. "She knows it's Christmas and that she needs to be home getting things ready with her family." My dad replied.

"Well, that's what I told her; that we still had gifts to get together for Christmas," Tyrone said, playing into my dad's reaction the way that he had planned. "I won't go down there and mess with her. She'll be mad if I do." Tyrone told my father.

"Well, she won't be mad if I go get her—and if so, she won't say anything." My dad said. Pleased with the outcome of his snitching, Tyrone let my father head down to the club where I was and get me.

"Leigh, your grandpa's out here." Said one of my friends who knew me.

"My grandpa?" I asked confusedly. "My grandpa's been dead since 1968!" I retorted. I kept dancing. No sooner than I said that, I felt a tap on my shoulder right there on the dance floor. I turned around, and there my dad was in the club. I was shocked and embarrassed.

"It's time for you to come home and play Santa Claus with your baby and husband. Come on." He said as he turned around and led the way back to the door. My mouth was wide open. I tried to play it off as I said goodbye to the people I knew and headed towards the door.

When my father and I walked in the door of my family's house, Tyrone sat there on the couch, waiting with a smirk on his face. That look that someone has when their diabolical scheme goes off without a hitch. I was pissed. Here he was, trying to paint himself as the picture-perfect family man by amping my father up to come to the club to get me when he only knew I was in the club because he was there himself! To add insult to injury, I knew he was probably up to way more than I was, even as far back as Louisiana went. I couldn't prove it yet, but I was suspicious. We spent the rest of the evening together as a family, wrapping presents for Tyronica and getting ready for Christmas.

That same year that Tyrone and I relocated to Louisiana, we talked about having another child—both of us hoping for a boy—to solidify our fresh start as a family. I was sixteen weeks pregnant before I actually knew I was. I decided to just go back to school since I was having difficulty getting pregnant on the timeline that I anticipated. I didn't feel any immediate changes in my body, and unlike with Tyronica, I didn't have morning sickness or symptoms that gave it away. It was a different pregnancy, indeed, yet still, fear started to creep back in. I went to the doctor and told them the history of my previous pregnancy with Tyronica, and they immediately declared me as a high risk. I saw the doctor every three weeks during my second trimester, and by the time I made it to my third trimester, I was seeing him weekly. At 28 weeks, I was ordered to partial bed rest. I started to dilate early again and ran the risk of having another premature delivery. The doctors stated that my pelvic bone wasn't strong enough to hold my baby full-term. At 32 weeks, once again, I went into premature labor and was ordered to complete bed rest. Remembering the agony and struggles of my first pregnancy, I was determined to do exactly what the doctor had said.

I ate my meals in bed, brushed my teeth in bed, washed up in bed, and even went to the restroom in bed with a bedpan. The only time I left the bed was to go to my doctor visits. Tyronica had preschool three days a week, and Tyrone would pick her up and drop her off before and after work. Even though I had to remain in bed for most of the time, when Tyronica was home with me, she was good at entertaining herself. She was going on four years old now and liked to read and do puzzles. I made sure to enlighten her about how our family was about to change and how Mommy needed her rest. We would read stories together about families with new babies, and she understood my need to be in bed a lot. We would have prepared meals and snacks for her, and other than that, she would nap.

In September of 1987, at 36 weeks, I finally gave birth to our second child, Tyrone Jr., who weighed four pounds. After my second difficult pregnancy, I knew I officially didn't want to have any more children. I had always wanted to have a boy and a girl anyway, so I was at peace that our family was complete. Unlike Tyronica, Tyrone Jr. was a planned pregnancy. When he was born, although I was still somewhat of a young mother at the age of 19, I felt that I had matured as a mother. In fact, I raised Tyrone Jr. altogether differently than I raised Tyronica.

I raised Tyronica like a friend as I was a mere 15 when I had her and raised Tyrone Jr. more like a mom. There was a four-year difference between the periods of time when I had them, and it marked subtle but certain differences over the years. I felt like I was still figuring myself out when Tyronica was born. I loved her but was insecure in my parenting. I was balancing a lot with school, being a mom, and still dealing with Tyrone's antics. It was a lot to deal with at once. By the time Tyrone Jr. came along, I felt more confident in who I was as a mother and even felt more nurturing. I guess it's just one of those things where age makes a huge difference. Perhaps in a small way, this is even telling of why Tyronica always called me LaFarris growing up, and Tyrone called me Momma.

Even though Tyrone Jr's birth brought great joy to our family, I began to have these intuitive feelings that gave me a pause about the real status of our marriage. Maybe I was just being suspicious of his old ways. Or maybe it was because we started our lives together so young and so fast that I had yet to discover knowing myself, let alone what love really was. Part of me still felt as if I didn't know how to handle love and the responsibilities of marriage, but I felt obligated to stand by his side as a wife and bear through our foundational years.

Rocky Road

That's what I saw husbands and wives do as I was growing up. From infidelity and abuse to alcohol problems and sickness, I observed that when times are hard, wives hung in there. I also wanted to try my hardest to raise my children within the confines of a traditional family unit.

While living in the mobile home park, we had a next-door neighbor named Marsha. Marsha lived in a mobile home with her friend named Katy. Katy was actually married but went through problems so often with her husband that she was with Marsha more often than not. I recall a time when they had fallen behind on their bills, leading to their water being cut off. I decided to do the decent thing as a neighbor and let the two of them come to our place and bathe, get water, cook, etc.

My conversations with Katy and Marsha began occurring somewhat regularly as we'd chitchat in passing while I was outside playing with Tyronica and rocking Tyrone Jr. I didn't have any friends, so I was grateful for the camaraderie. They even invited me to the NCO (Non-commissioned officer) Club with them one night. That would be the first and last night that I went, actually. They were nice, but in all honesty, a bit too wild for me. I would have thought that Katy would have had a little more sense to conduct herself better as she was married like I was. Not only that, she had a military husband—this meant people were always watching and waiting to report something back to gossip about just because.

After three months of waiting, our on-base housing was approved, and we moved out of the trailer into a three-bedroom quad that was much more spacious. Shortly after we moved, I started selling Mary Kay products part-time to have money of my own. My role as a housewife was my main business, but when the kids were at daycare, it was a good way for me to pass the time. Tyrone made it very clear that he didn't want me working outside of the home.

Dare to Dream

I, therefore, had to find something that fit into my schedule of being a housewife. Mary Kay was perfect for that. I enjoyed makeup, I could make my own schedule, and at the time, it was a booming business. It was perfect. I also around this time remember longing for a change in my appearance.

One day, I walked into a barbershop, sat in a chair, and told the man I wanted to try something different. For starters, he colored my hair burgundy. I had a Jheri curl, so next, he shaved my sides and left my curl somewhat full on top. I even asked for a Gucci symbol on one side and a Playboy Bunny symbol on the other. He showed me the finished look, and I approved. When I got home, Tyrone just looked at me. He didn't have words. One way or the other, it didn't matter. I liked it, and I thought it fit my Mary Kay image as well. Whenever I left our house, I was dolled up and ready to represent.

I couldn't help but notice that Tyrone was having more and more field time during the week. One day while at home, I received a phone call from Marsha.

"Hey, Marsha, how are you?" I answered, pleasantly surprised.

"I'm fine." She said, sort of dismissively. "Well, this is not a social call." She said as she proceeded to her real point. "I'm calling to tell you that Tyrone and I are in love, and he's leaving you." I was shocked. And then almost immediately, I became irate.

"Wait, what?" I stammered. She repeated herself, and it set me off officially. "You mean to tell me after all I've done for you—feeding you, letting you shower and stay over, this is how you repay me?!"

"Well, I wanted to let you know that I'm also pregnant." She added. She let me know that he was on his way down to Jasper to visit her and that she would have him call me once he arrived. I was psychotically cordial as I told her goodbye and my real anger began to surface. I picked up the phone and called the mess hall where Tyrone worked on post. When the voice on the other end answered,

I didn't say who I was but simply asked if Tyrone Burks's shift was working this weekend. The voice on the other end told me that his shift was off for the weekend. "Thank you," I said as I hung up the phone. I couldn't believe it. My mind began to think back to all the times when he said he was going to the field. Had he been doing this all the while? How did I miss this when Marsha was right under my nose—well, had been anyway before she moved back to her hometown in Jasper, Texas.

That weekend, he came home acting as if he had been working in the field. He had on his BDU and all. He came into the house, greeted me with a kiss, and hugged the kids. I played the game right along with him. I tried my best to keep my composure when our kids were awake so that they wouldn't have to witness their parents arguing. I had never recalled my parents interact with each other in an aggressive or harsh manner, and I didn't want that for my children. He hadn't seen the kids since Thursday, so that day, he spent time playing with them outside and washing the car. I was glad for that. It made it easy for me to avoid him. When night came, however, and the children had been put to sleep, I was ready. He was seated on the couch in the den with the TV on as I stood in the kitchen, washing dishes. All the while, he must have been able to sense my glaring at him as he would occasionally look up.

"What's your schedule like tomorrow?" I asked nonchalantly as I continued to wash the dishes. "Do you have to go to work early, or are you going back to see Marsha?"

"What are you talking about?" He said off-guard.

"Marsha called me and told me that you have been seeing each other for about six months. She told me that you're in love, that you're going to be together, *and* that she's pregnant."

"I don't know what you're talking about! You're talking about Marsha who used to live next door?" He said as if he was insulted.

"Yeah, the one who I used to let come and wash her ass when they didn't have any water—the one who I used to let come by and eat when they didn't have any food in their refrigerator—yeah, that's the one! You didn't even have the decency to find someone to mess around with that I didn't know or didn't know me!" He got up and started to walk towards me in the kitchen.

"You always believing some trick's word over mine!"

"Oh yeah, well, she called here and knew your schedule. I also called the mess hall, and they said that your shift wasn't working because y'all had the weekend off. So if you left here on Thursday and didn't come back till Monday, where were you at?" I asked in a satisfied tone, knowing that I had all ends of his lie exposed. He walked up on me as his eyebrows furrowed and his forehead wrinkled. He slapped me.

"Don't you ever call my job asking no questions about me!" He said, raising his voice. I pushed him with all the might that I had as his anger quadrupled, and he punched me in the side of my head near my temple. I heard an immediate ringing in my ear, and a knot slowly but surely began to form on the back of my ear.

I went out for my birthday and met a man named Henry. He was a white officer in the military who was incredibly fine. We began chitchatting, and I told him that it was my birthday. "Why are you out here by yourself on your birthday?" He asked me. "Where's your husband?"

"Probably somewhere with his girlfriend," I replied. He looked shocked, but his facial expression broke slowly into a smile.

Henry began inviting me to lunch, and I would oblige. He was sweet, and I was lonely. Though on the same base, I never worried about the two of them crossing paths. Tyrone was an NCO and a cook, and Henry was an Officer and military attorney. Tyrone never knew of our rendezvous as I didn't change a thing about my routine.

I just made Henry fit into my world. I took Tyronica to McDonald's every day after school. I told him if he wanted to see me, that's where he could find me. Henry had an apartment off-base, and after a few months ended up giving me a key. I'd go over, and we'd talk, laugh, eat, and just have a good time.

I remember one weekend while Tyrone was off in the field, Henry and I were at the club one night and Keith Sweat's "Make It Last Forever" was playing. The next thing I knew, I passed out right there on the dance floor. Turns out that the knot on the back of my ear was something to be concerned with. I was rushed to the ER, and the doctors determined that the loud music had made my eardrum rupture. I would have to have surgery and all. The doctors assumed the loud music was solely to blame, and I certainly wasn't about to tell them that the real cause was from my husband's punch to my head. I was not about to risk losing my military check.

On more than one occasion, Henry alluded to the fact that he wanted me to leave Tyrone, but after the eardrum incident, he became increasingly concerned. "You need to leave him." Henry firmly suggested.

"Henry, it's not that easy," I told him. "We're married, and I have two kids by this man."

"It is easy—you pack your bags and walk out. He's abusive to you." Henry challenged with care. The truth was, while I had grown to love Henry, I wasn't in love with him, and I definitely wasn't about to leave my husband. If I had left Tyrone, it wouldn't have been to get with Henry. He was a supplement to what I needed at the time. Tyrone was very financially in tune, but emotionally, he would always go so far and then run. I cheated with Henry for emotional reasons. I had the best of both worlds. Tyrone took care of our family and our financial security, and Henry appeased to my wants. He'd draw baths, cook me dinner, buy me flowers, give gifts on special occasions, and even just because. Though Henry's chapter in my life was short-lived, it was a boost to my self-confidence and made me realize that I was wanting and needing more in my marriage and my life.

I remember getting a phone call while Tyrone was in the field one day. It was from yet another mistress that he had started sleeping with. She was 38, and I was 21. At that point in my life, it scared me. This woman on the phone told me everything about me. She told me where I lived, she told me about my husband's work in the field, what I did, where my kids went to school, where they caught the bus, and so on and so forth! She told me she was a KP (Kitchen Personnel) in the same mess hall on base that Tyrone was. She knew everything about me and my family, and I knew nothing of her. It scared me so much I decided to purchase a gun. I needed to have protection for myself and my family in the event she wanted to walk up on me. I didn't know her or what she looked like, but apparently, she knew all of this about me. I called rear detachment and asked if it was possible that I could speak with Tyrone.

"Is everything alright?" The person at rear detachment asked. I assured him it was and that I just needed to speak with Tyrone. The person told me that he was in the field still and asked if what I needed could wait until tomorrow. I told him it could, thanked him, and hung up. I started to think about all that his mistress had said. I wondered who she must have been and started thinking of women's faces that I apparently had overlooked or paid no mind to. I was enraged. I had no more tears left for our situation as I was sadly used to his games by now. I couldn't keep up. So far since we had been in Louisiana, we were on two and a half incidents. Marsha and her false pregnancy claims, this new woman that had called my house, and a failed attempt from one of my neighbors in our building. We started to invite a few couples in our building over to our house for cards, dominoes, and hanging out from time to time.

Rocky Road

One day, I invited one of the usual couples over and the wife, Lily, told me that they regrettably couldn't make it because their family was attending a movie. When I saw her a couple of weeks later, I casually asked her how the movie was.

"Movie?" She asked, seemingly lost.

"Yeah, remember you said you all were going to a movie," I said laughingly, trying to jog her memory. She looked uneasy. "Well, Leigh, actually…" She came closer to me and looked around, checking our surroundings. "We didn't go to a movie. I just feel a little uncomfortable coming to your place after a particular incident." She said.

"What incident?" I asked, tuned in.

"Well, a few weeks back as I was going into the house and Tyrone was sitting outside in your garage, it looked as though he had quite a bit too much drink. He said, 'I wouldn't mind hitting that.' It threw me off, and I uncomfortably tried to laugh it off as I went inside."

I immediately believed her. If he had slept with a woman next door whom I considered a friend, why wouldn't he have made a pass at Lily? I knew who I slept with at night—in fact, everyone can say the same! You may not want to admit it, but in the back of your mind, you know the characteristics and ways of the one you're most intimate with—and I knew Tyrone's ways.

"So, I'm sorry, Leigh. I probably should have said something right then when it happened. But that's the reason I've been distant—I just didn't feel comfortable being around."

"I understand," I told her. "And thank you for telling me." Tallying up all of the incidents—that I knew about anyway—only gave me fuel to lay it all out on him as soon as he came home.

The next day when I heard the garage open, I knew he was back. He unpacked his gear and came inside.

"Man, I'm glad to be home!" He said with a light smile. He walked towards me and greeted me with a kiss. I was in the kitchen cooking.

Dare to Dream

"Smells good in here." He said. I looked at him nonchalantly. "I'm about to hop in the shower. Can you make me a drink?" He asked as he went through regular motions of just getting home. "Sure," I said. He went and got into the shower, and I fixed him a drink like he asked. When I heard the water go off, I made sure my cooking was in a good place to step away briefly and grabbed his drink. I walked into our bedroom and handed it to him. "I need to talk to you about something." He sighed and threw his head back as he dried off.

"I knew it; I could tell by how you were acting when I came in." He said smugly.

"Yeah, so who's Sheila?" I said as I handed him his drink, pushing it into his chest."

"What? Who the f**k is Sheila?" He said, trying to play dumb.

"Yeah, your new one called my house. She told me everything about me—where I work, where my kids go to school—all of that. Why would you have that discussion with her, leaving me at risk to be walked up on with our children?" I asked, growing more furious as more words spilled out of my mouth.

"I don't know what you tripping about. I told you nothing's going on." He said, still maintaining his lying demeanor.

"Well, since you don't know what I'm talking about, I got her number, let's go ahead and give her a call." I picked up the phone and dialed her number. His face looked like he had seen a ghost as I put the receiver to my ear. I stood there for a while as the phone rang, but she didn't answer. No surprise there as he had probably covered his bases enough to tell her to never answer a call from our number; on the other hand, those precautions didn't seem to count anymore as she had made the first move and called me!

Suddenly with anger, he slapped the phone out of my hand. This, in turn, officially angered me, and I pushed him. After he bounced back from my push, he then slapped me. I began to cry.

"Look at what you made me do!" He said. "I'm tired of you always believing something some tricks say over me!"

"Yeah, you right, because the things they say always seem to be true!" I yelled through tears. I started to call out all the things that had happened since we had been in Louisiana—the time when we were supposed to be working on our marriage and building a life together for our children. I threw out everything from his disrespect with Marsha, his inappropriate statement to Lily, and now the audacity of a second unknown caller to our house. I told him if he didn't want to be married anymore to just say it so that we could end it and move on with our lives. I was tired.

Ever since we had been together, there was always something. Always lies, always other women, always the fighting, and it was old. "I'm tired. I want to be happy, and I understand we started when we were younger, but I can't keep going on like this." Suddenly, I heard the door fling open downstairs. It was one of the kids coming in from playing outside. Tyronica appeared in our bedroom door.

"Momma, Man got ice-cream off the truck without any money again!" She hadn't noticed that Tyrone had come home and ran up to hug and kiss him.

"Daddy! You're home!" He picked her up, hugged her, and swung her around like she loved. With my back turned as I tried to get my face together, I couldn't help but think to myself how crazy it was that he had just slapped the piss out of me and now was lovingly swinging our daughter around as if nothing had happened. I didn't want to interrupt moments like that, even though all the while, I was hurting. I guess in some small way, it gave me a glimpse of his strong point as a father—which he was great at—versus how he was as a husband.

"Tyrone, give her the money so they can get the ice cream," I said, trying to hurry the scene along as I was still fixing my face from crying. He handed her some money.

"Tell Man to come here," Tyrone told Tyronica as she ran back outside just as quickly as she had come. With an awkward period of briefly being alone, we both knew our argument would need some kind of finality—especially since I had just declared that I didn't want to be married anymore.

"So, if you don't want to be married…. let's just—"

"No, no, I still want to be married!" He said.

He insisted that he still loved me and didn't want to end our marriage and poured out all of the apologies and love. It was typical of a man who had a lot to lose and was really only sorry that he had gotten caught. He even suggested that we go to counseling. Actually, I had brought it up previously after the Marsha incident when I found myself struggling with trusting him. At that time, however, he never agreed to go, and I was left to my own devices like clocking miles on the car. Now that he was bringing it up on his own, maybe he had given it some thought. He seemed genuine, so I agreed.

A couple of weeks later, I made our first counseling appointment. There was counseling available on-base, but he didn't want word to get back to his unit that would potentially follow him for his military career—or so he said. So, I found a marriage counselor off-base in Leesville, about 10 miles away, and we began going. I told the counselor flat out that I was tired of the abuse, I was tired of the way he treated me, and tired of the cheating. I told our counselor that if he did anything else to hurt me, that I was going to shoot him. I meant it and, our counselor knew I did. Our counselor reiterated the seriousness of my scorn to him.

"If you don't work on your marriage, she indeed is going to harm you," he told him. When it was his turn to talk, he admitted to the affair with Marsha. However, as far as everything else that we were dealing with went, he put on quite the show. He lied and downplayed so much of what had happened between us that the doctor believed his lies because of his calm demeanor and false sincerity. I literally just started crying out of frustration. When he asked Tyrone about the abuse, he even spun that. "She hits me, so I hit her back." He said plainly. My eyes widened like saucers.

"When he consumes alcohol, he becomes a totally different person—to the point where I am fearful of him," I argued. "So, if I confront him for staying out all night, I become the bad guy! Next thing I know, I'm being pounded on." I retorted in my defense.

"Do you have a drinking problem?" The doctor asked him.

"No, I don't have a drinking problem, she gets mad at me, starts yelling, screaming, and pushing me, and then I retaliate." The anger rising up in me had me emotionally undone at times as I was recounting various situations to the doctor. From tears to raising my voice, and boisterous hand gestures, in he came to the appointment in one of his uniforms from work. There he was in his military whites, pressed and starched. The session played against me like I couldn't have imagined.

On top of that, my age and flamboyant appearance at the time made me seem immature and unhinged. Here I was, with my burgundy hair and playboy bunny and Gucci symbols cut into my head, and my husband appeared to be some sort of poster child for reverse abuse. By the time we left the doctor that day, this man had the doctor convinced that *I* was the culprit of the problems in our marriage. The doctor ended up prescribing me a calming medication called Lorazepam that I had to take three times daily. What I couldn't figure out was, *how come I was the one who had to medicate, and I wasn't the main source of the problems in our marriage?* Funny all the ways we enable the negative behavior of others.

CHAPTER 6

Next Level Crazy

Counseling or not, the abuse continued and was always more so physical than verbal. We seemed to constantly fight, and he was the kind of person who couldn't own up to his shortcomings. Black eyes and bruises were a usual consequence of his anger, and I grew used to fighting him back as a fed-up means to defend myself. Though he was abusive, I never felt like one of those "victimized" women who just took his hits. I defended myself and got hits in of my own. That in no way excuses his actions, but I didn't feel helpless per se, just stuck in this unhealthy situation that I had sadly gotten used to over the years.

Tyrone came home one night, drunk from hanging out in the streets with "his friends" and wanted to fight. By this time, I had started clocking the miles on our car and taking note of any discrepancies in his miles traveled versus the miles that should have been represented based on where he said he was going. Earlier on this particular evening, I called a taxi. When it arrived, I got in and blatantly asked, "What part of town would you go to that would leave red mud on your tires?" The driver told me a trailer park. I told him to take me there. I can't necessarily explain it in instances of natural understanding, but having never been to his mistress' house, something on the inside was leading me directly to where it was. As the driver turned down a few streets as I directed him, I saw our car was parked in one of the yards. I told him to let me out a few trailers down so I could approach the house unsuspected. All the lights of the house were out as I went up to the door and knocked. A few minutes later, the door opened.

"I'm Leigh, the wife of the man whose car is parked in your yard—the wife whose house you called a few weeks back!" The same woman that had boldly called my house and ran down the details of everything she knew about me, stood there in a shirt and some booty shorts looking dumbfounded while trying to act oblivious. If she wanted to play games, it was no problem for me. I told her plainly, "Every time I see you, I'm going to whoop your ass. Not for f**king my husband, but for calling my house and disrespecting me and my house." Her face looked shocked as she tried to play it off.

"I don't know what you're talking about; I don't know a Tyrone; that's my friend's car."

I rolled my eyes and almost chuckled. "Nevertheless, tell your friend—Tyrone—to come up out of there." Suddenly, I heard some footsteps run down the back steps of her trailer. I hurried around towards the back in hopes of catching Tyrone making an exit but was too late. He had maneuvered through the lots of the other trailers and disappeared. I walked back toward the front of her trailer, and she had gone inside and locked the door. I got in my car and headed home, looking around for him as I drove. I never ran into him, however, and went home and waited for him to show up.

A couple of hours later, Tyrone stumbled into the house, drunk as can be. He came in through the garage, and I was seated in the den with the TV on, though I wasn't paying it much mind. I was stewing in what I was going to say when he came home. He opened the door, and I immediately went for it.

"So you ain't stopped seeing her, I see?"

"What are you talking about?" He said, slurring his words. "I was at my friend's house!" He said, raising his voice.

"I went to your little girlfriend's house, and our car was in the yard. I heard you when you jumped out of the back door!"

"I let my friend use the car so he could go to his girlfriend's house." He said. I grew amusingly annoyed.

"So, where were you when your friend was at the girlfriend's house?" He stumbled in his words as he tried to keep from giving me a direct answer. "How did you get home then?" I continued to pile on questions to his baseless lies as he got more and more angry with having to come up with answers that weren't true. I attempted to walk away from him as he grabbed me. "You don't walk off from me!" He said furiously. "And you don't come and get my car after I've told somebody they could use it and leave me stranded!" He pushed me.

He pushed me and I fell to the floor. Fueled by anger, I leapt to my feet and pushed him back. He slapped me, and then I slapped him back. The next thing I knew, I was on the ground from a punch to the face. As I was down, he kicked me in my side, and I winced in pain. He looked at me with a glare of rage. I began to cry. Though he slapped me around here and there, he hadn't punched me dead on in my face since that first time back in high school. I felt the fear rise up in me again. That was the night that I made up in my mind that it would be the last time that he ever laid his hands on me again. I lay there on our kitchen floor in pain, crying, as I could feel my face swell up. The longer I lay there, I hoped he would just go away. He was standing there over me, his face still painted with a strange, indescribable fury. I made an attempt to get up, and he reached down and helped me. "I don't want your help," I said as I did my best to snatch away and get up on my own.

"I'm sorry, I didn't mean to—you just kept pushing me, and screaming, and taunting me—"

"Nah, you know what? You need help." I said. "When you drink, you are a different person. Not the person I married and not the person I love."

I walked past him and went to our bedroom to get a change of clothes. The clothes I had on now had blood on them from my burst face. I went into the bathroom and closed and locked the door behind me. I sat on the toilet and cried heavily. My sobs were so hard that they were inaudible. *How did I get into this?* I wondered to myself. On top of that, I wondered, *how would I get out*? I looked at my reflection in the mirror. I had a broken blood vessel in my eye and an overall puffy and tight face. I cleaned myself up so my appearance would be as normalized as possible once my kids woke up. I took inventory in that very moment and realized that this altercation had all stemmed from his acts of indiscretion—solely. He had stayed out all night with some other woman only to come home and beat me up for confronting his infidelity. In my mind, I didn't need another marriage counseling session, no intervention, no more apologies or promises to change—I was done. His behavior wasn't going to stop, and therefore, the violence wasn't.

I was in the kind of relationship that I couldn't just walk out. I couldn't call the police or the MPs—my husband was in the military, and reporting incidents like ours could jeopardize his military career. If he got put out of the military, how would my kids and I survive? I had more than one mouth to feed now—I had two. I was scared to just up and leave with my kids as he had told me numerous times during altercations after I threatened to leave, "You can do what you want, but you are not taking my kids." Though I'm sure my father would have welcomed me back with opened arms, I didn't want to go home with a failed marriage and two children on my hip.

One day, I was sitting down and contemplating all the things that Tyrone had done to me. Tyrone had inflicted emotional and physical abuse on me that I could never have imagined from the beginning of our love story as teenagers. What we had together could no longer be called "love." It was a far cry from that by now. For him, it was about the thrill of new women and escapades while still being able to come home to his family. For me, it was about keeping my guard up and anticipating what new form of disrespect he was going to come up with, next. It was toxic and turned me into a person I didn't like or know. He was out cheating on me, and rather than showing any kind of remorse, he acted out on me physically, out of anger of getting caught. I would contemplate what was so wrong with me that he couldn't commit to acting right. It hurt me, no matter how much I tried to act like it was "our norm." It even drove me to dark thoughts of killing him so I wouldn't have to endure his painful cycles anymore. I started to contemplate how I could kill him while avoiding going to jail.

During that surgery, where part of my eardrum had to be removed in my right ear, left me partially deaf permanently. That wasn't supposed to be part of "happily ever after." All the abuse, all the black eyes, all the times I got dragged across the floor, all the women—everything—drove me to desperate measures. I decided that I was done and that it was time to do something about it.

One night, I helped him get totally drunk to the point of being wasted. This wasn't very hard, considering that Tyrone was a drinker, anyway. I wrapped something in a towel and used it to hit myself hard enough for bruising to occur. It was a crazy idea, but I had found myself in a crazy place in my marriage. I wanted out by any means necessary. I called the Military Police (MPs) and told them that he had jumped on me. By now, he was practically passed out drunk. They bought it, and I was going to use it as documented evidence of his physicality if I ever had to do something drastic to him in self-defense. One of the MPs who came recognized Tyrone from the mess hall. They saw me all bruised up, did a report, and took Tyrone with them—though it wasn't so much an arrest as it was a trip from the house to let him sober up. All the while, he was too drunk to remember the scene ever taking place—just as I had planned.

It was getting close to the Fourth of July weekend, and Tyrone and I were planning to travel home to Arkansas to visit family as we tried to do during the holidays. The Fourth of July is usually a time marked by family fellowship and summer fun; here I was, though, at my wit's end. I was nervous all the time, crying, unhappy, and miserable. What was I to do? I had two kids to think of, regarding any decisions that I made about my marriage, and they mattered most.

On the night before we were planning to travel, Tyrone told me that he was planning to go to a friend's house for a drink and would be back home before it was time for us to head out in the morning. I said okay, and even ironed his clothes and helped him to get dressed. If I didn't have such a keen sense of observation, he could have perhaps left that night without me suspecting something awry. However, I notice everything. Where he made his mistake, was he poured a drink to go for his "friend" in the same cup that he had been drinking from previously. What guy does that for another guy? Anyhow, I took my Lorazepam and went on to sleep. The funny thing was, even though I felt being put on medication for Tyrone's behavior in our marriage was ridiculous, I did find that it helped me sleep versus being up all hours of the night wondering where he was.

Around four in the morning, I heard the garage raise and the sound of the car pulling in. It was him creeping back in from his "friend's." I wasn't having it. I got up out of bed, grabbed my gun, and made my way towards our backdoor where the steps came up from the garage. I stood in the doorway and watched him as he began climbing the stairs unsuspectingly. I fired the gun and aimed for his head. He ducked just in time as the bullet shot right past him. He ran back down the stairs screaming, "You crazy b***h, what's wrong with you!?"

I stood at the top of the stairs, un-phased. "I'm sick of it," I said. "I've had it; you ain't coming up in here, go back to wherever you've been all night." It was the first time that I think I had him scared for his actual life. I watched him run and get back into the car, heard him back out of the garage and speed off. I went back to my bedroom and had a mix of various emotions. I felt empowered, yet I somehow felt scared of myself. Had I allowed him to drive me to such crazy actions as firing a gun with my children in the house? He went to a local gas station and called me. I answered the phone.

"What's wrong with you? Are you f**king crazy?" His voice had a mixture of both anger and fear. I told him I was done with him and for him to leave me alone. I hung up the phone, and since I was awake, decided to get dressed for the day. I showered, made up my face with some Mary Kay products, and after doing so, left my sleeping kids at home to go on a mission (that's how I knew I was crazy). I called a cab and told him to take me to Tyrone's mistress' house--in the trailer park with the red mud. When the cab pulled up, Tyrone was underneath his mistress' car hood with our car right next to it, apparently giving hers a jump. I got out of the cab, walked up towards the door, and he didn't even notice. She, however, was standing in the doorway, and as I walked closer towards her, I hit my purse. Back in the day, I'd hit my purse when I was in the club or out and about to let any and everyone know that I was "packing." I snatched her out of her house and commenced to whooping her ass. Tyrone finally noticed that I was there and stood there, shocked. "Let's go!" I said as I walked to the passenger side of our car, and he walked to the driver's side. We drove off. The whole ride home, we argued, and he fussed talking

Dare to Dream

smack. All the while, I'm sitting there thinking to myself like, *"Wow, you're the one who was caught in the wrong and have the nerve to be running off at the mouth?"* It was crazy. No remorse whatsoever, no apology, just audacious nerve to try and argue with me! When we arrived at the house, we continued our arguing. Tyrone peeked in on the kids who were still asleep. While he was, I b-lined straight for the kitchen to place my gun back in its secret hiding place that he knew nothing of. After doing so, I checked in on the kids for myself and headed back down the hallway to finish packing and getting the kids' clothes out for the trip.

"So you got caught up again at her house?"

"Man, I gave my friend a ride to her house because her car wouldn't start!" I was pissed. Here he was, caught once again and was still lying to my face.

"So where's the friend?" I challenged him.

"He was in the house!" He said as he yelled back. I shook my head and walked away. I went to the bedroom to finish packing so we could get ready to go. I was still going home as planned. He came into the bedroom, *still* going on and on.

"You're supposed to help people who help you," he said smugly yet seriously. The trigger word was help, H-E-L-P and I will never forget it as long as I live. I turned around sharply.

"Help?!" I said in angered disbelief. "What has that b***h ever done to 'help' us besides further help destroy our marriage and our home?!" I turned around while he was still standing there talking, went into the kitchen and reached inside my canisters on top of the refrigerator where I had just placed my gun moments before. It was high up, and out of reach from my children.

I went back into the bedroom, and he was still talking and turned around, facing the opposite direction.

Next Level Crazy

"She helped us? She HELPED US?" I repeated myself. "HELP THIS mother*****r!" I said as I pulled the trigger to the gun and fired a bullet from the magazine in his leg as he fell to the floor. I had snapped, and it was almost as if I was a whole different person. I didn't even see him at this point; all I knew was I was enraged. I was pulling the magazine, trying to put the rest of the 5 bullets in him but the magazine was stuck, and the gun wouldn't fire. I was literally going to kill him. He laid there on the floor, yelling for me to help him. "Tell that b***h to help you," I said. He was angry, and he was, of course in pain, but more than anything, I think he was frightened. "Call my momma then!" He exclaimed in pain. Coolly, I replied, "Sure, I'll call her." I dialed his mom, she answered, and I said, "Lil Momma, I just shot Tyrone, talk to you later," and hung up the phone. I got in our 1989 Ford Escort GT and left him lying there on the floor, kids still asleep in bed. I drove to Sears & Roebuck in Leesville, Louisiana because I was still going home to see my daddy that weekend as planned. I got to Sears & Roebuck and ran into Tyrone's First sergeant's wife. She was always overly bubbly and friendly in a way that got on my nerves.

"Hi, Leigh. How are you?" She asked.

"I'm fine," I told her. "Are you guys still going home this weekend?" She inquired.

"Yes, we are," I said.

"Where's Tyrone?" She asked. I looked at her calmly and responded, "I just shot him." She looked at me, and her smile faded as she began to slowly realize that I was *not* joking.

"Leigh, you need to go home. Someone heard that gunshot—you need to go home right now."

"Okay," I said, still un-phased by everything. If I never believed in the opposing forces of good and evil, I believed it then. It was like I was being dealt with by both sides. I got back in the car and headed back to our house. I felt like I was in the middle of a spiritual tug of war. I heard an audible voice say, "*When you get to the house, tell him to do exactly what you say or else you'll kill him.*" I got back to the house, and he was still lying there on the floor. I could hear the police sirens in the distance. I stood over his body with the gun. "If you don't tell the police what I'm about to say, I will kill you for real, do you understand?"

"Yes." He said while nodding.

"You're going to tell the MPs that while getting ready to go to Arkansas, we were trying to get the magazine out and the gun backfired, do you understand?" I sternly asked him.

"Yes." He reassured me.

At that time in the state of Louisiana, you couldn't have a gun and the magazine in the same place. When the MPs got there, he told them what I had instructed him. He had to be taken immediately for emergency surgery, and I stayed behind at home with the kids.

By this time, our families were on the way to Louisiana from Arkansas due to the phone call that I made earlier to Tyrone's mother. She called my dad and told him about what was happening. I was at home, still un-phased with no plans to go to the hospital. Shortly after, the First Sergeant's wife came by to check on things. She told me that I needed to go to the hospital so that the incident didn't look intentional. "They'll wonder why you're not there otherwise. It will look like you tried to kill him." She warned.

By this time, Tyrone was calling me to bring his military identification and paperwork to the hospital, and I was so done that I paid none of it any attention. I eventually went ahead, though, as the First Sergeant's wife suggested.

"I'll see after the children while you go. Is there someone I can call for them?" She asked. I told her that I would ask my downstairs neighbor named Tonya. Tonya agreed, and so I left and headed for the hospital. When I arrived, I told him that I was done, and I wanted a divorce.

He said, "Well, if I knew you wanted a divorce, I would have told them that you shot me on purpose so that they could send you to jail!"

"Tell them if you want to," I said, "and you'll end up dead." His mother arrived later and talked with me while he was in surgery. I remember her telling me, "If you all can't get along and do right by one another, you need to go your separate ways and leave one another alone. I don't want you to relive my life." She told me. She had shot Tyrone's father in his own past saga of drama. By now, she was saved and living a life for Christ, but our present was paralleling their past. She too endured infidelity and heartache from Tyrone's father. She too had been driven to the point of crazy after trying to keep things together for her children when all the while she was falling apart.

He was shot in his right calf. The doctors said if he had been shot an inch higher, it would have hit a major artery and he would have potentially died. In fact, some of the bullet fragments, they were unable to get at all for that very reason—just attempting to retrieve them might have put his life in jeopardy. He stayed in the hospital for a few days after his surgery. He had a complete cast from his hip down to his feet with only his toes exposed. For the few days that he was in the hospital, he wanted me to be there and acted like nothing had happened in the first place.

I stayed overnight with him while he was there. I remember while he was asleep, sitting in the hospital recliner and watching him, just thinking about everything. I replayed in my mind all the things that had led us up to this point. I thought how crazy I was to have shot my husband—the man I supposedly loved. I wondered why we couldn't get our relationship on a healthy course. I wondered what kind of life we were living that I would be driven to have a gun in my house, let alone fire it inside the house while my children were home, or get up

Dare to Dream

and leave my house to go on a creep mission to find my wayward husband. What was this life that we called "normal?" And what would come of it after he got out of this hospital?

When he was released from the hospital, I, of course, had to drive him home as he was unable to drive himself. We got home, and he transformed back into an attentive and lovey-dovey version of himself. All of a sudden, he had placed a premium on quality time. He wanted to watch TV together, play card games, and listen to music. For me to have just shot him, his behavior seemed strange to me. So much so, that I began to wonder if he was plotting some sort of revenge on me for what had transpired. Shortly after being home from his surgery, Tyrone received orders to relocate to Bamberg, Germany. In light of his cast, however, his orders to move were pending until his doctor announced his total recovery. As soon as we got word of his orders, I immediately made up in my mind that I wasn't going anywhere. If anything, I was going home to Arkansas. I refused to move halfway across the world in a marriage that was on pins and needles. On top of that, I had just shot him! Things weren't okay between us, no matter how "normal" he tried to play them down.

True to my word, every time I saw his mistress thereafter, I beat her up as previously promised. It didn't matter where we were—I didn't care. One day when going to Tyrone's job to pick up some paperwork for him, I noticed her on the back dock. I walked up to her, caught her off-guard, and slapped her. She grabbed her face in shock.

"I'm not even seeing him!" She yelled. She couldn't retaliate much, as doing so would have put her job in jeopardy. On top of that, Shift Leaders weren't supposed to be fraternizing with KPs. If someone by chance had seen me slap her and inquired about what was going on, the sheer possibility of me getting angry and telling that she was sleeping with my husband would have created problems for her career

Next Level Crazy

as well as his. So, she said nothing, and I walked off. I had her by the balls, and she knew it.

Another time, I saw her at the gas station, and this time, I pounced on her in full force from behind. The same way that she called my house with all of her information and felt like she could bombard my life, I felt the same—let's see how you like it when I walk up on you—was my mind frame.

"What is wrong with you?" She screamed.

"Nothing is wrong with me," I said.

"I'm not even seeing him!" She maintained.

"Well, you shoulda been—because every time I see you, this is what's going to happen." I walked back to my car, got in, and drove off. I was fed up and sick of everything. I became relentless at getting even. I didn't care how long it would take; I just knew that before it was said and done, I would get my revenge.

I remember once; I was out grocery shopping for a farewell BBQ get-together that Tyrone and I were having with friends. It would be our last get-together in Louisiana before packing up our family and moving back to Arkansas for Tyrone's 30-day leave prior to going to Germany. I guess I had been gone shopping too long for Tyrone's liking because shortly after returning home and hopping in the shower for our get-together, I prepared to get dressed and made a shocking discovery. As I opened my drawer to get a pair of panties, I noticed that the seat was missing. It was peculiar. I grabbed another pair and realized they were cut too. I frantically scoured my entire drawer and discovered every pair of underwear I owned, and every bra as well, were ransacked. My bras were cut in half, and the seats were cut out of all of my panties. Every single pair except the ones I had just taken off. I went to my closet, and my clothes were the same way.

"Tyrone!" I screamed in anger as he sauntered in the room, drunk with his cast. "What is wrong with you?" I asked in disbelief.

"What took you so long?" He said. "Don't take nobody that long to go to the store and pick up a few items for a party." I looked at him in annoyed astonishment.

"So, you did all of this because you thought I was out with somebody?" I asked for clarity.

"Yeah, won't nobody be sniffing those panties!" He said crazily. The only thing he didn't cut up was my coat. He even alluded to this "courtesy" by saying that he didn't want me to be cold when the season changed. *How crazily considerate.* He walked back out of the room like nothing happened as I was stuck there in limbo. I quickly washed the clothes that I had taken off so that I could put them back on and go grab a new outfit for our get-together and a few items to start my wardrobe over. I literally had nothing left intact but my coat. The thing about it was, at this point, I had already made up in my mind that I was on my way out of this relationship. Tyrone's orders in Germany were for three years. Since he had to go ahead of us to secure housing for our family, my plan, unbeknownst to him, was to stay put in Arkansas. When he sent for us, I would put it off for as long as I could and then finally tell him that I wasn't coming at all. By then, I would have a job, I already would have my family's house back, and I would be independent enough to be able to take care of my kids on my own. That was my plan, and I was sticking to it.

The military packed our house up in one day and the next day divvied our belongings up between storage and shipping to Arkansas. That same week, Tyrone finally got his cast removed, and we packed up our car to head home to Arkansas. I was back at the very place that I wanted so desperately to be away from. On the other hand, for the new start that I was planning *sans* Tyrone, home was where I needed to be. Trish Ann lived in our family house now, and we moved back in alongside her.

Next Level Crazy

Once back home, after we had caught up with both sides of our family, it didn't take long for Tyrone to get back to his old shenanigans. He started staying out late and coming home at odd hours of the night. The thing that was different this time was I didn't care. In the back of my mind, I had to stick to my plan of preparing to walk away from this toxic relationship.

One Friday night on our first weekend home, we were staying over at his mom's house when Tyrone mentioned that he was going out. I told him okay, and the kids and I settled in and spent time with Lil Momma. Hours passed, and we all turned in for the evening. The next morning, I woke up and Tyrone still wasn't home. I wasn't even surprised. I fixed the kids some cereal, and they ran off to watch Saturday morning cartoons. I cleaned up after them and prepared to fix me something to eat. Suddenly, I heard footsteps behind me as an arm came around me for an embrace. Immediately knowing it was Tyrone, I pulled away. "Where you been?" I asked.

"I told you last night that I was hanging out with my friends!" He said defensively.

"No, you're just getting in, and it's morning." I retorted back.

"I've been here!" He said, lying quickly as he was used to doing.

"No, I've been up, and you're in the same clothes you had on when you left here last night." I pointed out to him.

"Don't get started in my momma's house!" He said as he slapped me. As soon as he did that, I grabbed the small black cast iron skillet that I had placed on the stove in preparation to cook and swung around, attempting to hit him.

"I told you, you're not going to be hitting me anymore!" I said as I prepared to connect with his face. He grabbed my hand just in time to avoid getting clobbered.

"I said, don't start this in my momma's house!" He said, getting closer to my ear. He loosened me with force and then walked out of the kitchen. I went into the bathroom and started to get dressed so that I could get my kids together and go back down to my family's house. I wasn't in the mood to deal with his games for the day.

I went and enrolled Tyronica in school. Per Tyrone's relocation to Germany, the list for housing usually took anywhere from 90 to 120 days to get approved. This meant once he left, the soonest timeframe we were to go over and move with him wouldn't be until about the first of the year. That's what he thought, anyway. As far as I was concerned, I was finding a school for her entire first-grade year, as I, of course, wasn't planning to move at all.

Our second weekend home rolled around, and on Sunday afternoon, the kids and I were outside playing. I was anticipating Tyrone's arrival home soon so that I could switch places with him, take the car and run some errands. When he pulled up in the yard and got out of the car, I noticed that he practically stumbled out from being drunk as a skunk. I did a double take at him. As I approached him to get the keys, he reeked of alcohol.

"Have you been drinking?" I asked, already seeing that the answer was obvious.

"I had a couple of beers with Joe Harold." He said as he tried to walk past me and head towards the porch.

"You've had more than a couple of beers!" I said matter-of-factly. "You don't think!" I said. It reminded me of an incident a couple of years prior when we were driving back to Fort Polk after one of our weekend visits in Arkansas with our family. He had been drinking before we got on the highway with the kids. He had been speeding and zipped past a police car that was driving in the opposite direction along the heavily wooded two-lane highway. It was nighttime, and the policeman's lights flashed, and his siren came on as he slowed down to make a U-turn to follow us. My mind raced. If Tyrone got pulled over and charged with a DUI, not only was he going to be affected, but I was too. A DUI charge for an NCO in the military was great grounds for losing his rank, getting an Article 15, and even being put out altogether. I thought of having to put up the money to get him out of jail—something we didn't have the luxury to waste during that time. I sprang into action to switch seats with him. Thankfully, at that time, we were driving a Deuce and a half—one of those old schooled big-bodied cars that had a one large front seat uninterrupted by armrests or consoles. If not for this, switching seats with him while in motion would have been impossible and who knows how things might have played out. We so happened to be going down a pretty steep hill as the officer tailed behind us in the distance. This gave us just enough time to make the switch while being temporarily out of sight as we were approaching the top part of the hill while the officer was still at the bottom. After we successfully made the switch, I pulled over. The officer gave us a ticket for speeding, but we both knew we had dodged a far greater charge. So, when he stumbled out of the car that day, I was livid as I thought back quite clearly to that instance.

"You're getting ready to leave, and you're riding around with these out-of-town plates while drinking and driving like you won't get arrested!" I fumed as I opened the car door and got inside. I looked up, and he had blatantly ignored me to go and play with the kids. The window was already down as I yelled his name. "Tyrone! Do you hear me talking to you?" He became angry from my nagging and whipped around and walked back towards the car and stood there, staring at me. "You know what?" I said, fed up, "I'm not going!"

"You're not going where?" He asked, thrown off, as I believe for a moment or two, he must have thought I meant I wasn't going to run my errand anymore. But I wanted to make it clear for him.

"I'm not going to Germany!" I retorted spitefully. Tyronica and Tyrone Jr. were still on the porch playing. "I don't plan on going with you anyway, so I don't care what you do! I'll have the household goods, the money, the car—everything I'll need, and I'm going to cheat, cheat, cheat, and CHEAT just like you while you're gone!" In saying that, I rolled up the window and put our stick shift in first gear. His eyes grew wide, and he became enraged.

"Yea, I'ma show you what it feels like!" I said through the glass. Suddenly, he punched his fist through my driver side window as hundreds of pieces of glass shattered in my lap and on the car floor. I screamed, and he reached inside the car and grabbed my neck with both hands and began to choke the life out of me.

"Oh, you gone cheat, huh? You gone cheat?!" He said vengefully as I hit his hands with all of my might as I couldn't breathe, and his grip grew tighter. I panicked and pressed my foot on the gas to drive off. All the while, he maintained his grip on my neck. He started to move alongside the car, refusing to let me go until I applied more gas and the car's speed outdid that of his footsteps. I gasped for breath and kept driving. I looked in the rearview, and he had stopped dead in the street, no longer trying to come after the car. I frantically tried to get my composure as I drove around aimlessly for a while before beginning my actual errands.

Ever since news of the gun incident had died down among our family, I didn't want any more suspicions about the true nature of me and Tyrone's relationship. Having said that, I didn't want to go to anyone's house to vent, and I didn't want to be questioned. So, I kept driving for a while until I was calm enough to focus back on my errand trip. By the time I was finished, I figured enough time had passed for his temper to calm down so I could drive back home. Thankfully when I returned, he was passed out and my sister Trish Ann was feeding the kids. As usual, once he passed out, by and large, the worst part of his drunkenness was over. He would wake up in the morning sobered up, and chances were, he would act like nothing had happened, which he usually did. The only thing was, now, I had spilled the beans about my true intentions of not going to Germany and with only two weeks left before it was time for him to leave, I knew I had to play nice and convince him that my confession was merely a bluff to get him to act right. All the while in my mind, I still knew one thing: I was NOT going to Germany.

CHAPTER 7

Germany

From the moment I dropped Tyrone off at the airport, I felt a sense of release. As far as I was concerned, for the next three years, I would be at peace. I wouldn't be fighting every weekend, wouldn't wonder where he was or wonder what he was doing if he stayed out all night.

One weekend, Tyrone's mom had invited me and the kids to a Friday night church service. I went. I went up to get prayed for, and I passed out under the glory. When I came to, everything was crystal clear. Even my perception in the room was different. The first noticeable change was that I didn't have a vengeful spirit in me anymore. I didn't have the desire to inflict harm on behalf of being hurt. I felt calm and refreshed—a newness. I was always constantly unhappy within myself, and the moment that I got up off the floor, that melted away.

I started reading my Bible and learning about this new person that I was. Tyrone called me and told me that he had made it there safely. I told him about the experience that I had. "Yea, okay." He said nonchalantly. He brought up my coming over, and for the first time, I looked forward to the idea. That's another reason I knew I was changed. I felt like since I had become better, maybe we could be better as a couple based on that strength. I felt like I could be a better mother, sister, friend—just an overall better person. The love that I had been searching for, I had stumbled upon. I had found it in Christ, where I should have been looking for it all along. Receiving Christ into my heart helped me find wholeness and peace. I knew I was loved, and therefore, I didn't seek it in someone else for validation or security. In fact, I could bring greater love to my relationships, having experienced the true gift of love.

You want everyone else around you to feel it as well—especially those close to you—your children, spouse, siblings, friends—everyone. With new eyes, I was able to stop being so consumed with what Tyrone was doing wrong and focus on my own actions. I'm in no way excusing his abuse, but for the first time, I was taking ownership of my role in our marriage. My arguing, my selfishness, and my anger. I had shot the man, for crying out loud, and could have killed him! Seeing who I had been allowed my healing process to unfold. I was no longer a victim. I was now a survivor. That's a place of power versus a place of hopelessness.

As the time drew closer for my family to transition, leaving my family in Arkansas was one thing, but leaving the United States for another country was altogether different. My family warned me the whole time never to go. While Tyrone no doubt was the root of their warning, I think a lot of it also had to do with the lifestyle in general. I, on the other hand, had no real hesitancy about going. My relationship with God had grown to be my foundation of peace and reassurance. As long as God was in Germany, I would be just fine. My first real experience witnessing God move in my finances was around this time. Looking back to when I had watched my mother prepare her "dues" as she called it, I remember how she would give me an envelope, and I would write on it and put my money in it. I'm not sure if she knew it or not, but she was teaching me the power of giving.

Germany

Just before we were to depart for Germany, I only had $600 and needed to pay $60 in tithes. I thought twice about it because I really needed all of the money to use for odds and ends for our trip. I heard God say, "Pay that money, and I'll double that money before you leave." I was obedient to what I thought was His leading, and sure enough, before I left the church, people were giving me money and I had $120. I heard my mom talk about it as a child, but from that day forward, having had my own experience, I made up in my mind that I wasn't going to cheat God.

Tyrone had gone ahead of the kids and I to get our living arrangements squared away. A month or so later, and it was finally time for the kids and I to head over. It was now January, and 1991 had made its debut. I rented a car and drove to Illinois from Arkansas—the longest road trip I had taken by myself with just my kids up until that point. From there, we took a rental car from Illinois to St. Louis and then prepared to board our flight to Frankfurt, Germany—the last flight leaving American soil before the war Desert Storm began. I have never liked to fly, so I was nervous, but once I prayed, my nerves settled a bit. My excitement started to outweigh my nerves as I looked forward to seeing Tyrone and beginning this new chapter of our lives. I was different, and I prayed that God would move on his heart like he had mine. That he would save him and bring our marriage back together.

When the kids and I got to Germany, everything was going pretty good for the first two years. We traveled a lot and spent quality time together visiting castles, the beautiful green countryside, and other points of interest in Germany. When Tyrone went ahead of us and moved to Germany, I had begun attending church pretty regularly back home, and my spirit was a little stronger and a bit more optimistic. I had found a new sense of strength in my faith through prayer and being around people at church.

One of the first things I did once I moved to Germany was to discover the church on base and begin attending the services. I recall inviting Tyrone one Sunday, and he agreed to go with the kids and me. This Sunday was very special, as he answered an altar call for salvation and gave his life to Christ. I was beyond excited. It seemed like a sign of a turning point in our marriage, as we were no longer unequally yoked in our beliefs. He had enjoyed the person I had become. I wasn't always on the defense now and operated with a bit more optimism when it came to our disagreements. In fact, our disagreements were minimal. Instead of fighting my battles, I had learned to turn to God in prayer. When I had formerly tried to deal with things on my own, we would end up fighting. My new mode of operation was to let my husband be himself—minus the nagging or complaining. It never did any good, anyway. My new line of defense was prayer.

In 1992, Tyrone received an urgent Red Cross message from the states, granting his temporary leave for an emergency back home. Turns out, the emergency message was for me. My sister, Sue-Baby, had a brain aneurysm and was in the hospital. Immediately after receiving this message, I had another strong spiritual occurrence happen—probably one of the strongest I had ever experienced up until that point. It was an out-of-body experience, similar to déjà vu. I was lying in a La-Z-Boy all the way in Germany and had a clear vision of my sister Sue-Baby's spirit leaving her body. It was so real to me and honestly a bit disturbing. I could sense something very pressing about her being sick.

We packed the children and were back in the states within 12 hours of receiving the message. From Frankfurt, we flew to Dallas, and from Dallas, we flew to Little Rock. I had traveled the furthest and somehow got to the hospital before all of my family members. When I arrived, she was unresponsive. I wasn't sure of my sister's

Germany

salvation, so I earnestly prayed to God and asked Him to use my mouth to intercede on her spirit's behalf for the gift of repentance. I knew her spirit was still present, even though she was physically unconscious. I wanted someone to go into the hospital room with me, who was in faith with me. The only person who was with me was Tyronica. She was young, and it wasn't the best idea given the circumstances, but I knew the faith of a child would at least be pure.

After I prayed for her, I had a sense of peace. I met with my father and siblings after that. The doctors wanted to run one more test to see if they could identify any brain activity. If they could not, the decision to keep her on life support or take her off would be on us. It was a tough decision to make, but we agreed to take her off. Her organs were deteriorating and therefore, so was her quality of life. My siblings and I had to take the lead on the decision, as my father would have never come to that conclusion alone. My sister would have been on life support forever if it was solely up to him. And I suppose as a parent, that hopefulness is completely understandable.

After my sister passed and we returned home to Germany, Tyronica began to see her everywhere. In her bedroom, in the bathroom, while she was in the bathtub, and other peculiar places. The transference of spirits is real, and I knew that it had happened while we were in the hospital. She had a dream once that Sue-Baby wanted to walk with her to the Cracker Box, the convenience store that was down the street from our home back in Arkansas. I began to regret taking her into the hospital room with me that day back in Little Rock. She was becoming terrified of these frequent sightings with my sister. I told her, "The next time that you see her, tell her that you don't want to go with her and that you don't want her to visit anymore." She told me that she tried that but still was seeing her in places. I didn't know what else to do, so I called my Pastor at our church on base and told him what was going on. He agreed to come to our house to pray. After he did so, Tyronica never saw my sister again.

By now, both of the kids were in school, and I didn't want to sit at home all day. I got a part-time job at the kids' school on-base that aided in helping to pay back the loan we incurred for traveling to my sister's funeral on emergency leave. I was paid in marks—German money—and at that time, every American dollar was worth 1.54 marks. I wanted to be an active participant in my family's finances, so having this job came in handy for shopping on the German economy, travel, and for accommodating my phone bill for calling home to the states, which I did at least once a month.

There was a park that was walking distance from our house in the center of our housing complex. Tyrone would take the kids there regularly during the week and sometimes on the weekends.

One day, when Tyrone and the kids got home, I randomly asked Tyrone Jr., "Did you have fun at the park?" I said as I prepared dinner.

"Yeah, me and Ms. Terri's kids had fun, we played together! They're my new friends."

"That's nice," I said as I continued cooking. I thought nothing of it at all until the next few times when they would come home from the park. I casually would ask Tyrone Jr. how his time was, and he would consistently allude to playing with Ms. Terri's kids. Around this same time, I noticed that the time at the park was becoming more frequent, and the duration, longer. At first, it was once a week when Tyrone was off, and then it started increasing to taking Tyrone Jr.—who got out of school before Tyronica did—practically daily during the week.

"Who's this lady Terri that's always at the park when you guys go?" I asked, generally.

"Oh, she's married to Sgt. Gray." The way that he talked about him, I didn't think any more of it, really. I was mainly being inquisitive for the sake of knowing who my kids were playing with, on what was becoming a more frequent basis. The park seemed like a random place to *always* run into the same kids unless it was pre-planned. This prompted me to join Tyrone and Man at the park one day. Though I had joined my family at the park at times before, I hadn't gone lately as it had sort of become Tyrone's quality time with the kids—which I thought was good. But this day, I decided to make a cameo. I got to the park, and when I walked up, I saw Tyrone sitting on the bench with a lady. They were smiling and laughing and excessively chummy. Like I said before, everyone knows who they sleep with at night—having said that, I observed that Tyrone's behavior and actions were way too friendly. They were so engrossed in talking that they hadn't even noticed that I walked up. "Hey!" I said.

As they both looked up, there seemed to be a bit of surprise from my greeting. The woman on the bench flashed me a light smile.

"I'm Leigh, Tyrone's wife," I said as I extended my hand to her for a handshake. "We live right up the street from here." She shook my hand.

"Oh, I'm Terri, nice to meet you." At this point in the introduction, that I had to self-initiate, Tyrone was still seated there saying nothing. *"Hmm," I* thought to myself. No sooner as I had arrived, Terri was preparing to leave.

"Well, you all have a great evening, and it was nice to meet you." She said as she wrangled up her kids and prepared to walk away. Shortly after her departure, Tyrone called the kids over, and we all walked home together.

All the while, I wondered what exactly it was that I walked up on at the park. After we got home, I got straight to the point.

"So Tyrone, what's going on with you and Terri?"

"Oh, so something's going on with me and Terri?" He said defensively. "I knew all this going to church and stuff would be too good to be true." He said, trying to deflect the question.

"No, I'm not accusing you. It just seemed that when I walked up, your laughter and chatter stopped—almost as if I was interrupting something," I replied simply.

"That's Sgt. Gray's wife—they live down the street!" He retorted. I let it go. Old me would have pressed the argument and even perhaps had confronted her that day, but that's not who I was anymore and not who I wanted to be.

A few weeks later, he started to go down to Sgt. Gray's house to play cards. "Oh, well, do you mind if I go with you?" I asked.

"Nah, church folks don't play cards." He said.

"Just because I go to church and love God doesn't mean I can't play cards." I mused.

"Well, we'll be drinking and smoking and carrying on, and I don't want to put you in that type of environment." He said, trying to be done with the conversation.

"Well, you're my husband—I'll be with you—that's okay, isn't it?"

"Nah, I think you should just stay."

"Okay, Tyrone," I said and left it alone.

The next weekend came around, and he said once again he was going to Sgt. Gray's. This time, after he left, I waited a while, about an hour and a half, and decided to go down to their house anyway. Before Terri and I had officially met in the park that day, I had seen her from time to time around the military base. I didn't know who she was then, but after meeting her, I observed what car she drove. Having said that, I knew which apartment hers was, by seeing her car parked in the assigned parking space, which had the corresponding units painted in them. So, I got the kids together, and the three of us walked less than ten minutes to their house, which was in the same division as ours. I knocked on the door, and Terri answered and looked surprised.

Germany

"Hi," I said. "I'm Tyrone's wife; we met at the park, remember?" She looked puzzled.

"Oh…oh yes, I remember." She said.

"Well, I was at the house, and since my kids play with your kids, I just decided we'd come on down, and I'd play cards with you all tonight." She forced a smile, it seemed.

"Oh, yes, come on in." She opened the door, and I stepped inside to see about four or five people, including Tyrone and Sgt. Gray whom Terri introduced me to. Tyrone did a double take and started walking towards me.

"Everyone, this is Leigh, Tyrone's wife," Terri said. They all gave their echoed hellos and greetings. Tyrone placed his hand slightly around my waist and pressed his head near mine to discreetly ask, "What are you doing here?" He looked surprised.

"Well, I just thought, if the kids play with her kids, and you said you all are playing cards, that we'd join you," I replied. He studied my face and looked confused.

"Are you checking up on me?" He quizzed.

"Not at all," I said peaceably. He walked back to the table and sat down as he was in the middle of a card game.

"Is it okay if the kids go play with your kids?" I asked Terri. "Sure." She said as she called one of her children to the front and Man ran off to play. Terri's daughter looked at Tyronica, "Come on!" She said whimsically. Tyronica shook her head no and looked up at me. I looked at the little girl and smiled. "It's okay; she'll just stay up here with me." The little girl smiled and ran off with the other kids. Tyronica never left my side as we both had a seat on a couch near the card table. I looked around. Their home was very nice, but I could observe that our tastes were distinctly different as far as décor and furniture went. I also observed that they allowed their children's toys to be scattered around casually in common areas. I wanted my children to of course enjoy playing in our house, but I was very stern about everything having a place and things being in proper order—a room lent itself to looking cluttered and junky otherwise. Not long after I had arrived, the other guests began to say their goodbyes and left the Gray's home.

Pretty soon, only the four of us remained in the living room. Though the card game had ended when the other visitors left, Sgt. Gray and Tyrone remained at the table, drinking and chatting casually about various aspects of the military and life. Sgt. Gray also politely engaged me in casual conversation—especially since Terri wasn't engaging me very much at all. She would walk to the kitchen and straighten things, back to the card table where her drink was and take a sip, and then go back and check on the kids who were playing. She was rarely still enough to have a conversation, in the first place.

After about a half hour or so, Tyrone looked at me and asked if I was ready to head home. "Sure, I'm ready if you are." With that, we stood up and exchanged our goodbyes. Terri went to where the kids were playing to get Man for us. "It was nice meeting you, Sgt. Gray."

"Nice to meet you as well!" He said as he walked Tyrone and I to the door. Man ran to the front, and we headed out of the door.

"Nice to see you again, Terri!" I yelled towards the back where she had remained. Tyrone had driven our car down to their house, so we all got in and headed home.

After we got home, the kids ran to their rooms to play since it was the weekend and they could stay up a little later. Tyrone and I went to the living room. Just before fixing himself a drink, Tyrone turned on our stereo and started playing Gerald Levert.

"I had a nice time," I remarked of our visit. "Terri seemed a bit nervous by my being there, though. It seemed like once I came, the party stopped." I said.

Germany

"Well, you weren't invited." He said as he moved around the kitchen, pouring his drink. I looked over at him in disbelief. *"Was he defending her?"* I thought to myself. *"Was it really Sgt. Gray that he was friends with—or was it her?"* Noticing the abrupt pause on my end, he looked over and saw the expression on my face. He then attempted to compensate for his first answer with an even poorer substitute. "Maybe she was uncomfortable because you go to church and she didn't know what to say to you." While his second answer was even more suspicious than the first, I was still stuck on his initial comment.

"Wait a minute; if you're invited someplace, I should be invited—whether I decide to come or not."

"All I'm saying is, maybe she felt uncomfortable because you're in church and she didn't know what to talk to you about."

"How would she had known I was in church?" I thought to myself. This was only the second occasion that I had ever encountered the woman on a formal basis, and neither time had she engaged with me long enough to barely even know my name. I cut to the chase and asked him outright. "Okay Tyrone, who are Terri and Sgt. Gray, and how do you know them?" He chugged his drink and went back to the kitchen to make another.

"I met Sgt. Gray through Terri." He said nonchalantly.

"Okay, how do you know Terri?" I continued.

"She was a KP in my mess hall." He said.

"Wait a minute—you told me that you met her at the park with the kids," I replied as I walked closer to where he was in the kitchen. "You said she was there with her in-home childcare children," I said as my memory jogged.

"No, I didn't!" He said defensively.

Dare to Dream

"Yes, you did; you said that you struck up a conversation with her while she was at the park—now you're telling me that you've known her for longer than that?"

"She was a KP before she started her childcare." He said with his patience for my inquisition fading by the second. I knew Tyrone—well. Between his shoddy answers, Terri's awkward behavior that evening when we were at their home, and a thorough track record for being able to sniff out Tyrone's tendencies, I was zoned in on getting to the bottom of the real truth about the Grays.

"So, are you sleeping with Terri, Tyrone?"

"Here we go!" He said.

"I told you no, I'm friends with her husband." He replied, trying to move past the conversation.

"No, it sounds like you are friends with *her* before you were friends with her husband," I answered quickly.

"As usual, you're going to believe what you want to believe, so I'm through talking about it." He said as he grabbed his keys. "I'm about to go; I'll be back later." He said as he threw back his last drink and walked towards the door. I stood there and watched him walk out the door. The old me would have fought and cussed and made a much bigger scene from what was happening. The new me, however, wasn't about to do all of that. I promised myself long before I got to Germany that no matter what happened, that I would never allow a man—or anything—to take me out of my character again. I asked God to sincerely help me with that. I knew that God would reveal to me whatever I needed to know about Tyrone. I also knew that no matter what happened, God would show Himself faithful in my life. With that, as he walked out of the door, I headed to my kids' rooms and began to get them ready for bath time, a story, and bed.

Over the next few months, Tyrone's visits to the park with the kids continued until the colder fall weather started to settle in. He also continued his card games and hangouts at Terri and Sgt. Gray's house. After that first visit to their home, I never again accompanied him down there. I thought it in my best interest to keep my mind off the speculation of what was potentially brewing between him and Terri. A small part of me hoped and prayed that given our long dramatic history of mistrust and infidelity—not to mention my shooting him—would be enough incentive for a sincere and real turnaround in our marriage. After all, he was always the one who begged to hold on to our marriage when I found myself at points of wanting out. I didn't have any proof about him and Terri, but I honestly didn't want to search for it, either.

In the past, I had my fair share of taxing heartache from the cycle of suspicion, accusation, broken trust, and the difficult road to reconciliation—which was always harder to travel down again the more his cheating occurred. I decided to occupy my mind with prayer, going to church, and of course, raising my children. After attending the church on base for a while, I ventured out and found a church in Schweinfurt, Germany, which was about 40 minutes away from Bamberg. The pastor was an African-American man named Johnny R. Butler, who was one of the first people who taught me truly about growing in my faith. He taught me how to believe God when everything was against me. Going to his church was my sanctuary while in Germany. Though I was far away from the States, missing my family, and trying desperately to keep faith in my marriage, I was determined to let nothing disrupt my faith walk. I had come to a place where I was no longer consumed by trivial things like worry, suspicion, and revenge—I was consumed with living my life for Christ and being a good mother and wife.

I recall one Saturday night preparing to get ready for church the next morning and wanting to press Tyronica's hair. A week or so prior, I had let my girlfriend Gail borrow my hot comb and needed to walk to her house about 15 minutes across post to go and get it back. I asked our downstairs neighbors, Sgt. Huff and his wife, if they would mind if Tyronica and Tyrone sat at their home briefly as I made the quick walk. Tyronica and their daughter were about the same age and would play together frequently, so they obliged with no problem. I bundled up and walked to Gail's as snow began to fall. I walked as quickly as I could so I could get back home to the kids and out of the snow. As I was walking along, I heard what sounded like the familiar hum of my car driving behind me in the distance. The high beams flashed briefly as the car passed by, and I looked up to realize that it was indeed my car! The car never slowed, so I chalked it up to Tyrone not realizing it was me. Though it wasn't too cold out, it would have been nice to have hitched a ride versus walking the full way if he had seen me. However, I didn't think much more of it and arrived at Gail's shortly after that. After grabbing the hot comb, I started the journey back to my house.

As I walked towards the back parking lot of our complex, I walked past our parked car that was running in the driveway. Just as I was about to climb the stairs to our door, I happened to look over at the running car and saw a woman seated in the front seat. I about-faced and walked towards the passenger side. As I got close, I saw none other than Terri. She was sitting in *my* car in *my* driveway, waiting for Tyrone to come back downstairs. I remember thinking to myself with disgust, *"How disrespectful."* Funny how I also thought to myself how much I had changed. If it had been just a few years prior, I would have swung open the door and whooped her like I was prone to do with his other mistresses. I gave the window three hard knocks as she peered at me through the glass. She rolled the window halfway down.

"Get away from my house, and I don't *ever* want to see you here again," I said to her sternly. Here I was, about to give him the benefit of the doubt for not seeing me when he passed by, only to realize the real reason he didn't stop. He had her in *my* car while *I* was walking. On top of that, her being in my car was one thing; her being in front of my house was quite another. As far as I was concerned, there was nothing more to say to her—the culprit in this was Tyrone—the person who had been bold enough to bring her to my house. The same person who had sworn up and down that there was nothing going on and that I was the crazy one. I turned to walk up the stairs, not even stopping by to get the kids first. I prayed within myself for strength and calmness to combat the familiar feeling of anger from when I shot him rising in me again. I reached the top of the stairs and couldn't get my key in the hole fast enough. I unlocked the door and flung it open. He was in the kitchen with his coat on, with a poured drink in one hand and the bottle to go in the other. When he heard the sound of the door fling open, he looked up with stunned eyes to see me walking towards him full speed ahead.

"Tyrone Burks, how disrespectful can you be?" He froze as he looked at me like a deer that had been caught in headlights. "Terri is the woman in the book of Proverbs who can't keep her foot in her own house! She's going to wish that she never heard your name and you're going to wish that you had never heard hers. You're going to end up losing everything that you have and have worked for and may even end up losing your own life." It was the first time that I could remember ever confronting him with an overall calmed demeanor. Though I spoke firmly, I didn't raise my voice or yell. The look on his face was stark confusion. He too was used to my former days of violent and boisterous confrontations, and here I was now, calm, cool and levelheaded, simply getting straight to the point.

"Get her away from in front of my house," I said, bringing finality to the conversation. He was expressionless and didn't speak a word. He walked past me, out the door and down the steps as he got in the car and drove off. I was angry, worked up, and took a few minutes to simmer my emotions before going back downstairs to pick up my kids. Though I was hurt, I somehow had to find a balance in peace and sanity. We had about six months remaining in Tyrone's tour before it was time to go back home to the U.S. I refused to let his incessant extramarital affairs take me back to my old nature. I had worked really hard to become someone better. Someone that my kids could respect and that I could respect myself. Not only that, I had to use wisdom when it came to my anger as I was in a foreign country with different laws and customs that I was unaware of. I couldn't afford to let my emotions get the best of me and risk losing my children or my freedom. Deep down, I was comforted by the thought that what Tyrone was sowing; he was sure to eventually reap.

CHAPTER 8

Same Old, Same Old

I continued to feed my faith by regular church attendance and praying. Around this time, I became acquainted with two soldiers on base, Sgt. Hill and Sgt. Davis, who attended the same church as I did. Sgt. Hill worked in the mess hall with Tyrone, and Sgt. Davis knew him, at least. I began to give them regular rides to church, and they grew to be like brothers to me, always there when I needed to talk or doing nice gestures for the kids.

After I had confronted Tyrone about Terri, he started to become vindictive. He played on my insecurities about my body and how I had gained weight and used manipulative insinuations that he would be more attracted to me if I weren't so heavy. I was going to great lengths to still try and save my marriage. I found myself starting all of these fad diets trying to slim down and walking daily to aid in the process. I knew that Sgt. Davis was big on working out regularly in the gym, so I started tagging along with him for tips on how to navigate the weight room.

The night I confronted Tyrone at the house about Terri didn't slow down a thing for the two of them. While she never came to my house again, their affair continued, and both were becoming bolder with their rendezvous. I remember one day stopping by the PX to shop. The kids were with me, and we walked in. As I got a basket, the next thing I knew, I saw the two of them in the distance—together. I was upset but didn't have the time to be as I nervously became concerned with the possibility of my children seeing them. I frantically placed the basket back and told the kids that we would have to leave as I had forgotten something at the house. I grabbed Man's hand and told Tyronica to come on as I hurried them out of the store but kept my cool so they wouldn't suspect anything was wrong. Later, when he came home, I couldn't wait to bust him out.

"I saw you today at the PX with Terri," I said to him.

"What? I wasn't at the PX today. I was at work."

"No! I saw you at the PX—and I had the kids with me. You might have gone to work, but I saw you at the PX!" He chuckled. "It wasn't me, must have been my twin." He said sarcastically.

"Your twin? I've known you for half of my life and now all of a sudden, you have a twin, huh?"

"Yeah, next time you see me somewhere, come and tap me on my shoulder then." He said in smug tone and went to get in the shower. I stood there feeling insulted and humiliated by the whole ordeal. Riding around with her was one thing, but being out and about with her in public, taking no thought for me running into him, or anyone else for that matter, was a new level of disrespect—though it was far from the last. After that, one Saturday morning, after pulling one of his typical all-night escapades, only God knows where, he casually strolled into the house, plopped down on the couch, and made a phone call. At this point, we had become more like roommates. He was doing what he wanted to do, and I had resolved within myself to save my breath as far as confrontations went. I was coming out of the bathroom when I overheard him in the living room on the phone, pouring out his love to whomever was on the other end. I assumed, of course, that it was Terri. His back was facing me, but there was no way for him to mistake me not being home.

In other words, he wasn't concerned with whether I overheard him or not. At this point, he just didn't care. I stood there and listened for a moment as he sat in *our* living room, telling another woman how much he loved her, was going to miss her, and plans of their being together soon. I sighed. I had developed the spiritual maturity by now to look past his actions for the spirit that was really behind them. I felt like it was the devil's attempt to get me unhinged and distrusting in my faith in God. I felt tears well up in my eyes and a lump rise in my throat as I headed for our door and left. There was no way I was going to stay there and continue to be humiliated and hurt by his blatant disregard for who I was, and all I had been to him. I decided to just take my morning walk right then, as the tears began to fall, and I began to sob. I prayed to God through my tears for strength as I didn't know what else to say. As far as God was concerned, I knew my crying was communication enough to express what I couldn't in words. I was so overwhelmed in my tears that I was walking aimlessly and not necessarily according to my usual morning routine. I had no destination, to be honest—I just knew I needed to get away from there. As I continued walking, I eventually arrived at the shopette—an on-base convenience store and gas station. As I was walking by, Sgt. Davis, who was coming out of the store, saw me. He walked towards me, and I was finally coming down from my crying spell. "Hey!" He said as I tried to fix my face. It was too late though; he had noticed my red eyes and puffy face. "What's wrong? Why are you crying?" He asked, concernedly. I sighed, and without being able to help it, began crying again.

"The same old, same old," I said, mustering my speech through weeps.

"What happened?" He asked. He was aware of the rocky state of me and Tyrone's relationship as I frequently confided in him when issues arose between us. I told him what had just happened with my overhearing Tyrone's phone conversation. I told him how Tyrone had used my weight gain as an excuse to defend his cheating and how it all made me feel. Listening to my lament and seeing my tears, he became upset on my behalf and interrupted me.

"—Just stop." He said as I paused. "You gaining weight has nothing to do with it. That's an excuse to make him feel better about what he's doing. There are men who would be glad to have a wife that loves God and her family—he just wants to do what he wants!" He added. I went on to tell him how Tyrone was staying out all hours of the night and how I couldn't figure out where he could have possibly been during those hours since his mistress was married.

"Well, I've seen him over at the barracks with other soldiers from time to time, Leigh, maybe he's not always up to no good." He said, trying to ease my mind. He and I both knew as he said it, that Tyrone was more than likely up to no good. "What's her husband's name?" Sgt. Davis asked me. "His name is Sgt. Gray," I told him.

"Oh, okay. Do you know his first name?" He continued.

"Well, no…" I replied.

"Where does he live?" He followed up. I mindlessly retorted the address. He let the questions subside as I was emotionally drained, anyway. He walked me back home, and I thanked him. When I walked upstairs, Tyrone was passed out and asleep, and the kids were still playing in their rooms just as they had been before I left.

The following week, Tyrone arrived home from work one day and began confronting me. "Why did you tell this man to go confront Sgt. Gray?" I looked at him first in confusion and then disgust from his audacity.

Same Old, Same Old

"What are you talking about?" I asked him, annoyed. "Don't come in here confronting me with nothing Terri's said to you—I don't want to hear it," I told him adamantly.

"Oh, yeah? Well, your so-called brother from the church told Sgt. Gray that he needs to check his wife and keep her out of my face!" My mind put two and two together as I realized what he was saying must have stemmed from my talk with Sgt. Davis, days prior. I didn't expect Sgt. Davis to go and say anything, to be honest. I actually could have cared less about any of that as I couldn't get past Tyrone's gall for checking me on behalf of his mistress. I found it offensive, to say the least. I walked away as I refused to entertain another second of his boldness.

For the first time ever, Tyrone had slacked up on his responsibilities, as far as our family went. I was used to him disregarding me, but ever since he had been running behind Terri, he had neglected his family time with the kids, as well as changed our normal routine for handling financial responsibilities. What had always worked for us was that Tyrone would make the money, and I would be in charge of making sure everything got paid for and taken care of. The more he became engulfed with Terri, he began to blow money on his lascivious lifestyle of drinking, partying, and entertaining her. Everything came to a head one day as I remember waking up early one Sunday morning and feeling overwhelmed from the moment I opened my eyes. The first thing I realized was that he wasn't in bed—which was of no real surprise to me, as this was his norm for the weekend. I was a wreck, and trying to hold things together amidst raising my children, being in a foreign country, and having to act like I was immune to my breaking heart, had taken its toll on me.

I found myself at my wit's end and felt defeated and hopeless. I pulled myself out of bed and went to the closet to attempt looking for something to wear to church. But I couldn't even do that—I ended up sinking to the floor in a corner near my closet. I pulled my knees to my chest in an upright fetal position and rocked back and forth as I began to cry quietly as my kids were still asleep. The kids and I were in the house with no groceries, and he, of course, had the car. The car really didn't matter as much as the fact that I didn't have any money. In all of the things that Tyrone had put me through, he had never left me feeling insecure as far as our family's well-being went. I couldn't take another thing. This particular day, I will never forget, as it was the first and only time that I can ever recall in my life, entertaining thoughts of suicide. I was trying to keep my faith in Christ and live a life for Him, but there was too much going on in my natural world. I didn't know what to do. My mind was in a daze, and I was crying from a reservoir that didn't even have tears left to give. I couldn't even find the strength or willpower to pray. I had no words, and the fact that my children were still asleep permitted me this moment to sit and lament. I took a long look over my life up until that point and all the decisions I had made.

All I had was a high school diploma. I was unemployed—and only had a string of odd and end jobs that didn't align with a specific career trek. I had taken a few college courses, but by in large, I had spent most of my married life being the backbone for our family and his thriving military career. I was thousands of miles away from home and had no family support. I had a great church family, but the support I found amongst them as a community was temporary—we were all likely to end up back in the States at some point. I contemplated the fact that perhaps it was really time for my marriage to end. I realized that I had been dealing with this man for almost half of my life with nothing more to show for it, other than my children. They were the only things that kept me moving forward. I sat there and started to think about what would be next for me. No matter what, I

Same Old, Same Old

had two little people sleeping in the next room who were depending on me to make the right decision.

I stayed there, seated on my floor for what seemed like an eternity, though it was perhaps no longer than 30 minutes. The next thing I knew, I heard our doorbell ring. I literally gave it no reaction as I continued to sit there, rocking and exhausted from my cries. The doorbell rang again. I remained seated there in what best can be described as a zombie-like state. Nothing mattered at that moment. I didn't care who it might have been or what they may have wanted. It wouldn't have mattered either way, as I had no energy to exert to even attempt to move. The doorbell rang a few more times before finally, whomever the visitor was, eventually left. I felt relieved. I didn't have the energy whatsoever to be social.

A few minutes after the doorbell stopped ringing, Tyronica quietly was standing in my doorway. I suppose the doorbell ringing had awakened her. She saw me seated there on the floor and noticed my crying state. She walked to where I was quietly almost to get a clarification that I was crying—something that she had rarely, if ever, seen before. The expression on her face was mixed with an innocent look of bewilderment and concern. She sat down next to me on the floor. "Are you okay, mommy?" She asked in a gentle tone as if she knew that it would be appreciated. I kept rocking. She placed her arm around me. I mustered up the strength to speak. I didn't want one of the kids to find me there, but since she had, I couldn't fake the moment, just sort of basked in it. "I'm okay, baby. I just don't feel good this morning, that's all." She stayed there as a quiet comforter. She may have been too young to fully understand what might have been going on, but the basic humanity in her could sense that silent support was better than none.

I finally gathered enough willpower to get up from the floor and try and begin my day. If for no other reason, I didn't want to remain in such a dejected state in front of Tyronica, nor risk Tyrone Jr. coming in to see. I had to get myself together. "Come on, let's get up and get ready for church," I said to her as I stood to my feet and she did the same. She exited my room to go begin her morning routine. Regardless of wanting to stay there on the floor, I forced myself to stand up. It took everything in me to get ready for church. I helped them get dressed as we were preparing to get a ride with one of my fellow church members. When I opened the door to leave, I noticed that there was a bag full of groceries positioned right there in front of the entryway. I looked down in awe and then looked around, left to right to see if there was a trace of anyone. Then I recalled the doorbell ringing earlier. I picked the bag up and noticed that it had chicken, milk, snacks for the kids, my favorite Cap'N Crunch cereal with berries, and other grocery staples for us to eat. Considering how my morning had started, the groceries were just the reminder that I needed about God's faithfulness to provide for me.

On top of that, as soon as I set foot inside of the church sanctuary, Pastor Butler called me out during service to come down for prayer. He told me that he could see a spirit of suicide and destruction on me and commanded that it go in the name of Jesus. I couldn't help but cry as it confirmed to me yet again the power of God and His faithfulness to be involved in my life. No one could have possibly known what was going on with me that morning. As soon as he prayed for me, I felt an immediate sense of release. After church, I felt revived. Since the current status of my life felt like I was jumping from one frying pan to the next, it was nice to have a fresh wind for whatever awaited ahead.

On a weekday evening not long after my church refresher, I heard Tyrone come in the house late after I had gotten into bed. The children were long asleep, and as I heard him approaching our bedroom, I closed my eyes and lay there motionless so that he would think I

Same Old, Same Old

was sleeping. Falling for it, he went to the bathroom and dialed a number. He called Terri, and I could overhear his responses. Based on whatever she was saying, he told her that it wouldn't be long before he was heading to the States too—meaning she and her husband must have been heading there shortly. He also said that he was planning on getting stationed at Fort Benning so that they could be together. I lay there unsurprised but felt a small flicker of relief as I could finally see an end coming to what had been one of his longest-running flings to date. As far as I was concerned, as long as she was far away from Germany, she was far away from wreaking havoc on my family, and maybe we could finally get on with our lives.

Terri and Sgt. Gray finally moved to Fort Benning in Georgia, and the normality for our household started to resurface. He started staying home on the weekends again and spending more time at home during the week. I wasn't about to be swayed by it, one way or the other. I kept on going to church, being a mother, and being present for my family. The fact that he now wanted to be more attentive seemed phony to me or, at the very least, insulting. He was only acting right because his mistress was gone. But in reality, it was all good. I had learned to play the game and sit back and collect information from his sloppy phone calls. The tidbits that he dropped would potentially be helpful in supporting my case for divorce if it came down it. In my mind, I bookmarked his comments to Terri about planning to relocate our family to Fort Benning where she was. I wasn't too concerned with that, however. In the military, just because a soldier puts in a request for a particular duty station, doesn't necessarily guarantee its approval. I sincerely hoped, however, that it wouldn't come to that.

I can recall frequently praying and asking God to never let anything suddenly come up on my children or me. To reveal to me anything that Tyrone was doing underhandedly that would hurt or devastate us. It wasn't 24 hours later that I got my answer right away to that simple prayer. Tyrone took training in Grafenwohr, Germany, which was about an hour and a half from Bamberg. While at home one day, I went to check the mailbox as usual, and amongst the usual junk mail, I saw a letter that Tyrone had attempted to send that had been marked "return to sender." I also noticed that some other address was on the envelope and not our home one. What was most interesting of all, however, was that the letter was addressed to Terri Gray in Columbus, Georgia. "Well, well, well, what do we have here?" I said aloud to myself as I went inside the house with mail in hand. Terri and Sgt. Gray had only been back in the states for a few weeks, and the lovebirds were still determined to talk to one another. I opened up the envelope and found some money wrapped up inside of the letter. It was about $50. I read the letter, and within the text, Tyrone asked her how the doctor's appointment had gone. I wondered what doctor's appointment he could have been referring to as I read on.

He poured out his love for her and remarked about how he'd be home in the States soon, and that was about the gist of it. I was sick to the stomach as I read his heartfelt confessions of love for her as he still laid in our bed in the night as if we were working on our marriage, and everything was okay. I took the $50 and placed it in my pocket with immediate intentions to go to the PX and buy a bottle of Amarige perfume that I had been eyeing for the longest time. But first, I put my detective hat on. I analyzed the address that he had sent the letter from originally. I'm not sure what happened on the receiving end of Terri getting the letter, but the fact that it had made it to my house, and it wasn't even the original sender address, was all the confirmation that I needed to dig deeper. It wasn't a residential quarters address, but I could tell it was a base location because the zip code had an APO prefix. I sat and thought for a while about what building he would be comfortable enough to send a letter to his mistress from. After a few minutes of contemplating, Sgt. Davis' comments about seeing Tyrone frequently in the barracks rushed back to my mind like a ton of bricks. The barracks were dormitory-style living quarters for unmarried soldiers. Married soldiers with families, of course, were privy to housing quarters and therefore didn't live in barracks. Had Tyrone somehow managed to obtain his own barracks room? I wasn't sure whose room he might have been using or what kind of strings he was pulling, but I knew for a fact that it was against the rules for a married soldier to have a barracks room in addition to housing. In fact, the only way a married soldier would have a barracks room was if he was on an unaccompanied tour—meaning his family was not deployed with him. This, of course, was not Tyrone's case. If the address on the envelope were indeed a barracks room, that would indeed explain how two married people were able to spend so much time with one another without being in either of their own homes. I sat and contemplated for a while if Tyrone had left his keys at home while away at training. He indeed had. I found them and looked at every key on the ring. As it turns out, I could readily identify every key, except for one. I made up in my mind that I would drive to the sender address on the envelope that evening and check things out. I figured it would be best to go while it was dark out so that I could minimize the chance of running into any men as I tried to enter into an all-male barracks. I called my friend Gail and asked her if she would briefly babysit for me. She, of course, obliged. I drove to the address on the envelope, and just as I had suspected, it was the location of a barracks. I parked my car and got out. I had Tyrone's keys with me and pulled them out to try the unidentified key in the lock. I checked my surroundings and placed the key inside the lock to give it a turn. The key unlocked and the door opened. Part of me couldn't believe it, but I didn't have the time to stand there and bask in my surprise. I hurried inside and went to the corresponding room number that was on the envelope. I got to the door, unlocked it, and went inside. I closed the door behind me and turned on the light. I looked around, and all of the belongings that were in the room belonged to none other than Tyrone Burks. The closet had a few pieces—mostly uniform attire, but a few casual dress items that I readily recognized as being his. By now, my adrenaline was pumping as I could barely believe that I had stumbled upon the room in the first place. This room was undoubtedly where he and Terri had spent most of their time together. I started going through drawers, his wall locker, and desk. I resolved to leave no stone unturned as I searched for more concrete evidence of his affair. When I opened the desk drawer, I came across a stash of about 2 or 3 more letters between him and Terri. This time, all of the ones that I found were from her writing to him. I grabbed the letters, put them in my pocket, made sure the room was put back like I found it, and left. I picked the kids back up and headed home. My anticipation for reading the letters reeled within me as I hurried to put the kids to sleep so I could take my time and read each letter. Once the kids were finally down, I went into the living room and sat down on the couch. I pulled the letters out of my pockets and looked at the postmarked dates to see which order I needed to read them in. The first one was her notifying him that they had arrived safely in the States. Further down in the letter, I also learned that Terri was pregnant before leaving Germany—pregnant with my husband's baby. I was stunned. I paused for a moment and reread the words to appease my need for confirmation, but it read the same. Not only was she pregnant, but the letter made mention of her taking care of the abortion. I put the letter down, as there was really nothing else to garner from it. I sat there, speechless for a moment. I snapped out of it, though, and reached for the next letter. In this one, I learned that Sgt. Gray had actually been stationed to Fort Rucker in

Alabama. Before moving there, however, he moved Terri back to her hometown in Georgia, made sure she was settled, and then headed to Fort Rucker as their divorce proceedings began. From the third letter, she spoke of the mounting excitement from seeing Tyrone soon. We were finally down into the weeks before our move, so she spoke of the excitement of the two of them being reunited. After I finished reading the letters, I realized that I finally had written proof of Tyrone's infidelity. I created a loose floorboard in our living room under our area rug and opened it up to make a spot for the letters to be hidden. By now, I was anticipating that the subject of divorce would come up between us; if it did, I would be ready. Having never been divorced before, I didn't know the ins and outs of what would be needed to expedite my case and just figured if I were ready, I wouldn't have to get ready. Our base was fairly small in the first place, so in this case of his name being on a return-to-sender envelope, the mail system was familiar with where he lived in the housing quarters and therefore routed it to our house.

In the fall of 1993, it was finally time for us to prepare to move back to the States from Germany. Tyrone came home one day and announced that his new duty station was to be in Fort Benning, Georgia. The thing that irked me more than anything was the fact that I knew that he had made this request for his mistress, and he presented to me as if it was merely an assigned location. He still was unaware that I knew this tidbit from overhearing his conversations with her, months prior, as well as the actual letters between the two of them. He hadn't mentioned divorce, so it was clear that his plan was to move our family there and continue his cheating ways with Terri. When I got by myself, I prayed earnestly for God to intervene. What was I going to do in Georgia? Again, I would be in a situation there where I knew no one and worse than that, I already had the inside track on how things were going to be for me and my children. It was

Dare to Dream

going to be the same story in a different location—that's it. I knew deep down that I couldn't just concede to the plans that he had for us.

Days went by, and I continued to pray and look for God's loophole in this ridiculous fiasco of moving our family to where Terri was. God had come through for me so much while in Germany that I knew one way or the other, He would show up in this situation. One thing that I knew for sure, was that I would never do another overseas tour with Tyrone ever again. The distance, the loneliness from being so far away from family, and the trials and tribulations that my marriage had endured were all the experience that I needed as far as overseas living was concerned. Knowing this would be my last time in Germany—ever—I made an intentional point to take advantage of Germany's retail price point one last time. There were high-end furniture items that were practically a steal there, compared to their pricing in the U.S. I purchased a grandfather's clock and a German shrunk; these were among the staples that American women were known to bring back to the States. The other common staple was a baby—and I for one wasn't about to do that—in fact, Terri had that covered for me.

When we got down to the last few days in Germany and had our house all boxed up, ready for the movers to come and load everything, Tyrone came into the house, fuming. "What have you done, and how did you do it?" He asked me accusatorily.

"What are you talking about?" I asked, unsure of what he was trying to pull. It turns out that his orders were suddenly changed from Fort Benning in Georgia to Fort Riley in Kansas. For some reason, he blamed me for the "interference" of him and his mistress' plans. I didn't know anyone in the U.S. army who could have even helped me with such a task. Then again, I knew someone bigger than the U.S. army. Upon hearing the news and taking a moment to think about it, I realized that God had heard my prayer. It was like a tremendous weight had been lifted off of my chest. The bonus about moving to

Fort Riley was that my niece Robin was there. She too was an army wife, and moving to Kansas at least meant that I had family support that I could rely on.

It was the third week of November, and we officially touched back down on U.S soil just in time to spend Thanksgiving with our family. I was so excited to finally be back home. I hadn't seen my family face-to-face since our emergency visit for Sue-Baby's funeral a couple of years back. In the midst of being exciting about being home, I still felt unclear about the prognosis of my marriage. After all that he put me through, I still loved Tyrone. The thing was, I wasn't about to beg him to stay in a marriage that he no longer wanted to be in. Once again, we returned back to Arkansas and moved back into my family's house—our old house—where Trish Ann still lived. Tyrone took 30 days of leave, which allowed us to spend time with our family during the holiday season, but more purposefully, it would allow him time to go ahead to Fort Riley to secure our housing—or so I thought. He spent the first week home with us in Arkansas and got us settled in. Our family wasn't due to move to Fort Riley until January when it was time for him to officially sign in for duty. The following week after the holiday, he told me that instead of waiting until January, that he was going to head to Fort Riley and sign in for duty early and also take advantage of signing us up for housing early. This would at least help in the possibility that we would get our housing sooner, as there was a waiting list, either way.

After going to Fort Riley for a week, he returned home the following week just in time for us to begin our Christmas shopping for the family. After he got in off the road, he poured himself a drink or two and laid down for a nap to rejuvenate before it was time for us to head to some stores. While he was asleep, I took it upon myself to clean out our car from his traveling and also the trunk to make room for the Christmas gifts that we were going to buy. Though the kids were at school, I didn't want to put things in the actual car itself as we might have needed to go pick them up by the time our shopping had ended. Tyrone had a bag of dirty clothes on the inside that he had yet to take into the house from his week's travel. I took the bag inside and decided to throw the clothes in the wash before heading out to shop as I'm the type of person who hates for laundry to pile up. I figured by the time I came back from shopping; they'd be ready to throw in the dryer. I took the clothes out and started checking his pockets, as usual, so that no paper, tissue, etc. would get into the load. As I checked the pockets on one of his pairs of jeans, I felt a folded piece of paper. I took it out and looked at it to make sure it wasn't something important. When I unfolded the paper, I realized that it was a recent gas receipt—a gas receipt from Columbus, Georgia. There was also a number written on the back of it. I was stopped in my tracks. My mind started to compute on overload. What reason was Tyrone in Columbus, GA—where Terri lived—when he was supposed to be at Fort Riley in Kansas getting things in order for us to move? I felt my blood pressure rise as I went to grab one of our cordless phones and dialed the phone number on the receipt. As the phone rang, I couldn't wait for it to be answered on the other end. I could feel the heat rise up from my neck.

"Hello," the voice on the other end said. Immediately recognizing that it was Terri, my eyes rolled.

"Hello Terri, this is Leigh. I just wanted to call and confirm for myself that *my* husband had been to Columbus." I could tell by her pause that I had caught her completely off-guard. She sighed.

"Maybe you need to be having this conversation with Tyrone." Terri said smugly.

"You're absolutely right, Terri, I will have this conversation with *my* husband."

Same Old, Same Old

With that, I hung the phone up in her face and headed straight to our bedroom where Tyrone was taking an afternoon nap. I shook his shoulder vigorously until his eyes squinted, and he woke up slightly hazy. "So we back on this again?" I asked, angrily getting right to the point. "You know what, at this point, you're gonna have to figure out what you want to do because I'm tired of this." I said. "I dealt with it while we were overseas since we were in another country and I didn't know the laws, and I didn't have anyone to rely on, but now that we're back in the States, I'm done playing this game with you. I want a divorce!" I said, fuming from anger that I could practically feel in my body. Still trying to come to from his nap, he squinted at me, looking lost as he sat up fully and then stood up.

"You're always accusing me of doing something. I told you, I haven't talked to her since we left Germany." He said.

"Oh, you haven't, huh?" I asked with a sarcastic chuckle. "Well, let me jog your memory and help you to quit lying, then." I said as I immediately handed him the receipt. "So, that magically appeared in your pocket from Columbus, Georgia with her phone number on the back of it, huh?" He looked at the receipt. "And don't bother denying it, because I already dialed the number and spoke to her." I said as I could look in his face and decipher that he was preparing to calculate a lie. "So all this time you told me you were up at Fort Riley supposedly getting things ready for us, you've been in Georgia, Tyrone?" I demanded in disgust. He looked at the receipt and then back at me. He paused for a moment.

"Well, okay then, you want a divorce? Fine." Said Tyrone. I felt the immediate sickening of my stomach from his words. With that, he walked past me and started repacking one of his bags with clothes.

"What are you doing?" I asked sharply.

"I'm leaving." He said as he continued to move around the room and gather things.

Though I had initiated the suggestion at first, I knew that *my* words were really being spoken in haste—I really didn't mean what I was saying. I expected his reaction would be to change. I wanted him to feel convicted enough to stop seeing her once and for all—not to be okay with ending our marriage because of *his* indiscretions. After all, we had been here before on more than one occasion. His usual role was to fight for our marriage and beg for another chance as I determined whether or not to give it to him. This was the first time, however, that he had ever agreed to my declaration to end things between us. "You want a divorce? Okay, then." He said again as I watched him pack and felt a frantic mix of anxiety from not wanting him to leave, yet at the same time, a strange sense of dignity that said, "let him leave then!" He left the room, grabbed our keys, and went out the door.

Once I heard the start of the engine and the car backing out of the driveway, I sank to the floor right there in our bedroom and started to cry. I didn't know what I was supposed to be feeling in that moment, but I felt a little bit of everything. I felt a bit of release, if this indeed was the end, and then I felt resentful for even saying anything at all. I almost began to entertain a sense of guilt from having uttered the word "divorce" first and wondered if I should have just let the incident be. I heard my sister Trish Ann coming down the hallway, so I quickly tried to pull myself together. I got up off the floor and sat on the bed. She knocked on the door and waited briefly before cracking it up open and peeking her head in. "Are you okay?" She said as she stood in the open door. "I heard the commotion." She continued. Tears pooled up again in my eyelids. She came all the way inside and stood closer to the bed where I sat.

"What's wrong?" She asked concernedly.

"He wants a divorce," I said as I put my face in my hands to stifle the audible cry I could feel about to escape from my chest. She sat down on the bed and put her arm around me. I began to give my sister a synopsis about what was going on with Tyrone and me. No one from either side of our families had ever known the full depth of what I and Tyrone's relationship was like—only bits and pieces. I began to tell my sister all about Terri and how she was a soldier's wife that Tyrone had started seeing while we were in Germany. I told her about finding the gas receipt, having just confronted him with it, and his agreeing to a divorce just before leaving.

"Well, if that's what he wants, give it to him then, you deserve better than that." She said as she continued to console me.

"Don't tell Daddy, please. I have to figure out what I'm going to do first." I requested. She agreed. My family didn't really believe in divorce, only "figuring it out." At that point, however, I couldn't bring myself to want to figure out anything else.

About a week later, my sister Carla, who had been sick, needed someone to ride with her to the hospital in Pine Bluff, Arkansas, for an outpatient kidney stone surgery. The drive was about 50 miles from Warren and gave us plenty of time to have an official catch up with one another. As she drove, I told her how beautiful Germany was and gave her the highlight reel version of what our life was like over there. I went on and on until the topic trailed off. Without missing a beat, she said, "Well, I'm glad you came back in one piece." She said with a light laugh. As soon as she said those words, I was triggered by the truth that I actually was anything but one piece. On the contrary, I felt like my life was in a trillion pieces. She glanced over at me as tears began to fall from my face. "What's wrong with you?" She asked as she tried to study my face between glances at the road. I went into a full-blown cry as I tried to talk between sobs and tell her everything that had been going on with us as of late. Though I had vented to Trish Ann, venting to Carla was different. Carla was the oldest of all of us, and I always valued her opinion and respected what she thought

Dare to Dream

of me. She was among my many family members who pleaded with me not to go to Germany before we left. I knew that venting to her now would possibly mean having to listen to humbling remarks of "I told you so." I didn't want to have to endure that kind of disappointment, and for that reason, I always imagined that telling her details of my relationship with Tyrone would have been humiliating.

But in that moment when she asked, and my tears began to flow, I started to get the feeling that she was exactly who I needed to be venting to. "Calm down, Leigh, I can't understand you when you're crying and talking fast." She said to me, mildly. I told her that at the very moment, Tyrone was most likely in Georgia with his mistress when he was supposed to be getting our family ready to move. I told her about confronting him with the gas receipt and telephone number the week prior, and how he had agreed to a divorce. Once I hit all of the points, I continued to cry. "Okay Leigh, shut up all that crying!" She said sternly, still stealing glances at me while focusing on the road. I tried to reel myself back in. "I'm not going to let you keep carrying on like this—it's time to put on your big girl panties!" She said adamantly. Carla was always so strong because she had to be. She was a single mom of four children, and because there were so many years between us, she was in a lot of ways like a mother figure to me. She wasn't the type of woman to be dependent on a man. She had come out on the other side of two divorces happy and whole, and she knew I could too.

"I don't know what I'm going to do. I don't even know how I'm going to tell the kids." I said, hopelessly trying to finally bring my cry under control.

"You're going to tell them the truth!" She said plainly. "The truth is always better than a lie." I continued to look at her and listen. "This is the best thing that could have happened to you." She said. "You can't see the forest for the trees right now is all—but you'll look back

Same Old, Same Old

to this very conversation that we're having right now, and you'll help someone else going through the same mess later." She said. It sounded like a notion filled with hope for the future, but in the present moment, I just couldn't see how.

Before I knew it, the week of Christmas was finally upon us, and I hadn't heard from Tyrone since he had packed up and left about a week and a half prior. When we moved back to the States, we had to close out our overseas bank account that I had access to. Since being back, we knew that our staying in Arkansas was going to be temporary, so we, of course, didn't bother to set up one here locally. However, since we had returned, he had to have set one up somewhere in order to receive his direct deposit. Wherever it was, he hadn't taken me with him to be added to the account and, therefore I was in Arkansas with no money, and still no progress made on beginning Christmas shopping for the kids. Man had recently turned 6 at the time and made it known that he wanted a Sega Genesis. I was trying my best to make Christmas happen but didn't see the possibility in sight.

Regarding Santa Claus, I told my children from day one that while the notion was fanciful, it was false. In my personal opinion, I didn't want my kids to be looking towards someone else to provide for them, especially someone based on fantasy. I was frank with my son. I told him, "If you want a Sega Genesis, pray and ask God to send me the money." It was difficult for me to say, but it was all I had to tell him. If nothing else, I thought of it as an excellent way to start instilling faith in my children. I wanted them to know that God was the most important person for them to depend on—even aside from me. I wanted them to understand that at some point, even I as their mother wouldn't be able to give them what they truly needed.

While visiting Lil Momma's house one day, the two of us were in the kitchen while she was cooking over the stove. I was seated at the table, picking some greens for her when she asked me, "Will Tyrone be home in time for Christmas?"

"No, he'll probably be spending Christmas time with his girlfriend," I said as I continued picking. She paused and turned around to look at me full-on. "What are you talking about? What girlfriend?!" She asked astonished. I looked up at her and let my expression confirm what I had said the first time. "I thought things were going well for you and Tyrone." She followed up with her hand rested on her hip, stunned. I sighed. "We're still having some struggles—just continue to pray." I was brisk with my response as I really didn't want to delve into so close to the holidays. "She stood there in thought for a few more seconds as she shook her head. "Well, if you need to talk, I'm here." She said as she turned around and carried on cooking.

Christmas Eve came, and my dad came over to the house to visit. "Here," he said. He handed me some money, and I couldn't believe it. "This is to help with the kids for Christmas." I hugged him tightly. "Thank you, Daddy."

"If you think you'll need anything else, I put your name on my charge account at Otasko." I was so grateful to him as he literally saved Christmas that year. The kids had gifts under the tree but nothing from Tyrone and I, and nothing particularly big or that they had requested. It was already the middle of the afternoon on Christmas Eve, so I threw on my coat and dropped Daddy off to him and Dorothy's house as I took his car and did my shopping. Needless to say, when my son woke up on Christmas day, he opened his Sega Genesis. His excitement will be etched in my memory forever. His face lit up, he screamed for joy and told me, "See momma, God gave me my Sega Genesis!" My son prayed, and God made a way. That Christmas, God showed Himself mighty in not only my son's faith but mine as well. He made a way for my children on my behalf and reinforced my faith in Him at the same time. It was one of the best Christmases that both of my children had ever experienced.

A few days after Christmas had passed, I sat and thought about how things could play out for my family in the coming days. According to our original plan, it was almost time to make our move to Fort Riley. Since our blow up that had preceded the divorce conversation, however, I didn't exactly know the status of things. There was still no word from Tyrone—not even so much as a call to tell our kids Merry Christmas. I wasn't about to get up and go to Fort Riley if we were going to go through with a divorce. There would be no point to drag my children there, only to possibly have to come back. Also, divorce or not, I wasn't going to up and go to Kansas at all until Tyrone had established housing for us. Since we weren't speaking, though, I didn't know if that was still even a plan. I was in desperate need for answers, and so I decided to fast and pray. Carla's daughter, my niece Robin, who I had grown up alongside and always been close with, was stationed at Fort Riley with her military husband who was doing a tour in Korea. I felt led to call her one day as we hadn't had the chance to catch up since I had been back in the States. As soon as she heard my voice on the other end, it was like no time had passed at all. I began sharing with her in so many words what all I was going through. She told me plainly, "Look, you can't fight for yourself and your marriage from Arkansas, so you need to come up here." Her advice was simple, but she had a point. She reassured me that I also had her to rely on as a support system if I came to Fort Riley. As I continued to fast and pray to God for some kind of sure leading to what I was to do next, one day, I felt like I had a breakthrough on an answer. In my spirit, God clearly spoke to me, saying, "I will not let the devil destroy your marriage." I also heard Him say, "I give to you the promise of Joshua 1; that everywhere you tread your feet, you shall possess the land. No man will be able to stand before you." At the time, it was enough of a Word to keep me going. I thought about that divine message in addition to the comforting words that Robin had given me. Thinking that both of these instances were a form of confirmation, I settled it right then and there: I was going to Kansas.

In the natural, I actually wanted to stay in Arkansas with the kids where at least I had a multiple tier support system in my dad, sisters, and Tyrone's mom. It seemed like the most sensible decision, but I knew there was something supernatural about being led to move. That and, I didn't want to give up the fight for our family to be restored. I still loved Tyrone in my heart and resolved within myself to stick out the fight for my marriage. My daddy and even Tyrone's mom swore up and down that I was making a foolish decision, not only as far as I was concerned, but for my children's sakes as well. With the money I had left over from buying the kids Christmas gifts, I bought bus tickets for the children and I to Junction City, Kansas, where the base was located, and afterward, had only $50 left in my pocket. My Dad begged me to stay. "I'll give you the house," he said. "You won't have to pay a thing—just don't take the kids." My brother even tried to convince me. "Just come up here to Michigan with me and Beverly. We'll get you a house, you can go to school, and we'll help you with the kids," he contested. Tyrone's mom was also against it. "Don't go up there." She said. "Don't take these kids away from a support system that loves you." Given the tales that they had either heard or known about Tyrone and I, I understood their concern. But this was an act of faith. God was leading me, and I knew it. "I'm going to Kansas," I told them, and I did just that.

CHAPTER 9

New Beginnings

Three days into the New Year, I got on the bus and was so scared that I couldn't stop my legs from shaking. I remember it vividly. It was the annoying kind of repetitive shake that you don't even notice until you do. I literally had to still my legs with my hands. No matter what, though, I kept feeling an unction that simply was saying, "Go." It was nothing but the Holy Spirit. I had never been more scared in my entire life. The best way to describe it is to say I felt like I was being propelled. I remember the bus ride being cold and my kids not having coats that were heavy enough. Their main things were shipped ahead in our storage from Germany, and all they had on were the items that they received for Christmas. I kept them close to me for body heat, and thankfully, they slept for most of the way. My niece Robin picked the kids and I up from the bus station once we arrived in Kansas. After a while of catching up and laughs, she cut to the chase.

"So, what's going on?" She asked me. I gave her a look as if I didn't know where to start. Interpreting it well, she laughed warmly. Robin felt my hopelessness, I suppose, as she immediately sprang into action with words of encouragement and a tangible plan to help get me out of my rut.

"I need to stay with you for 30 days," I blurted out. Thirty days was all I needed, and she enthusiastically agreed to my request.

"Now, I need to stay with you for 30 days afterward." She said without missing a beat.

I laughed. "You need to stay with me?" I asked. I couldn't help but chuckle at the thought as I of course didn't have a place to stay.

"Yes, Ronnie's coming back from Korea, and our orders are for Fort Hood, TX. We'll be getting ready to move when he returns." 30 days didn't seem like a whole lot for me to be able to keep my end of that bargain, but the funny thing was, I was confident it would all work out. I knew that if God had told me to come, He would most certainly provide.

My focus was to first find a job and a place to live as 30 days would come and go before I knew it. At this point, I still had not communicated with Tyrone, whatsoever, let alone about coming ahead to Kansas. He was under the assumption that I was still in Arkansas. After a few days of being in Kansas, I wanted to get myself together and clear my head, so I went upstairs in Robin's house, got alone and began to pray. After I came out of prayer, I told Robin quite confidently that Tyrone was bringing his mistress to Fort Riley. Robin, thinking I was overreacting, tried to assure me otherwise. "Tyrone wouldn't be that stupid, Leigh," she said. I told her again firmly. "No. I just *saw* him bring her." She looked puzzled. "Huh? What do you mean you saw him bring her?"

"He was on the turnpike and pulling a U-Haul," I replied to her again. She seemed intrigued at my certainty but still disagreed with me. "I'm telling you, nobody's that stupid." She kept saying. In my mind, I begged to differ. It was one of my visions. Just like the others that I now know were spiritual premonitions, I knew that what I saw was about to happen.

Later in the week, Robin had to drive Ronnie to the airport in Kansas City, Missouri, for his departure. When she was on the way back to Kansas from the airport, she spotted Tyrone on the Topeka Turnpike. As soon as she pulled up to her house, she couldn't open the door fast enough.

"I just passed him!" She said with heightened excitement. I was seated in her kitchen when I looked up at her. I was caught off-guard at first by her abrupt entry, but immediately, my mind deducted who the "he" was. I was surprised, but not really. I was more so shocked at the dead-on accuracy of the vision that I saw.

"A gold escort, right?" She asked.

"Yep," I replied. "I was in a white escort and looked dead at him, but he had no idea who I was," Robin said. "You're right, he's coming to Fort Riley—and pulling a U-Haul behind him!" I swallowed, and all I could get out was, "Okay." I could see Robin's shock and curiosity at how the vision I shared with her was so spot-on. Composing herself from being captivated, she immediately switched gears when she noticed my demeanor had turned melancholy.

"Are you okay?" She asked.

"I'm fine," I replied.

Robin seemed even more adamant about helping me get a plan together. "What are you going to do?" She asked. In my own heart, I didn't know what exactly, but I was holding on to what I heard when I got aboard that bus; the words to simply, "Go." I knew I needed to get on my feet, have a place to live, and make money.

"How are you going to get money?" Robin asked. I told her that I was going to pray and ask God where to go and get it. "He's going to tell me exactly where it's at," I told her. "Everything I'm going to need; I'm going to have." At this point, Robin was seeing a side of my faith that she had never known before. We had grown up for the most part side-by-side, our lives mirroring one another, even down to being pregnant in our teenage years. I could tell that the confirmation of my vision and the confident faith that I had when telling her how I was going to get by piqued her curiosity if nothing else. "How much money do you have?" She asked.

"Not enough," I replied. "But something's going to have to happen."

I had been in Junction City for a little over a week and had one and a half of my main objectives checked off thus far: I had enrolled the kids in school on the base, and I found a place to stay with my cousin for the time being—that was the "half" part—but at least, we were ok. On my birthday, January 13th, I remember planning to drop off the kids and afterward continue putting in applications and inquiring about who was hiring. Robin let me use her car to get around, which was extremely helpful. I was making a left onto the military post after dropping my children off at Fort Riley Elementary when I looked up as Tyrone was turning right, leaving post. I honked my horn at him and motioned for him to pull it over. I scared him to death practically as he was still unaware of my being there. He looked as if he had seen a ghost but pulled over like I had motioned. As I walked up on him, I wasn't even angry. All I could think about was the fact that I didn't want my daughter to be me, and I didn't want my son to be him.

We got into a heated argument. I called him out on the fact that he had left his family, been AWOL for Christmas with the kids, and was playing house with his girlfriend and hers. He had used his allocated moving resources from the government to get Terri and her three kids settled, while leaving his wife and his own two kids to hang. I asked him how he expected us to get by when he had opened a new bank account and neglected to place me on it. On top of that, he knew we only had one car between the two of us, and if he had it, that meant I was walking or having to hitch rides with his children in the cold.

Looking at me seemingly unphased by what I was saying, he told me sharply, "You came up here, you figure it out!" I looked at him, stunned. He really had lost it this time. He felt as if he was holding all the cards and wanted to make sure that I knew. "At this point, I'd rather live in a cardboard box while eating peanut butter and jelly sandwiches than to keep putting up with you and this." He had a smirk on his face and his lips were pressed as if to emphasize that he wasn't listening to what I was saying. He began to tell me that I wasn't going to be anything without him and tore me down verbally, saying that I wasn't this and that. His anger, for the most part, was based on his getting caught by surprise. See, Tyrone banked on "knowing me," and figured he had time to get Terri settled first since he knew I wouldn't make any irrational moves or decisions without making sure my children's living conditions were set in stone. Per his usual manipulation, he tried to make me feel guilty, as if I was the one who had done something wrong. The thing was, though, I wasn't going for it this time. "Let me tell you something," I said. "I will drive better than you. I will live better than you, and I will always make more money than you—take that to the bank!" The irony was that I didn't have a bit of a job at that moment nor a place to live. But I meant what I said. I proceeded to tell him that when the dust settled with all the mess that we had created, that I was guaranteed to walk out on the other side and be the better of the two of us. I told him that God would make all of my enemies—including him—be at peace with me. I told him boldly that no matter what, my two children would be taken care of before her and hers would. My children would never ride on top of the van; they would always ride on the inside. My kids weren't going to go without for Tyrone to take care of someone else's. After I said those things to him, I turned around, walked back to

Robin's car, and drove off. For the first time, although I was hurt by him, I felt strong. I felt like I had taken my power back.

I stepped out on faith and I continued to look for a place to live. I found a basement apartment located at 415 West 15th street. The landlord told me that the apartment was 2-bedrooms and that it was $285. I didn't even have $285 yet. I told Robin about it and she asked me what I was going to do. I told her that my plan was to go and talk to the landlord and to be straight up when the time came for him to ask me about signing the lease. I went to meet the landlord and he was a little old white man who showed me the inside of the apartment for the first time. He recounted the price to me and before I knew it, I was crying. I caught him off-guard, no doubt. I told him that I didn't have the money but that if he would give me a chance for the sake of my kids, that he had my word about me paying him the money. I found myself spilling a condensed version of my life's current chaos to him. From my husband bringing his mistress, to my children and I staying with my niece and needing a place of our own—the whole nine, basically. After all of that, he reached his hand out to me and said, "Here are your keys." I looked down at my hand and couldn't believe it. I almost felt a new onset of tears coming when he said, "I'm giving you this apartment because you look like you'll pay your rent on time."

I didn't have a dime to my name when he said it, but if he had faith in me, surely, I could get in agreement. I was surprised on one hand, but on the other, I wasn't—I was in faith. When I got settled in Fort Riley, I made sure that I called Pastor Butler and updated him on my location—as he was adamant about staying connecting with members who would come and go because of deployment and duty. To my surprise, Sgt. Davis and Sgt. Hill contacted him for my contact information. While in the field on active duty, they said that God told them to send me some money. The money that the two of them sent combined was the exact amount of my first month's rent! Getting the apartment and God using the two of them to cover my rent was all the confirmation that I needed as a reminder that no matter what I was facing, God was going to make a way for us, just like He led me to believe when I first prayed about coming.

At this point, my niece, Robin, was suspicious of how all my chaos was seemingly working itself out. "I need to know a little bit more about Jesus for real cause money is coming out of nowhere for you!" She said. "You just go and pray, and it happens!" She said in disbelief. I was happy for the opportunity to be able to talk about Jesus with her in depth. The Jesus both of us had known growing up, was based on good works and not relationship. We were literally taught that if we did good and treated others well, that we would go to Heaven. My life was an example for her because she knew my old nature very well. God works things together so well that even my life's ups and downs were drawing my niece to want to have her own deep relationship with him.

I landed a job at Burger King and was grateful at least to have some form of income coming to me and my kids. I needed money next to see a divorce lawyer. I had visited a lawyer when I first moved to Kansas, but having not been a resident for at least 60 days at the time, there was nothing official that I was able to do. What I could do now was go before the judge and file for temporary support from Tyrone to help out with the kids and bills. I also told my lawyer that I needed transportation to and from work and to get my kids to school. My lawyer also informed me that we could get a car arrangement. We went before the judge for both and Tyrone showed up, but without legal representation. The judge approved the temporary support in the amount of $600 per month and created a court order for both of us to share the car. Truth is, I never would have taken him to court if he had just agreed to do what he needed to do on his own. By now, it was March, however, and I went to begin the official process to file. I didn't have the money up front to officially start the filing process but the next thing I knew, someone sent me some money! This time, I wasn't even sure where it came from! God was supplying me and my kids' needs, and at the same time showing Himself mighty to my niece, who was witnessing it all. God's so awesome like that. He can take one person's lesson or story and use it as a tool to draw others unto Him.

Though I felt like a significant weight had been lifted off my shoulders, believe it or not, now the tables had turned, and Tyrone was trying to reconcile things between us. For one, Tyrone's name was still on our vehicle, so we had split custody over a car! We were court ordered to split our car in such a way that one person would have it on the weekends and the other person would have it on the weekdays and then it would alternate weekly. It looked like he was getting away with murder, and I was just struggling. He had two cars at his disposal and by court order, I had to share my one.

On the weeks where I had the car on the weekend, I struggled to figure out how I was going to get my kids to school on post during the week. It was an annoying situation, to say the least. Fortunately for me, I ran into some of my church family from Germany who also were stationed at Fort Riley. Sharon Goodin and I had attended Pastor Butler's church together, though we didn't know each other well during that time. While church searching in Kansas, we ran into each other again and from there became good friends. All of this to say, on the weeks when I didn't have access to the car during the weekday, she started to give me regular rides to get back and forth to pick the kids up from school. Sometimes, she'd even take them without me. I was grateful for that. When it would be time for Tyrone and I to trade off on the car, he started leaving notes for me on the inside, asking if we could talk and suddenly wanting to work things out, but I couldn't do it. He had left our family and our two kids to go and start a family with her and her three! Apparently, his math wasn't very good.

I had been in Kansas for about 3 months now. Though Tyrone did not live with us, he, of course, found opportunities to play with my head and try his usual "back and forth" antics when he made time to visit the kids. I was vulnerable, and we, of course, were still married, so it was hard not to lean towards missing him and longing for him to be at home with us at times. Deep down, I was still in love with him, even though I knew he was no good for me. I felt like I needed one more official reason to be totally out, and then I could go through with the divorce. For some, the turnpike and the U-Haul story would have been enough of an out. But this was my high school sweetheart, and furthermore, he was my husband and the father of my children. I had too much vested in our relationship and I wasn't ready to let it all go just yet. That is, until one day when Robin and I were shopping at Dillon's Grocery Store in Junction City. I turned down an aisle, and lo and behold I saw *her*. "Her" was none other than Terri, the mistress, and a whopping pregnant belly to boot! That was it! *That* was my official reason to be out! I became so overwhelmed with emotions that I almost started to shout right there in the middle of the grocery store. Robin saw her and looked at me and looked at her and then looked at me.

"Beat. Her. Ass!" Said Robin. "Beat her asss right now!" She said with borrowed offense, trying to egg me on.

I peacefully stood looking at Terri and told Robin quite calmly, "No. I'm not going to beat her up."

On the contrary, I walked towards her and said, "Hi Terri, how are you?"

She had an undeniable deer in headlights look on her face, and nervously responded. "Oh, I'm doing good." From her expression, I'm not sure she knew I was in Kansas.

In the distance, Robin's eyes were ripe for me to get a sudden swing on her, I could tell. "Well, I've moved here, and if you need anything, let me know," I said to her.

Robin's eyes were the size of saucers. Once more, she looked at me and looked at her and looked back at me as I turned back around and walked back over to where she was observing. Seeing her and that pregnant belly was a stepping-stone for me to walk away.

When it was official that Tyrone had left the kids and I—Tyronica blamed me and was upset. She was 12 around this time and Tyrone Jr. was 7. Like most adolescents, she processed the transition of our divorce with difficulty. Tyrone Jr. and Tyronica were also both struggling in school. I knew fully well the academic potential of both of my children, and therefore, knew their academic changes were based on the emotional climate that was happening around them. Tyrone never sat the kids down and said anything regarding why he wasn't in our home anymore as their father. One day, he was there, and the next, he wasn't. In my mind, I never tried to press the issue. I knew as they got older, they would put the pieces together for themselves and discover the character of their father while growing up.

CHAPTER 10

Breaking the Cycle

I desired a fresh start in every sense of the word. Burger King had been a blessing, but I knew my destiny and desires extended long beyond that. I began to search my heart for what it was that I was called to do, and I was brought to the idea of children. I always worked with children in one capacity or the other, and so, I decided that I would start a childcare facility. I didn't have the startup funds for all that I needed, but I did have children myself, so some of the resources were already present in my house. I met a lady from my church, who was a childcare provider. I inquired of her what were some of the steps on how to get it off the ground, and she graciously told me. I learned that I first needed to apply for a childcare license, which took about 30-60 days to get approved.

After I completed that step, I could officially start operating my business as a registered home childcare facility in my basement. I utilized my kids' toys to meet the state's minimum requirement. I decided to call my business Loving Arms Learning Center. I was ready to start posting flyers and information about accepting new clients. I made flyers and distributed them in the Laundromat, grocery stores, apartment buildings, churches, school PTAs, hair salons, barbershops—wherever I could.

Once the divorce proceedings got underway, Tyrone seemed to suddenly have a change of heart. I was standing in the court lobby with my lawyer, and Tyrone tried to get me to stall the divorce until after he and Terri's baby was born. I finally had called his bluff, and he was using any excuse available to prevent our divorce from being official. "I need to talk to you—in private." He said urgently. I looked at Robin, and she looked at me. She rolled her eyes and pressed her lips. "Okay," she said as she walked off to allow us time as he requested. I looked at him, waiting to hear what he possibly had to say.

"Why haven't you been responding to my notes?" He asked.

"What for?" I said, looking him square in the eye, "There's no point." I then told him that I could deal with the abuse and cheating, but I knew myself, and having to help raise another woman's baby was a request I could not accommodate. I knew a baby meant having to deal with the mother, and that was my deal breaker, of all things.

"We can work it out though, Leigh—"

"No, we can't," I said, cutting him off.

In my mind, there was literally no coming back, and the only thing to do now was to end it. When the recess ended, we both had to take the stand and testify. My lawyer examined me on the gist of why I wanted a divorce. He painted the picture of what our military life had been like with Tyrone's cheating, alluded to the letters between Terri and Tyrone, the baby on the way, and how Tyrone had left his family; basically, he set up the case for the court to see why I wanted out. When it was time for Tyrone to take the stand, he was compliant with the questioning and took it upon himself to volunteer statements of how he loved me and was sorry and didn't want to go through with signing the document that would put our divorce in motion.

"Sir, you should have thought this through before you took on the responsibility of another family." The judge said emphatically. When Tyrone stepped down, the judge said that he was ready to rule. The judge ordered that I would get 50 percent of his retirement if he retired from the military, his temporary support became regular child support that was to be paid up until the kids graduated from college or the age of 22. I was to receive spousal support up until an agreed period of time, all of our housing goods and full ownership of our car with his obligation to finish off the payments. He walked away with his hold baggage from Germany, which included his clothes, stereo, and La-Z-Boy. Sure enough like I had told him back in Germany, Terri would cause him to lose everything. He got what he wanted and lost what he had. He was now supporting three mouths with one on the way, not to mention our two. Our divorce was final in April of 1994.

By June of 94', I had acquired a decent number of clients and began to think beyond the basement of my apartment, which I wasn't particularly fond of anyway. With the onset of the summer, roaches and bugs were beginning to come out sporadically because of the heat. I knew that remaining in that apartment to live, let alone facilitate a business, was a no go. Financially, moving was not an option, but I diligently worked to make sure both the facility and quality of service I provided were excellent since that was the best I had at the time. I wanted change so desperately for my children, my business, and myself. Not being in the ideal location, not having the ideal funds, and outgrowing my basement, were all stepping stones for where God was eventually taking me. For whom much is given, much is required. I knew to qualify for the "much," I would have to be found faithful over the least.

After the divorce, Tyrone would come by my place on the regular to visit or see the kids. I had to check him after he did so a few times unannounced. I wasn't seeing anyone at the moment, but the principle was, we were no longer together, and things had changed. He was the only person who hadn't received that memo. He'd try to hug on me and kiss on me when he came by, and I tried to pull away from his advances. "Let's not go there," I'd say. He'd say things like, "You're still my wife," as I'd roll my eyes and shake my head. Since I was awarded the car during our divorce proceedings, Tyrone didn't have a car of his own. He now had to share Terri's car, which he didn't like.

When the summertime rolled around, I planned on going home to Arkansas to visit my family for the 4th of July holiday like we usually did. One day while dropping the kids off, Tyrone asked me if I was going home for the holiday weekend. I told him that I was. He asked if he could ride along with us so that he could visit his family too. That wasn't a problem, so I told him sure. Nobody from either one of our families, except Robin, knew that we were divorced nor about his living with Terri or their pregnancy. When we got home, he even stayed at my family house, though I made it clear that we were not sleeping in the same bed. While most women wouldn't travel home with their recent ex-husband, I honestly didn't think anything of it. Because we grew up together so young, in a small town no less, our being around each other was second nature—married or not. I'm really not sure what he told Terri as he left her at home over the holiday weekend, but I, of course, could not have cared less.

The weekend home was fun. We hung out with our families, caught up with old friends, and even hung out together—just the two of us. It was almost like old times. So much in fact, that before the weekend was over, Tyrone and I slept together. Part of me was still in love with him, and the other part regretted my vulnerability. It was like a flashback to a frozen moment in time; for that weekend, he was like the Tyrone I knew and loved in high school. I knew once we got home to Kansas, the reality of Terri and her pregnancy would put things back in perspective for me, but it was one of those things that just sort of happened. When we returned home to Kansas, Tyrone and I started to spend regular time together again. We would go shopping for the kids together, to the movies, out to dinner—wherever. Some nights, he even would fall asleep at my place. Here I was again, back playing these games.

My nephew Darion and his wife Michelle had moved from Arkansas to Kansas to stay with us temporarily. One day in August, his wife and I decided to stop by the Army Community Service building on post. It was basically a hub of information for servicemen and women and their families. As Michelle and I went inside looking for information about miscellaneous military spouse benefits, there was a man on the inside who was doing a horrible job at hiding the fact that he was repeatedly glancing in our direction. We continued to browse various displays of informational pamphlets and handouts, grabbing ones that piqued our interest and left. As we walked out to my car, the staring man from the inside followed behind us a few seconds later. "How are you ladies doing today?" He asked as we prepared to get inside the car. "We're fine!" Michelle said, immediately instigating the man's attempt to make my acquaintance. "My name is Kevin, and I hate to bother you—"

"Oh, no bother, Kevin. I'm Michelle, and that's LaFarris." My niece-in-law said all too enthusiastically, cutting him off. He smiled. I stood at my car door plain-faced, but not rude, as I forced a smile in exchange for his introduction. He continued with his former sentence. "I was wondering if I could have your telephone number?" He asked, looking directly at me now. Michelle's eyes might as well have been light bulbs as she lit up, standing at the passenger side door. Not having the energy to even get into why I was about to decline, I rolled my eyes with a slight smile. "Thanks but, no thanks. I'm not really into dating right now." I replied as I put the key in the car door to finally attempt to unlock it. Michelle about had a fit. "Um, no thanks?" She asked, looking at me demandingly across the hood of the car. I shot my eyes at her. She was unbothered by my glare and continued her inquisition. "He ain't asking you to marry him, dang! Just your phone number." Kevin stood there and watched our back and forth banter with a patient smile and giggle. I rolled my eyes at her and looked back at Kevin.

"Thanks, but no thanks," I said again as I finally opened my car door and got inside. Kevin respectfully nodded but never stopped his subtle smile. Though uninterested, from what I could see, he was light-skinned, tall, handsome, and did have a nice smile. From this brief encounter, his countenance did seem polite, but I just had too much going on in my world. I was fresh out of a bad marriage, still playing on-again, off-again games with my ex-husband, had just started my business, and was trying to be focused. Michelle opened her car door but hadn't gotten inside yet. From the windshield, I could see that Kevin was looking in her direction, but neither of them was saying anything audibly. "Chelle!" I said as she still stood and placed a foot inside the car as if to appease me. Her head was still out of my view. "Ok, Kevin, it was nice to meet you," Michelle said as Kevin nodded at her and then looked at me through the windshield. "Nice to meet you, LaFarris." He said with a mysterious yet innocent smile as he put his hands in his pockets and took a few steps backward on the sidewalk as we pulled off. I rolled my eyes, and Michelle was tickled at my annoyance all the way home.

A few days later, when I had pretty much forgotten about the Kevin incident, my phone rang. I answered. "Hello," I said. "Hello, may I speak to LaFarris?" A deep and unfamiliar voice said.

"Who is this, and how did you get my number?" I asked, trying to decipher the voice still.

"This is Kevin from the ACS Building—I met you with your friend the other day—she's the one who gave me your number." I couldn't believe it. That slick heffa had given him my phone number without me knowing. I couldn't help but giggle to myself. "Hello,

Kevin," I said sarcastically with a laugh. He could hear my giggle over the phone, and it broke the ice a bit.

"Hey, listen, I don't want to keep you too long, I just wanted to reach out and formally introduce myself and wonder if you'd like to go out Friday?"

I sat there quietly on the other end. Part of me wanted to totally dismiss the thought altogether while some small part of me was feeling a bit daring. I was single. That, and an even pettier part of me wanted to prove to Tyrone that I was still a hot commodity. Hearing my initial pause to his invitation, he readily offered up plan Bs and Cs just in case I was leaning towards declining. "Now, if you can't do this Friday, we can do Saturday—or even next Friday. You just let me know when you're free." He said. If nothing else, he was insistent. That got my attention somewhat, but I still wasn't entirely enthusiastic to say yes. Still, Michelle's words came back to my memory about how it wasn't marriage that he was asking for—just a hangout. I finally agreed to meet up with him the coming Friday. He solidified our plans, and we hung up.

When Friday came, he knocked on my door, and I welcomed him in briefly before we headed out. We got in his car headed to a local park. We sat in the car for a while and exchanged tidbits about one another—where we had grown up, what we did professionally, what our interests were, and so on. After a while, we got out of the car and casually took our conversation to the swings. It was the early evening in August, so it was still fairly hot outside, even though the day was winding down. "I hate this hot weather," I commented as I plopped down on the swings. He looked at me. "Me too! I prefer the colder months myself." He said as he sat on the swing next to me. I looked at him and agreed. "I know, I love the chill and snow." We discovered other commonalties like sharing purple as our favorite color, both being parents—he had two girls and a boy, and both having been married. Well, I was, of course now divorced, but he still was. He told me that he and his wife were in an open marriage, and I had never heard of such a thing before. He told me that per a mutual agreement between the two of them, that on Friday nights, he went out to have his fun, and on Saturday nights, she went out to have hers. On Sundays, they would alternate, depending on what week it was, and on Monday through Thursday, they were both home with their family. I was perplexed at his explanation, but it wasn't my business. Hell, I had an ex-husband who treated our marriage like it was open, so it wasn't the most far-fetched thing I could imagine. We talked about various things for about an hour or so, and the conversation was easy flowing and pleasant. We headed back to his car, and he dropped me back off at home. Before I got out, he told me that we should have another date soon. Politely, I told him thanks but no thanks. He looked a bit disappointed but still maintained his gentleman-like demeanor. I thanked him again and quickly got out of the car, not giving him a chance to walk me to the door. I had fun and all, but just wasn't interested. And besides, for a first date, the park wasn't exactly a spectacular first impression. When he said date, I thought we would be going to dinner somewhere, or at least a movie. If I was going to jump back into the dating game as a grown woman, I had expectations and wasn't about to settle.

The following Monday after closing out the day and all the children were picked up, Michelle emerged from my living room with a small gift bag and a mischievous smile on her face. "What?" I asked, wondering what she was up to. "Oh nothing, just that *somebody* dropped this off for you." She thrust the gift bag forward, all the while still smiling. My forehead wrinkled. "For me?" I asked in curiosity. I grabbed the bag from her as I looked inside. She stood there, waiting to see what was inside. I pulled out a bottle of Elizabeth Taylor's White Diamonds perfume. I was shocked as my cheeks couldn't help but rise into a slight grin. "Ooooh!" Michelle said in obnoxious enthusiasm.

"Who's this from?" I demanded.

"Girl, Kevin. He dropped it off a little while ago and told me to give it to you!" She said, pleased to make the revelation. My eyes widened. "Kevin?" I repeated back to her as my mind processed the fact. I looked back at the bottle. Though the gesture was thoughtful and a bit out of the box, I still wasn't sold on this Kevin guy.

The next day, once again, after closing out the day, Michelle brought me another gift bag. I was shocked. I opened it up, and this time, it was a bottle of Calvin Klein's Escape. "Girlllll, another bottle?" Michelle exclaimed as I rolled my eyes. Kevin had once again left a gift with Michelle. Wednesday came, and so did another gift. This time, it was Elizabeth Arden's Red Door, and he once again dropped it off to my door and left it with Michelle. Each time he had come by, I was preoccupied with childcare duties and never saw him. By now, Michelle wanted answers. "Ok so, remind me why you would never go out with him again? He obviously likes you!" She asked. By now, I had to admit; he at least had my attention. I guess he wasn't as cheap as I thought, and at least he was thoughtful. I sat there in my thoughts as Michelle demanded an audible response. "So, you wouldn't consider another date?" Her question seemed to be a part of a covert offline conversation between the two of them — no doubt taking place during the drop-offs. I looked at her and then shifted my gaze, trying to stifle my smile. "I guess I wouldn't be opposed to going on another date with him." I finally said. Michelle smiled with satisfaction. "A real date!" I added as we both laughed.

Another bottle of perfume came Thursday, and this time so did a phone call. "I trust you've been receiving my gifts?" He asked. "Yes, I have. Thank you. That was nice. I would have called to say thank you, but I don't have your number, you have mine." I said with a chuckle.

"So why is it that you won't go out with me again?" He asked. "You want me to be truthful with you? I asked. "Of course." He replied. "Well, I thought our first "date" was distasteful, immature, and inconsiderate. We're not teenagers. And if that was someone's idea of a first date, there won't be a second one with me." He laughed at my surety of speech. "Wait, wait." He said as he composed himself. "How about you give me a chance to make it up to you? How about dinner tomorrow at 6?" I thought about it and told him okay as we hung up.

When Friday came, Kevin came by my house on time, but I was exhausted. I apologized to him and told him that I honestly wasn't up to going out as planned but that I was still down to hang out at my home if he wanted. He agreed and said that since we weren't going to dinner, that he'd bring dinner to me. Michelle beamed to see Kevin walk through my door.

"Heeey, Kevin." She said as she hugged him.

"Oh, Lord," I said with another eye roll. Kevin smiled. "Hi, Michelle." She introduced him to Darion. Kevin told us that he'd cook for the four of us. My kids were with Tyrone for the evening, so I would make sure our evening was wrapped up before the kids returned. I had never had another man around my children other than their father, and besides, I barely knew Kevin myself, let alone my children meeting him. He asked me what I wanted to eat. "Surprise me," I said as he smiled and accepted the challenge. "Okay, I'll head to the store and come back."

When he got back, he unpacked the groceries and got to work. He seemed incredibly comfortable in the kitchen and shared with us that he loved to cook. I told him conversely that I did not. I went on to emphasize that I wasn't the type to have dinner waiting when a man had a long day at work because I too had long days at work. That and, my ex-husband had been a cook, so he usually opted to do the same at home. Kevin was amused. I purposefully made comments and told stories that I thought would be off-putting as I still wasn't interested in officially dating anyone. He didn't seem to pay my attempts any mind, and the four of us talked, ate, and laughed the evening away.

After that night, Kevin and I would talk casually on the phone, and he would begin bringing me lunch and inviting me on random hangouts. I didn't mind the company, as long as he understood that we were just friends. He said that he did. I invited Kevin over to hang with me, Darion, and Michelle the coming Friday. At first, it started out as a spare time type of thing. Then it would escalate to for sure seeing one another once a week, then twice a week, and so on until it was a bit of a norm. On Fridays, it was nothing for Kevin to come over and hang with me, Darion, Michelle, and other friends of ours. We'd have fish fries, barbecues, play cards, listen to music, and dance—just good old fun. Sometimes we'd have movie nights, and I would end up falling asleep halfway through. He'd hang around for a bit watching me sleep or sometimes would fall asleep himself in a chair. Most times though, I'd wake up to find him gone and a blanket conveniently sprawled out over me. Kevin had met Tyrone Jr., and Tyronica, and the three of them got along well. Kevin would play ball with Tyrone Jr. and drop Tyronica off to shop or hang with friends if she asked.

The more time that Kevin and I spent around one another, the more it seemed that his perfect fit in my life was the friend zone. This wasn't a sentencing, but rather what seemed to make the most sense. He, after all, was still married, and I was still entertaining my ex-husband. I wasn't attracted to Kevin in that way, and even if I was, I wasn't in a rush to be tied to another commitment, having just freed myself from one that had been so taxing. Friendship was what I needed most at the time, and he was a great friend. He was loyal, kind, and always took a genuine interest in what I was saying or how

I was. Knowing him was refreshing and in many ways, reminded me of the connection that Mo and I shared back in the day.

One day, while having a typical Friday get-together at my house, my doorbell rang. I answered the door and saw a woman standing on my porch. "Hi, sorry to bother you. I'm Kevin's wife, is he here? She asked cordially, making the deduction from recognizing his car parked out front with a few others. "Oh, hi! Yes, he is." I replied as I turned to call his name from the door and looked back at her to invite her in. Her eyes seemed to study my face and vice versa. I had seen her before, and the expression forming on her face must have been registering the same. When I had first moved to Kansas back in January of that year, my niece Robin insistently drug me along to a barbecue gathering at one of her friend's houses. While there, I recall meeting the young lady that was now standing on my porch. I remember having a random conversation with her during the barbecue and her introducing me to her husband—which was *not* Kevin as I recall. "I know you." She said, finally breaking the silence of our mutual mental computing with an uneasy grin.

"I know you too," I said with a small smile as if to communicate that her secret was safe with me. "You can come in if you want." I offered as I opened the door wider to welcome her. She smiled and stepped over the threshold but still stood as close to the door as possible. Kevin walked up, slightly surprised to see her but introduced us.

"LaFarris, this is my wife, Irene. Irene, this is LaFarris." We smiled at each other as if we had never seen one another before this very moment.

"Nice to meet you, Irene," I said as I turned to walk back over to the social scene in my living room.

When my back was turned to the two of them, I raised my eyebrows in a sort of comedic shock to myself. Open marriage or not, she seemed very uneasy to learn that the stranger she had encountered at a barbeque—while with another man—was now at the same house as her *real* husband. While she didn't know me well enough to know how I knew Kevin, she certainly seemed to grow subtly fidgety in the few seconds that she stood there waiting for him to come to the door. I think maybe she worried about the possibility of me telling him that she was at a barbeque with another man. She had nothing to worry about, however, as that wasn't my business. Besides, Kevin had already told me about their unique marriage scenario, and I pretty much chalked it up to that.

The warning that I gave Tyrone not to pop up at my house unannounced after our divorce, kind of canceled itself out after we both started fooling around again. He'd pop up at my house at will—his most practical excuse being to come and see the kids. One Friday when he stopped by to drop the kids off, Kevin was at my house. Once he realized a car he didn't recognize was out front, he took it upon himself to accompany the kids inside. Darion, Michelle, Kevin and I were hanging out and listening to music. Tyronica and Tyrone came in and greeted Kevin, and I followed by Tyrone Sr. stepping his legs through the door. I cut my eyes to him and then rolled them to myself. He stood in my living room with this strange sort of alpha male glare at Kevin as if he was sizing up the scene. He had heard the kids speak to Kevin—which let him know that his children knew the stranger sitting in my living room. "How you doing man? I'm Kevin." Kevin said as he stood to extend a handshake to Tyrone. Tyrone looked at his hand and then over at me. I pressed my lips together and sucked my teeth at Tyrone's delay to return the gesture. "Yeah, I'm Tyrone…" He said in a bit of a smart-aleck tone. He finally returned Kevin's handshake, and it visually looked like an over exaggerated display of strength. "Can I see you in the kitchen for a minute?" Tyrone asked me. My nephew Darion cut a glance at Tyrone and then back at Kevin as he tried to hold in a chuckle. I excused myself from the social scene in my living room and followed him into the kitchen. "What's up?" I asked. "Who's ol' boy?" He asked with a condescending inference. Thinking he initially wanted to have a conversation about the kids or something of confidential substance, I was thrown off. "Huh?" I said. He shifted his gaze and then looked back at me. I stifled a chuckle. "That's my friend. That's just Kevin." I said dismissively. He pressed his lips together as if he didn't believe me. "Just Kevin, huh?" He said as he went back into my living room to meddle. "You know this is my house, right?" Tyrone commented in a casual bullying sort of way. He presented the phrase as a joke, though it had definite undertones of seriousness. Kevin rolled with Tyrone's punches and laughed, returning back to his seat on the couch. Kevin was a man's man too and wasn't intimidated whatsoever. Tyrone strutted about the house and called for the kids to say his goodbyes, but really, it seemed as if to scope out the scene and linger. After he was done saying goodbye to Tyronica and Tyrone, he walked back to the living room where all of us were still seated. His jealousy was evident, and I was very amused. Though nothing remotely sexual or romantic was going on between Kevin and I, I took great pleasure in playing into the ambiguity that might have been swirling around in Tyrone's head. "Bye, Tyrone," I said, as he seemed to be searching for another curt remark to hurl at Kevin before leaving. Kevin smirked to himself, identifying man-to-man the role of intimidation that Tyrone was trying to play.

"That's my wife, man," Tyrone said with a wry grin. Kevin held his laughter and looked Tyrone in the eyes with a look to communicate that he could take a joke, yet was in no way moved.

"BYE. TYRONE." I said again as I got up and opened the door for him. "Oh, I gotta leave?" He said, faking offense. I held my gaze at him to let him know it was time for him to go. Pleased with his display of foolishness, Tyrone let a sly smile grow across his face as he finally exited my front door. I rolled my eyes and shut the door behind him. Kevin, Darion, and Michelle laughed aloud as I couldn't help but let out a chuckle myself. "So that's Tyrone, huh?" Kevin asked. "Uh, huh, *that's* him," I replied, dismissing the little show that he had just put on as we all continued to enjoy our evening.

For months, I had begun looking for a new place that was more suitable for my business and family. Now having 3 months of experience as a business owner under my belt, when it was time to find a new location, I had a much more strategic mind for doing so. My apartment wasn't centrally located, and it was kind of hard to find as it wasn't easily visible from main streets. In July, I finally found a house to rent that was a substantial upgrade from my apartment. It was a 2-bedroom, had a huge backyard that sat far away from the street so that my kids and the childcare kids could play safely, it was near the area of elementary and high schools, and was a short ride from the military base. Tyronica and Tyrone Jr. were still young enough to share a bedroom during this time, and I, of course, took the other. The living room and the kitchen were the predominant areas for the childcare. When I moved to this house, I was able to increase my childcare capacity from 6 children to 10, and my title was now that of a licensed childcare provider.

One night while driving, I saw Terri walking down the street, crying. She was almost nine months pregnant at the time. I pulled over and asked her what was wrong. She, in turn, asked me if I had seen Tyrone. I didn't have the heart to tell her that he was at my house. I picked her up and took her back to their place. I knew then that I could no longer do any of this. All this back and forth foolishness with Tyrone caused me to backslide, and I didn't even realize it. I had a very real conversation with her that night. I asked her did she really think that he was going to treat her better than he did me? I told her that I hated what she was experiencing but in the same breath told her that karma was a b***h. She didn't say anything. I think she was so upset and in disbelief about how he had done her, that what I was saying was having very little impact at all.

November of 1994, I went and spent Thanksgiving with my brother and Beverly. I told them that Tyrone and I were divorced and even told them about meeting Kevin. I wanted to go back to school in the coming year and wanted to know if they would be willing to help out with the kids during the summer months. That would enable me to take a full course load of classes, and when the kids were in school, I could do part-time classes. They eagerly agreed to keep the kids as they didn't have any kids in their household. Beverly's daughter, Qui, still lived with her father ever since that fateful day when he had come to Aunt Athalean's in Cleveland to take her.

My first Christmas in business as a childcare provider was interesting, to say the least, as I recall having to put my foot down with the parents of my childcare. I gave every single parent with outstanding tuition balances termination notices for their children. People had all kinds of excuses about having to get their children's Christmas gifts and being short on holiday money when a thought occurred to me. I myself hadn't got *my own* children's Christmas gifts, either. I wasn't running this business for fun; it had become my livelihood. If I didn't get paid for services that I had already rightfully rendered, I wouldn't be able to make Christmas happen in my own household. That wasn't about to happen. Decisions like these early on developed tenacity in me and taught me a lot about the service industry and business in general. It was my first real experience having to let go of clients. Though I had a soft spot for children, I had to think like a mother who had children of her own. My operation had to be backed up with logic and business sense—not sympathy.

When 1995 came, my friendship with Kevin was still going strong. By now, Tyrone had figured out that Kevin and I were genuinely just friends and had come around to having an amicable interaction with him. Tyrone would start frequenting the social gatherings at my house with Darion, Michelle, Kevin, and our other mutual acquaintances and friends. During one of the smaller Friday night kickbacks at my house, Gerald Levert's song, "Rock Me All Night Long," came on over the radio. A few of our friends chatted and laughed amongst themselves and others were playing cards.

"Come dance with me," Kevin said to me.

I thought the gesture was cute and walked over to him to oblige him. He placed his hands around my waist and placed my arms around his neck. I laughed as he sang to me off-pitch, mimicking Gerald. Then a strange thing happened. Here we were, slow dancing in my living room, and it seemed like it was just the two of us there. Our eyes were locked, and he let his karaoke attempts cease, as we now just looked at one another. He smiled subtly, and I smiled back at him. He leaned in and kissed me. I wasn't expecting it at all, but I kissed him back. On the other side of his kiss, I could feel a tinge of passion that let me know this wasn't random—this was based off of feelings. On my side of the kiss, however, I thought to myself, "Uh on." What was this? What was happening? It was a very nice kiss, but I didn't know what to feel exactly when it was done. I mean, deep down, I felt twinges of something, but at the time, I don't think I was ready to yield to whatever it was that I might have been feeling!

That first kiss kinda opened the floodgates for other kisses to take place. I thought it would mess up our friendship or make it awkward, but I was enjoying this new level of intimacy that we had accidentally stepped into. About two weeks after our first kiss, Kevin came over one day, and it was just the two of us. We had planned to have dinner together, only we never got around to it. Instead, we made love for the first time. I don't know what I expected to eventually come from our frequent kiss sessions, but I can't say that either of us "planned" what happened that night. Well, maybe *he* had.

Though Kevin and I had slept together, the fact remained that we had no title besides friends. He was still, of course, married, and since he had an open marriage, I rationed that perhaps I was just the current "object of his open affection." It was sort of a gray area as Kevin never pressured a conversation about what we were or were becoming, and I stayed away from the conversation entirely. Having said this, my ex-husband wasted no opportunities when it came to asking me to seriously consider our getting back together. We'd have these fun-filled and rich moments when we came together to do things together with the kids. I couldn't help but wonder if things could be like that all the time if we gave it one more try as he suggested. Deep down in my heart, I still had love for Tyrone. I mean, if he had never gotten Terri pregnant, there was a possibility that we might not have divorced. But, because he did, and not only that, because he squandered the many chances I gave him to restore his trustworthiness, I never could fully allow myself to believe that another "this time" would be different. Terri had their baby the summer prior, and ever since then, Tyrone was working diligently to get back in my good graces.

When I started to feel myself leaning towards another reconciliatory path with Tyrone, I felt the need to tell Kevin up front. We had spent way too much quality time together for me to just keep my plans a secret or go ghost on him. I knew I owed him honesty. Above all else, I valued the friendship that we had, and I wanted to be upfront with him. Days after I settled on giving things another try with Tyrone, Kevin so happened to stop by my place, which by now wasn't out of the ordinary. He greeted me with a hug and a smile. "I'm glad you're here," I told him as I led our conversation to the living room to sit down. "There's something that I need to discuss with you." I felt somewhat unsure about how the conversation would go but knew it needed to happen. Kevin could pick up on the nervousness that I was trying to suppress. "What's on your mind?" He replied. I sighed and took a brief pause before blurting it out. "You know, Tyrone and I have been spending time together and doing things with the kids as a family." I started off. "Well, we've been sort of talking about working our relationship out, again." His eyebrows had slowly risen, and his lips had parted slightly. I swallowed as I noticed this body language and continued. "I didn't want you to hear it from some of our friends or pop up one day, and he's here, you know?" He nodded. "I just wanted to be honest with you," I said, finishing my spiel. He sat there for a moment before responding, trying to stifle his apparent disappointment.

"Are you...are you sure?" He asked. I looked him in the eyes and then looked down at my hands. "I'm not sure..." I said stammering. I had told Kevin an extensive history about Tyrone and I, from the abuse to the other women. I was embarrassed at my words because I knew I must have sounded like a fool. "It's just that...we have two kids and a family and...I just want to try and see if it could work." He blinked rapidly as if he were processing what I was saying. "Okay, but you've been on again and off again for a while," he stated.

"Yes, but we've never been back in the house together..." I said as if it gave my decision more support. He shifted his eyes briefly, and then there was a brief silence between the two of us. He looked at me in my eyes again and made himself smile slightly. "Ok." He said. "If that's what you want to do, I'm happy for your family. I have a family, so I understand." He was being genuinely empathetic, and I appreciated it so much in light of how difficult it was to have the conversation. He told me that he would respect the path that my family was choosing and give me some space. We said our goodbyes, and he left. I thought that after talking to him, I would feel a release, but strangely, I felt weighed down somehow. I couldn't explain it but had to shrug it off. I called Tyrone, and he came over to spend the night with the kids and me. Over the next week or two, he spent the night regularly, and by February, had moved in completely.

For the first time in our history as a couple, Tyrone was doing all the right things. He had moved in, and our home dynamic was surprisingly peaceful. He was contributing to the household again, being attentive to the kids and me, and had displayed a new commitment to transparency. The occasions when I asked where he was or where he had been, he was all too happy to give me details without conflict. It was all so strange, and yet, it was everything that I had previously longed for. Tyrone had been living with us for about two full months, and surprisingly, we had not had sex. It was weird, but for some reason, I just couldn't bring myself to sleep with him. I mean, physically, yes, we were sleeping next to each other each night. But there was no intimacy going on. Not that he certainly wasn't making attempts. Every time he tried to make a move, I would conveniently come up with some kind of excuse. I'd say I was too tired or stay up working late in the front room until he fell asleep. I'd sleep far away from him on the opposite edge of the bed and try to tuck myself in tightly at night. I starved it off for as long as I could until one day, he addressed it outright. He tried once again to make a move, and I resisted his advances.

"Is something wrong?" He asked me. I sat up in bed. I sighed. "I just…I just need some time." I replied. "Our past is…confusing. I just have to be totally sure that this time, things are different." Compared to how the old Tyrone would have acted about sex with his woman, I was very surprised that he agreed to respect my wishes so adamantly.

I looked up and six months had passed with me and Tyrone's new life. The moments I enjoyed the most where when we spent time together with the kids. It was the family life that I had always envisioned for them. During this time, I had talked to Kevin a few times here and there, but it felt different. He wasn't coming over anymore and, in fact, the only times I heard from him now were if I took the time to call him. The conversation was pleasant, as this was his general demeanor, but they were now more surface than they had been previously. I missed his friendship, and it was beginning to bother me.

The thing that I had wanted for so long—to reconcile with my first love and have my family be together—I slowly realized, that I didn't really want anymore. Maybe I never even wanted it, to begin with. Maybe what I wanted was a two-parent household for my children. Or maybe, part of me wanted to silently showboat to Terri that what goes around indeed comes back around. For six months, things had been better than they had ever been in all of our years prior. Because of this, I tried to give it time to see if the old spark would return. After all, with the full extent of our ups and downs and back-and-forths, I always seemed to be the one hanging on to the hope of another chance. Now that Tyrone was ready to offer it, my heart was somewhere else—with Kevin.

It became clear to me that somewhere during those Friday night gatherings, talks at the park, phone conversations, movie nights and the like, that I had unintentionally fallen in love with my best friend. And this time, the love wasn't based off of desperation or validation. It was genuine, it was natural, and it was mutual. The connection I was so determined to keep platonic now seemed to flood my heart. I decided to talk with Tyrone that night when he came home.

"What's up, Leigh?" He asked. Unlike the time when I was breaking things off with Kevin, this conversation with Tyrone seemed right and like a relief. "I love you, and I will always love you," I started, "But I am not in love with you anymore," I told him. "I'm in love with someone else." I boldly confessed. His face was blank as he hung his head and then locked eyes with me again to listen. I will always be your friend, and I will always cherish our growing up together, but

Dare to Dream

I can't do this anymore." I told him. He truly was a more mature Tyrone as there was no cussing, violence, or even anger in his reaction. Rather, he looked solemn as if all his past indiscretions had humbled him in this moment. He told me that he respected my telling him and that he would move his things out that night. I finally was at peace with the fact that we couldn't get our past back. We were two different people now. We had reached the point of no return, and our well had finally run dry.

With this new freedom from Tyrone, my mind kept drifting to Kevin. I was in love with him and now knew it, though I had yet to tell him that. I called Kevin that same evening. I asked him if he would agree to meet me at the park, and he said he could. Within a half hour, he met me, and I didn't waste any time.

"I just put Tyrone out." I sort of blurted out. "I just can't do this anymore. I'm not in love with him," I said as he listened intently. "Are you sure?" He asked. I nodded. He seemed to be analyzing what I was saying and trying to decipher whether this was for good. "You know I love you, right." He said. Though this wasn't the first time he said that to me, it was the first time that the context was different. All the other times he'd said it, I instantaneously interrupted it as a byproduct of friendship. This time when he said it, it seemed to mean something more. For that reason, though I was feeling the same, I held off on saying it back.

For months, Kevin had reason to believe that his wife was having a steady fling with another man. To support his suspicion, he had found receipts and mail at his house to and from another Junction City address that he didn't recognize. The receiving address on the packages was in Washington State. One day, he decided to take a ride to the Junction City address. When he got there, he noticed a vehicle with Washington state plates parked in front. He got out and looked in the window to see his wife and another man in the act. He knocked on the door, and his wife opened up in a robe. I'm not sure why he was surprised to see her with another man, given they had agreed to an open marriage, but perhaps, actually seeing her in the act, as well as the mail exchanges, indicated a level of commitment that he wasn't willing to compete with. It was hardly my business, but the amount of time that Kevin spent hanging with me was a plain indicator that their marriage wasn't based on quality time. Kevin and Irene came to the mutual decision to get a divorce. The love had left long ago, but he too was trying to stay in a situation for his children's sake. All that changed, however, when he caught Irene in bed with another man. The two found a "Do It Yourself Divorce Kit," paid a flat fee of $69.95, filled out the appropriate paperwork, took it to be notarized, went to court, and in 30 days, it was final. If only my divorce had been that easy.

I relocated to Indian Ridge Townhouses, which were a bit more modernized compared to where I had moved from. Shortly after that time, January rolled around, and I put my plan into motion to begin school and enrolled with the major of Early Childhood Education. I knew that I didn't want to just be a babysitter but that this was something that I really wanted to pursue professionally. I wanted to qualify myself with education and get the proper certifications to maximize the services I desired to offer to my clients. I was working 14-hour days and then going to class full-time on Monday through Thursdays, and then, one Saturday a month. I was determined to reach my personal and professional goals, and I didn't have time to waste. When I felt as if I couldn't go on anymore, I looked at my mirror where I had written a word of encouragement to myself in red lipstick. It said, "How bad do you want it?" This kept me motivated and focused on my goal to finish school.

Tyronica was now 13, so for the three and a half hours that I was on base in class, I trusted her to look after things at home with her brother. While located at Indian Ridge, I was qualified to become a licensed group homecare provider, and my childcare capacity increased to 12. I, however, didn't go beyond 10 children at this time, as I knew that would require me hiring additional employees—a step that I didn't want to take yet until we were in a bigger facility that didn't impose as much on my family's personal space.

Rosalind Wesley was my professor for early childhood education. She taught all of the early childhood education classes at Central Texas College's adjunct campus on post at Fort Riley. She was a middle-aged black woman with a sweet spirit who loved her job and was visibly passionate about the field of childcare and her role as a professor—but she was firm and didn't play. She didn't let anyone make excuses. I was rough around the edges as far as professional childcare went. I had only been running my business for a year and still had a lot to learn about the childcare industry. Nevertheless, Rosalind saw something in me. She asked me one day, "So what do you plan on doing?"

"I want to own a childcare center," I said. With that answer, she began giving me assignments and resources that she thought would enhance my goal. If we had an assignment to construct a childcare facility, she would insist that I focus on modeling mine according to center-based standards versus home-based—which I was already doing, anyway. I murmured and complained to myself and occasionally to her. Her response? "I'm going to need that assignment, LaFarris." And that was that. She was sharp and wasn't the type to accept or entertain excuses.

One day, I approached Rosalind before class and informed her that I was going to be late turning in an assignment that was due in a few days. It was one of those major assignments that carried a significant portion of our grade—the kind that professors start discussing on day one of reviewing the syllabus. "Why?" She demanded.

I told her outright; I was a single mother with kids in extracurricular activities, I worked 14 hour days, attended night classes three to four days out of the week—including a Saturday a month, and I felt I barely had enough time to rest, let alone the addition of this major project along with all of our regular assignments. She looked at me. "And? What does that have to do with your assignment?" She asked curtly. I stood there in disbelief. This lady had zero understanding of my life and all that was going on in my world. Yet still, she didn't budge. "Turn your assignment in on time, or it *will* reflect on your grade." I was annoyed yet tried my best to mask my response as professionally as I could. "Well…ok," I said as I left her presence and resolved in myself to get busy.

In all honesty, if I had paced myself from the beginning of the semester, I could have found pockets of productive time to get my assignment to a further along place. I just didn't manage my time well. Looking at my daily schedule at face value; however, I never saw the opportunity. I had to get my kids ready and off to school, get things situated for the day with the childcare, close out the childcare at the end of the day, get my kids to their respective activities, start dinner, and be heading out of the door to class. Only to get home and steal just enough rest to do it all over again. I had only a few days to turn a long-term project into a finished one. It was grueling, but I ended up turning it in on time. Not only that, but I got a good grade. As I looked back after the assignment was done, I was grateful that she didn't let up on the deadline. In all honesty, if she had given me an inch of an extension, I definitely would have taken a mile. She was mentoring me in ways that I didn't even realize. School gives you the education that people pay for, but the anointing actually opens the door and gets you the job. School teaches you how to work for somebody—rarely is its purpose ownership. Parent handbooks, staff handbooks, development of products, and trainings—school didn't teach me that. School gave me the background history and knowledge of the field. It didn't teach me concrete things for thriving in the business on a continual basis.

Kevin and I moved in together in the early part of 1996. That September, I took him home for the Labor Day holiday. When Kevin told my father that we were living together, my dad hit the roof again. He hit me once again with his favorite line—the same line he hit me with when he said Tyrone and I should have gotten married after discovering that I was pregnant: "Why buy the cow when you can get the milk for free?" Turns out that Kevin wanted to buy the cow. He proposed to me, and I was ecstatic. We made our plans simple and to the point as we were both divorcees in our 30s and wanted to get to the good part of happily ever after. We drove to Wichita and were married in the courtroom on Valentine's Day. Afterward, we headed to a Bed and Breakfast for our honeymoon.

In March of 1997, reality hit me hard as my father was diagnosed with lung cancer. When my siblings and I found out, he was in stage four and was pronounced with six months to live. The only living parent that I had was about to take his last breath, and this naturally shifted my focus for a while. I decided to temporarily shut down the childcare center and gave out a 30-day notice to my parents. I also interviewed a number of childcare providers that I trusted within my network. I didn't want to leave my parents hanging, so took it upon myself to find a quality replacement as quickly as possible. Once I chose a provider, I shut down the childcare in April and took a break to do all the things with my dad that he wanted to do before he died. He had agreed to do chemotherapy for his family's sake, but after two rounds, didn't want to anymore because he didn't want to be sick the last few months of his life.

In May, I graduated with my Associate's Degree, and I was so grateful that my father was alive to see me walk the stage. With the summer around the way, we spent our time doing whatever he could dream up. If he wanted to take a daytrip somewhere in Arkansas, that's what we did. We went to Chicago, to Michigan, to see his family that he hadn't seen in ages, and even Louisiana. I wanted his last days to be as peaceful and comfortable as possible. Some of our best memories were made during this time. We'd laugh, travel, and enjoy one another. By September, he was ready. Even though I knew my father's death was impending, I found it extremely hard to accept. Every time he would say he was ready, I'd say, "hang on a little longer, daddy." He died September 26, 1997. This was a bittersweet day as it was the same day that Kevin and I signed for our new house.

My dad's death took a tremendous toll on me. I decided to ride out the rest of the year with the childcare still closed so I could take time and sort through my grief. I still, however, was taking classes, and even that was a lot at the time. I couldn't even enjoy the fact that Kevin and I had purchased our first home together like I really wanted to. My life was transforming right before my eyes, and it all was because of faith. I told God that I wanted to move out into an actual building that wasn't affiliated with my home. He told me that I wasn't ready. I told him that I was. I heard again, "No." Though my dad's death was a down moment, I couldn't help but get a tad bit excited about the renovations that were underway in the basement of our new home that would become our new childcare site. I resumed the childcare downstairs in the basement of the home we purchased. We built a walkout entrance and used the basement as a group home childcare. I had expanded to the ability to have 12 children, and it was the first time I had hired my first employee. I wanted a part-time person who could help me balance my daily schedule. I had night classes for my bachelors, all sorts of activities and commitments for my children, and of course, being a new wife.

Dare to Dream

Around this time, I started to feel heaviness of heart, and I couldn't exactly pinpoint why. I would feel so alone and achy in my heart. I didn't know what was wrong. It definitely wasn't Kevin—he loved me in a special way—nothing like my first marriage. Then I thought about it and chalked it up to missing my dad. That was until one day I had this overwhelming sensation that just stayed with me. I woke up once in the middle of the night out of my sleep and cried. I even woke Kevin up. "What's wrong?" He asked. I sobbed and looked over at him. "I…I miss God," I said through weeping. He looked confused.

"Huh?"

"I miss my relationship with God," I said emphatically. I missed the constant communication and confirmation of things as a result of being close to Him. The proximity that I had grown so accustomed to had waned—and it was my fault. "I'm going to church," I said. I calmed myself and lay back down. When the sun came up, I got up, got dressed, and went to church as planned. I rededicated my life to Christ that day, and it was so refreshing. I recalled God's distinct words to me back in 1993 just before I made the decision to up and move to Kansas. He told me that He would not allow the devil to destroy my marriage. At the time I thought the marriage he was speaking of was between Tyrone and I. I came to realize, however, that He meant the marriage between He and I. It was our relationship that he promised to always keep and my heart was full at realizing that He always had. The next Sunday, Kevin came to church with me. He said that he saw demonic spirits trying to tear through the windows to get close to him. He said it scared him so bad that his feet were stuck to the floor in his pew. He felt as if he couldn't move. For the next few visits that Kevin came to church with me, the images that Kevin saw of demons trying to tear through the windows to get to him continued. I, of course, couldn't see anything—only the sweat beads accumulating on his face.

"What's wrong with you?" I would ask.

"Nothing, nothing!" He said hurriedly.

One day, after just visiting, he decided to answer the altar call for accepting Christ into your heart. After that day, he told me about the demon visions that he had been having. I was surprised that he had just continued to sit there through something so terrifying happening. He also told me that they stopped once he prayed the prayer of salvation that day.

From day one, Kevin had stated that it was important for him to win respect with Tyronica and Tyrone Jr. organically—not because I enforced it. A big part of making that happen was about getting to know their father and acknowledging that being in their lives included Tyrone Sr. as part of the package. Once Kevin and I married, there was a unique blended family dynamic present. After I had officially broken things off with Tyrone, he had married Terri, and the two of them lived together on post. Thankfully, when we parted ways, Tyrone didn't blow things out of proportion or try to create an uncomfortable environment for Kevin to be around. It was important, if for no other reason than, the sake of our children. Having said that, as time went on, Kevin and Tyrone seemed to foster a unique understanding with one another that never seemed to be rooted in awkwardness or ego. So much so, that Tyrone would still drop by my house unannounced from time to time—once or twice, I can distinctly recall with Terri tagging along. Things between her and I were surprisingly more cordial now. More often than not, though, he'd be by himself and would come over to visit the kids or shoot the breeze with Kevin and me.

Once, he and Tyrone Jr. played a typical boys' game of basketball versus Kevin and his son. From regular talking smack and the proximity it took to be around each other to play a game like basketball, one would be shocked to know that the two main players had a spouse in common. I'm not sure it was always as easy as they made it look, but I was grateful that the men in my life always were able to put the needs of our children ahead of their own personal wants or biases. Shortly thereafter, Tyrone would be stationed to duty in Georgia, and he and Terri moved away.

CHAPTER 11

Daring to Dream

In 1999, I was finished with my Bachelor's and began thinking that I wanted to start a center-based program. I applied for my director's license that authorized me to have a business with up to 100 children. At the time, our childcare operation was still in the basement of our home. Having my director's license would also allow me to expand my vision if I wanted to have multiple sites in the state. After having my director's license approved, I began the hunt for a physical building that was totally independent of my family's residential address. I prayed to God again—the same way I had two years earlier—about having a building for my business.

"God, am I ready for this now? Can I have a building?"

"Yes, you're ready." He said to me.

I found a building to rent, and it was different than being in my home as I, of course, had more room. I had a nameplate on my desk and all. "*"Ooh, I'm a director!"* I thought to myself. With the new building, we could have dedicated rooms for the children by age—from 12 months to five-years-old. The space had three bathrooms, one of which we tore out to expand the kitchen. The renovations and any required upkeep were our responsibility. When plumbing backed up, or things happened, I had to use my own money to repair and address issues. Since my lease didn't specify that I could only use the building during the weekdays, I made my landlord aware of my intent to begin using the building during the weekends. I envisioned parenting programs, parents' day out, behavior workshops, and more. I wanted to provide enrichment opportunities for the families whose children attended the childcare. The only thing was, my landlord was a licensed social worker who also used the building on weekends for his various programming as well. I tried to do a couple of programs during the weekends, but I noticed that the traffic from his classes upstairs was coming downstairs to where we were to use our bathroom. Not knowing the nature of the individuals who were in the building for his programs, which ranged from anything from AA meetings to child abuse counseling—I couldn't risk the chance of unknown persons using my space at the same time that children may or may not be present. I wasn't about to jeopardize anyone's safety or the integrity of my business. All the while, my landlord continued to go up on my rent.

In addition to my rent woes, I had stepped out on a limb and hired my sister Trish Ann as an employee at the childcare, which was proving to be a regrettable decision. She had moved in with Kevin and I after an unfortunate fire destroyed our family's home in Arkansas, where she was staying. Upon hearing this news, a part of me was devastated; this home was the last and largest tangible memory of my parents and their hard work. Not to mention, it was the first home that I brought Tyronica home to. My other siblings and I would later learn that the mysterious fire was actually set by someone that Trish Ann had hired in an effort to collect the insurance money. A few weeks earlier, she had "coincidentally" asked Carla if she could store some furniture and other possessions from the house in her garage. Not thinking anything of it, Carla obliged and even asked her to bring some chairs over that she had been wanting from the house.

Daring to Dream

Fast forward to two weeks after the fire, a neighborhood crack head, who our family knew growing up, stopped by Carla's house, inquiring where Trish Ann was with his money. When my sister asked him what on earth he was talking about, he revealed to her that Trish Ann had indeed hired him to set the house ablaze. My siblings and I were infuriated and called a family meeting. When the insurance check did come, I had to intercept it and pay for an outstanding balance on a new roof that was installed shortly after my father's death. After that, I told my sister point blank that I didn't care what she did with the rest of the money, but that roof balance would be paid, period.

I was the one paying taxes on the property, and my father left the ownership to all of us. Here she was, in her late 40s, and it seemed that her immature ways were as ripe as ever. During all the time she spent plotting, I guess she never stopped to think about where she would live afterward. She lived with Carla for a while, but that was short-lived as our older sister is even more of a "no-nonsense type" than I am. Somehow, Kevin's heartstrings got tied up in Trish Ann's situation, and he extended an invitation for her to come and live with us. I tried to help her out with the job at the center, but she ended up wanting to do her own thing. If she was supposed to be there at say 7, it was nothing out of the ordinary for her to stroll in at 9.

Then, when she did finally show up, she'd always have some sort of an excuse. After warnings that I guess she took lightly, I decided to ask Carla for advice. I felt so heavy about the decision that I was leaning towards and cried as I alluded to Carla that I was thinking of firing her. I told her about Trish Ann's antics, and she told me plainly, "Look, put on your big girl panties before you mess around and lose everything that you've worked for! Let her go." She said without a thought. Days later, Trish Ann was late again and left me with no other choice. I called her into my office. She was actually the first employee that I ever fired, and I cried the entire time. Trish Ann

Dare to Dream

was always there for me growing up, and a part of me felt guilty for coming to the decision that I had.

"I love you, and I'm sorry, but I have to fire you," I told her.

"Okay." She said as if she knew it was coming.

"Can we still have Thanksgiving dinner together?" I asked as I sniffed.

"Girl yeah!" She said as if nothing had happened at all. I felt relieved all around.

When I first started childcare, I had no idea I would enjoy it as much as I did. It started off as a means to an end. I needed money to take care of Tyronica and Tyrone Jr. in the midst of a nasty divorce, and I needed a form of stability for them. As time went on, however, it became much more than just an occupation. My vision for what the business was and all it could be began to outgrow the facility we were currently in. This was when I started the official hunt for what was next as far as facility space. I wanted to touch the lives of children, and subsequently, their families. With having to pay for upkeep at the current facility, having limited use of the building as I saw fit, as well as a constant increase in rent, I started to set my sights on buying a building.

I hired a business consultant named Kathy, whom I had been working with for the last year. During one of our meetings one day, I vented to her about my landlord going up on the rent and how paying an actual mortgage for a property would be cheaper when it was all said and done. She seemed to light up with an idea as I talked. "I know a place that could be perfect for you." She said. I was intrigued but emphasized that I didn't want another house.

"It's not a house," she said. She went on to tell me that when it was originally built, it was a commercial piece of property with a craft store, dentist office, and a preschool on the lower level. Kathy was familiar with it as her daughter used to attend the former preschool.

Daring to Dream

She gave me the exact address, and a few days later, I thought to drive by and have a look. Unlike my current building, it was surrounded only by a school and a neighborhood of houses. My current location sat on one of the main streets in the city with heavy traffic, but also visibility. I was near the doctor's offices, fast food restaurants, gas stations, the local high school and its administrative offices. I never got out of the car but glanced at it and then headed home. I was unsure about it, but not ready to count out the idea altogether.

About a year or so earlier, while praying, God told me to start getting my finances in order. He told me that a transfer of wealth was about to occur. I wondered what that meant. I knew money wouldn't just fall out of the sky but began to contemplate how it would happen. He told me to get my personal credit in order because it was tied to my business credit—which I didn't know. "Okay!" I said. When the opportunity to buy the building came, it brought back to my remembrance what God told me about getting my finances in order. My faith was stirred, and I thought to share this revelation with some of my fellow church members who had approached me and asked me for advice I had on beginning and/or growing their businesses. In addition to general inspiration, I was excited to share with them what God had told me a year or so prior about the transfer of wealth for believers. When I mentioned it, however, they tended to blow me off as if my advice wasn't concrete enough for them to run with, or maybe, just not what they wanted to hear. With these same people, I shared my plans about how I was considering purchasing the multi-level, commercial-building-turned-house for the relocation of my childcare center. They all seemed to laugh at my idea and condescended my faith. "I wouldn't get a business over there if I was you…" "You won't get any clients…" "How are people going to find you?" They asked in pessimism, disguised as concern. That didn't bother me, though. I knew what God had told me just like I knew he told me to get on that bus to Junction City with $50 in my pocket. Whether or not they chose to believe it was on them. God told me He was an organized businessman. I didn't know anything about pricing or marketing. I would just pray about everything. "God, what do I charge people in order to be able to fund this business?" He would tell me, and I'd go from there.

Before ever stepping foot on the inside of the building, I went one early morning just before dawn, walked around it, and prayed. "God, is this my building?" I asked intently. He said, "Do you want it?" I told Him that I did.

He said, "Well, go get it."

"But what about the money?" I inquired. He told me to pretend that it cost the same $50 that I had when I got on the bus and came to Junction City, Kansas. I didn't see how, but one thing was for sure, faith had always made a way for me. I made an appointment with the realtor by myself. She showed me the place in detail. The building—originally, a commercial space—was approximately 9,000 square feet with three levels that sat on 4.5 acres of land. However, someone had turned it into a residential house. On the first level, it had a huge open foyer, with a chandelier hanging down. Off to the side, you could see a space that was possibly made for a formal dining room. There was some sort of media room that had theatre style lighting and special sound accenting insulation. Another room looked like it had been turned into a walk-in closet. It had a huge open kitchen with an island, beautiful wooden cabinets, a stovetop range, a microwave nook, and a room that had been turned into a walk-in pantry. Further down the hall, there was a half bath and not too far from that was a full bathroom with shower, double sinks, a Jacuzzi, and an exclusive area in the corner that had a TV screen overhead for whoever was bathing to watch. It was incredible. I went upstairs, and there was a large open area, two bedrooms, a large bathroom, and a linen type closet.

We went downstairs to the lower level, which was used as an open garage space for cars. There was also a large area towards the back for storage. Off the side of the kitchen was a door with a carved-out doggy flap that led down a walkway to a huge outdoor area where a huge swimming pool was in the back. It sat on a nice chunk of land, and you could see the great lengths they had gone through with the amount of money that had been invested to make it look like a home. Knowing that it was formerly a commercial building, however, I could see various traces of the dentist's office in the layout. I asked her if I could have a little more time to walk around.

"Sure, take all the time you need." She replied as she walked to another part of the house to permit me some alone time. With that, I walked all the way outside to go back over the property from the entrance. This time, however, I would envision every part of the building as the future home for my childcare center. Starting outside, I saw my infant toddler playground; I saw my sign that said, "Loving Arms Childcare & Preschool." I went inside the door as if I hadn't just gone in moments before and I saw an entryway with security access to buzz in or buzz out. There would be a surveillance area, with a window where you could speak with a receptionist. The main floor would be an infant/toddler floor. To the right was a classroom, then a play area with fireplace, chairs, and another classroom that could be anywhere from birth to school-aged children if I decided to do a 24/7 care facility. I would have all of those rooms designed to specification in such a way that I could have the fluidity to later decide how I would utilize them. As I continued to walk, I envisioned being able to work with high schools and colleges, helping them be able to gain apprentice-type training experience for future career endeavors in childcare. I saw a warm spirit room for mothers who wanted to nurse their babies, or use the room for social worker meetings or private one-on-ones—it would be the only room in the building that

Dare to Dream

wouldn't have a camera. I saw an exercise room with a treadmill and a bike for my staff and parents to utilize on the side of the kitchen. On the hallway off of the kitchen, the half bath would be my staff bathroom. Down the hallway, the bathroom with the Jacuzzi and TV would be for parents to come and get some needed "me" time.

At this time, it hadn't been long since 9/11 had happened. A war had begun, and people were stressed out and needed relaxation—especially in a military-based town. I walked to the room with the fireplace as I thought it would be a great place for rocking babies. I would place a carbon monoxide detector near the fireplace, and further down, I would install a small bathroom for older toddlers and a changing table for children who weren't potty trained. I went downstairs and continued to pray and envision. I would have two preschool rooms, a laundry room, and a before-and-after school area. It was just a garage, but I saw it. I would put in another complete kitchen for my staff lounge. I noticed a big area of concrete towards the back and thought to make that a storm shelter. I had covered all the basics of child rooms and even amenities as I looked around and thought, "I need office space and space for training.' I went back upstairs to the main level and then up to the top level. I needed an entry door solely for the top level so that people could come and meet or train without coming through the childcare itself. I would designate a room for my cameras and computer servers. Then I saw the bathroom and thought it would perfect to keep in the event I had late nights there and needed to keep clothes and freshen up. After walking through the building twice now, I needed time to pray and envision what my business could be. I started to think about all the things that I had needed as a young mother and how childcare facility could address those needs for other mothers. I thought of military mothers who could use support systems being away from their families with young children. I thought about the space and how it could

Daring to Dream

enrich the lives of families in various ways. The realtor gave me the complete tour—still treating the space as a residence. All the while, I had already begun envisioning it again as a commercial facility. After I was done, I thanked the realtor and went home, sat down, and put my thoughts on paper. God had shown me every aspect of what I wanted in totality, and the space felt perfect for everything that I needed and wanted. I decided to call a special family meeting the next evening that involved us taking a trip together to look at the property. As we walked through, I told my family room-by-room what I saw and envisioned. Tyronica looked around, wondering how what I was saying would transpire. Tyrone looked around, and all he could think about was, "Am I going to have to clean this whole building?" He was currently my janitorial staff at our current building, and he couldn't help but notice how much larger this space was compared to where we were. Kevin was enthusiastic as I described in great detail what I believed God was saying was next for Loving Arms. I laid out the vision for my family as God had clearly shown it to me while walking around the day before. My kids had been front row witnesses at how God had moved in our lives up until then, so my vision of faith wasn't foreign for them to get on board with. After we were done looking at the space together, we went back home and resumed our meeting to discuss their thoughts. My children thought it was a great idea overall. I brought up the numbers for what the realtor was asking and asked both Tyrone Jr. and Tyronica if I could utilize the money I had put away for their college funds to facilitate some of the purchase of the property. My son, now fifteen at the time, was ok with it. My daughter sat there with a concerned look that tried to be positive in the midst of the budding excitement. She was twenty at the time and already working on her sophomore year at Kansas State University. Sensing her concern, I promised her right then and there that she would have all the money that she would need to get through school as I promised. As far as I was concerned, she was not going to be in debt after graduation, and I still was committed to that. After that reinforced assurance, she then told me that she was ok with the idea. When it was Kevin's turn to give his input, he was on board all the way. "Whatever you want to do, I'll support you." He said. With everyone on board, we decided that we had found the future home of Loving Arms Childcare and Preschool.

When I first started my childcare business, I used what was in my hands, from my children's toys to food that I purchased. But this time, I was attempting to buy a big old building, and I was somehow scared. I wasn't as scared as when I had come to Junction City with my kids, and I, of course, trusted the journey that God had been faithful to me on, yet at the same time, this was all new to me. I went to see Kathy again about approaching the bank. I told her my family was in agreement with me. She told me to make an appointment with a loan officer. I had never done that, but I was taking note of whatever direction she put out. At first, I went to the bank where my checking account had been for the last ten years. They weren't very helpful and told me rather quickly, "No." They also didn't seem very willing to help me along the process. They had all these requirements and documentation that I needed, and I was even more confused than when I had first walked in the door. "Okay God, where should I go now?" He told me about another bank, so I made an appointment there. I met with the lady. "Do you have a business plan?" She asked.

"What's that?" I asked straightforwardly.

"It's a document that tells us the details of your plans, your financials, and how you plan to utilize the loan money."

After I left, and she listed all of the information that I needed, I felt overwhelmed. I left there and went to the library to research business plans and called Kathy back. I told her what the loan officer said about the business plan. Kathy gave me reassurance about what

Daring to Dream

it was and what it entailed. She was a great source of guidance and walked me through the parts of what I needed, based on what the loan officer had told me and my brief research at the library.

"I need a board of directors," I told her.

"Well, who did you place down on your Articles of incorporation?" She asked. I told her that I placed myself, Kevin, Tyronica, and Tyrone Jr. "Ok, put those same names down."

I asked her if I could place her down as my business consultant. "Sure." She said. After about a week or two of drafting what each section would contain, how it would be worded, and visiting Kathy so she could help me put things in proper order and maximize flow, I had a 5-page business plan. The first two pages had my title, the third had my executive summary, and the last had info about my consultants and board of directors. I didn't know what I was doing. I didn't have detailed business knowledge, but I was determined, and I had a vision. After that, I went back to the loan officer with my business plan in hand, my articles of incorporation, my personal income tax statement, and the most recent financial statements from the business. She sat down and reviewed everything and told me about my options based on the amount I requested and what I qualified for. She told me about the Small Business Administration, which I had never heard of, prior. She told me that she would give me a call in the next 5-10 business days and that we'd go from there.

When she called me back, I was scared. I had never been responsible for paying that much money back. It was more money than the house my husband and I had purchased. Fears and doubts started to creep in. Then I thought about the promise to Tyronica for school. Was I going to be able to pay her back? I had to! In fact, for me, it wasn't an option.

We bought the property at the residential price that it was listed as—which of course was far less than what it would have retailed for

Dare to Dream

commercially. The building had been built around 1990, and it was now 2003. I'm not sure if it was because it had been sitting vacant for a few years, or they genuinely forgot that it was once a commercially valued building, but I benefitted greatly from it being transformed into a house. After I purchased the building, I had to get the building rezoned as a commercial property. After doing so, I could get it appraised for commercial use versus residential use. My property taxes increased by 25%, but the value of my building substantially increased as well. It also allowed me to get extra money from the equity to assist in renovating the property. It was at this point that the realtors realized that I was going to turn the building back into its original commercial use. When I was starting the rezoning process, the city council began challenging us in a variety of ways from traffic patterns, noise ordinances, and neighbor approval.

I had to go before them to refute the challenge after challenge that came up. Regarding traffic, they wanted me to submit a traffic pattern that outlined the proposed flow of traffic to and around the facility to assess the influx of potential traffic on the area. The only thing was, there was an elementary school nearby that was Kindergarten through fifth grade—in fact, Man had gone there when he was younger. How was a childcare facility going to bring more traffic than an elementary school was already? But I complied the pattern as requested. A few days later, they came back to us with results from a neighborhood poll regarding concerns for potential noise that the childcare facility would bring to the area. At this point, I was becoming frustrated with the politics that seemed to be involved in the process. The city was trying its hardest to stonewall us from opening the property as a childcare facility. I felt as if the message being conveyed to me was, "you can live here, but you can't have a thriving business here." I couldn't see any clear reason for their adversity other than the fact that I was a woman, African-American, or both. When I was before the city council the second time, I expressed myself calmly and professionally.

See, what they probably weren't counting on was the fact that I had done my homework. When Kathy had first brought the vacant property to my attention, shortly thereafter, I looked up the details and specs of the building. I saw that the county had appraised the property residentially, but I also saw the former zoning paperwork for when it was considered commercial. Having known this, I expressed to the council that the process for rezoning was actually unnecessary as the property was originally zoned commercially from the very beginning. In other words, I didn't need their approval this time around. However, it was important to me and wise to have an amicable relationship with them. It would behoove a business owner to have the backing of the city and political community—they can make life hard for you otherwise—as it felt they were trying to do. After making my case, the council voted and decided to grant my rezoning minus the additional hassle. I was relieved but knew that they wouldn't be able to stand in the way of what God had shown me all along.

Kevin, who was prior military, and had enlisted in the Reserves, had been called back to active duty by the 89th Regional Readiness Command in Wichita, Kansas. Wichita was only about two hours from Junction City, but this new assignment would require Kevin to be gone for extended periods of time. I thought my days as a military wife were over, and in all honesty, I had no interest in reliving that part of my life. Not that it hadn't been good to me—but now, I was trying to create a career for myself. As a military spouse, most of your life is centered around what your spouse and his or her career are doing. The mission is constantly above all else. Relative to the freedoms that were being protected for U.S. soil, I got it and appreciated it—it's just that a new season of my life was beginning to blossom, and I wanted so badly to focus solely on that. Not to mention that I myself was in need of Kevin's support. When he was around, it was excellent, but if he was going to be gone for extended periods of time, I was also back to being "married but living single." Kevin would hate when I made that reference, but it was the truth. I saw him "some" weekends, and during the week, we'd chat on the phone and update one another on pertinent things.

Other than that, though, if we needed something as a family, he was unable to be there to help. For him, that was the hardest thing. He had been a civilian for almost ten years and even had to take a leave of absence from his job at the post office, in order to resume active duty. Though he loved the military, it was a bit of an interrupt for the lives we were trying to build at present. While on reserve duty, he got mobilized and called to be a part of Operation Endure Freedom. Just like that, his status changed from reserved back to active. We didn't see that coming at all.

When the New Year came, we were still working diligently to finalize the paperwork for the building. In 2004, our official renovations got underway. I went and met with an architect about beginning the process for gutting out the building in its current state and restructuring it to create the childcare facility. He drew up the plan. After he did so, I called the state fire Marshall, the city, the code department, and the city fire department. For this project, I was my own general contractor—and I would never do it again. I got 3 bids from 3 companies in our region. All of them were in the excess of $300,000 for renovations alone. I knew that I only had about 150K to do everything with. I had to have my operating costs, my building renovation, and buy all of my furniture and supplies for this new location—all with the same 150K! I started to think whether I wanted to go back and get a bigger loan. I started to pray and ask God to show me favor and how to do this with what I had in my hand. I wanted it to be excellent; I wanted it to look elaborate, homey, and glamorous. I wanted it to have flair, yet be kid-friendly. I wanted it to be a place where both parents and kids could feel comfortable. I didn't want white walls—that gave an institutional feel, in my opinion. I wanted God to be able to get the glory for what I was doing.

On every bid, I would see a distinct place for a contractor and sub-contractor. I got to wondering what was the difference between the two and consulted with a fellow church member of mine who had professional expert knowledge in the field. I asked him to come down and take a look at the building. He agreed. He came down, and I showed him the property in detail, as well as the architectural plans. I asked him if based off the plans he was able to do this work. He told me that unfortunately, he was not a general contractor and couldn't take on that role. "You could be the general contractor, however." He said. I was intrigued. "You buy all the supplies and me and my guys can do the work." He didn't know what my bids were for specifically, but did know that I had expressed they were out of my price range. I asked him if he would consider putting in a bid so I could get an idea of what the project required in its totality. He told me the things that I would need to buy and other things that I would need to rent. He told me that he would recommend items that we would need to use long-term and regularly for purchase, and items that we would only need at present as rental items. He explained to me the main distinction of my role. "Basically, you're the go-between for communication between the actual construction workers and the various agencies that require specific paperwork and building specifications. Any problems between the various agencies like the plumbing agency or the state, you deal with, and I don't." He told me. But he was an absolute blessing. Everything that I needed knowledge about, he was right there to guide and steer me. I needed money to redo the building and

Dare to Dream

to get started and knew that it would pay off for all of us in the end. I went and got a credit card at Home Depot for $30,000.

For all the renovations we had to conquer, I realized that wouldn't be enough. I told Kevin to get a Home Depot card in his name for the same amount, and so he did. We started the remodeling, and the next phase of our business was beginning to take shape. I was taking the building from 3 rooms and an office to 9 rooms, 3 offices, and a training area. I was going from approximately 2,000 Square feet to 9,000 square feet. I had to repave the parking lot, get handicap space decals, erect a sign, and even build a fence—not to mention plenty more tasks. It was an absolute faith walk. If God had shown me all the components from the jump, I probably would have dismissed the vision entirely. But He knows what steps to give us and when. It was a lot more work than what I bargained for, and I would never do it again. But it was more financially feasible—I would have had to take out a bigger loan, otherwise. Not that I was afraid to, but there was future potential for me to do other projects, and I wanted to be wise and reserve that option for later.

CHAPTER 12

Faith to Go Further

With all of the renovations going on at the new building, not to mention the day-to-day operation at our current building, there was a lot going on in my world in 2004. Tyronica was in school and doing well, majoring in Family Life Communications. Though she didn't exactly know what she wanted to do professionally post-college, I couldn't help but notice that her path of study complemented the legacy that I was starting in childcare. As a little girl, she had always loved to help out with key childcare areas like arts and crafts and even developing curriculums. She actually had a knack for it. So, as she continued her trek through school, part of me was eager to see where those interests would take her upon graduation. Tyrone Jr. was getting ready to begin his senior year of High School. Even without applying himself fully, he was making mostly As and Bs. I knew if he had ever really put forth his full effort, he could have easily been a straight-A student. He was involved in every sport known to man and that, of course, meant my having to dedicate time to show my support at games. As far as high school went, he was, of course, beginning to date and found a girlfriend that he liked enough to bring home to introduce to me. Her name was Morgan, and she was a grade younger than him. I could tell he really liked her, and she was a sweet girl.

Kevin was still stationed in Wichita but would come on the weekends. It was trying on our relationship, as the more time went on, the more I realized that I really had a short fuse for doing round two of being a military wife. In fact, if we had to endure the distance, on top of the business undertakings and we were younger, our marriage would have probably failed. This was when I considered becoming a Certified, Family Life Educator. I started to construct the programs that would serve my clientele. I wanted to give guidance on parenting and finances and wanted a certification to back me up. I knew God had given me an anointing to do it, but for the world, you need a piece of paper.

Since 1999, I had taken it upon myself to go through a variety of certifications so that I could be a valuable asset to not only my staff but to others in my field that could possibly benefit from the knowledge as well. Anything that I was certified in, qualified me to teach it to others through training. Right off the bat, I saw the opportunity to save money by not having to bring in outside instructors and trainers for my staff, but rather, being knowledgeable enough to become an instructor for the required courses myself. I also envisioned being a hub for fellow businesses to be able to come in and train more conveniently. The various certifications that I possessed weren't necessarily required for my role as childcare center director, but rather, my forward thinking to set the stage for what I wanted to do 10-15 years in the future. I didn't want to be a center director forever. My main goal was to help train other people to become center directors. Center directors could own their own business, and that was key. The CFLE expanded my knowledge and training base in 10 core competency areas of family life education, including family resource management, family life education, and financial management, for

Faith to Go Further

example. These key areas would greatly benefit what I envisioned to do on a broader scale. I wanted to be able to show the credentials for the subject matter that I proposed to teach. So, on top of everything else that was going on, I began the journey for the CFLE certification.

I had to start penciling Kevin in for sex and date nights so that we wouldn't sacrifice the fire in our marriage. One weekend, he came home for his weekend visit, and I had an appointment. He arrived later than what he anticipated, so when he got there, I had to leave. We had been doing this routine for about a year, and it was solid. He had never been late before, but for whatever reason he was, it threw my schedule off. He was ready to spend quality time, and I was ready to head out of the door. "Wait, wait, where you going?" He asked, confusedly. "You're late," I said plainly. "I have an appointment and have to go now." To be honest, Kevin was committed to doing whatever it took to keep me happy. However, this was one of the first times that I clearly remember him putting his foot down. "Nah, not today." He said. I turned around and looked at him. "What?" I said, quite honestly surprised.

"You won't be going today. You're going to have to cancel." I was stunned as I kept looking at him, only being able to blink. "I'm tired of being penciled in when I want to spend quality time with my wife—that ends today." I wasn't used to Kevin telling me no by any means. Honestly, if he gave me an inch, I would take a mile—until that day. I was so wrapped up in my world and routine that I didn't consider that he, too, was bothered by the strain of our distance. I put my things down, turned around, and that was that. This was the first time that he outright asked me to put his needs in front of my own. It forced me to take more careful consideration into how important our marriage needed to be for the both of us.

December came, and one evening, Tyrone Jr. took me out to dinner for just the two of us at a local Chinese restaurant. I thought it was strange that he only wanted it to be just him and me going, so I sensed that something was up. We talked casually and ordered our meals. When the food finally came, he told me he had something to tell me. I looked at him as the moment I had been waiting for had finally come.

"Morgan's pregnant." He said. The words hit my chest like a brick wall taking my breath away. I sat there and looked at him, stunned. Then again, I really wasn't. I wasn't surprised or shocked because I had always prayed that God wouldn't let anything that would affect me directly come upon me suddenly. I always prayed for discernment and revelation to happen beforehand. In this case, about a month or so prior, Morgan was at our house visiting one day, and I couldn't help but notice her protruding stomach as she walked down our hallway to Tyrone Jr.'s bedroom. She was a small girl, so any sort of pudge was noticeable on her frame. I even told Kevin. "Kevin, I think that girl's pregnant! I think I just saw a big belly in front of her." I had no proof, but my intuition noticed it then. After that, I decided to let it go and wait on confirmation if that was the case. Here I was, at the Chinese restaurant, getting it.

"Do you have any idea how this is going to change your life?" I asked him. He looked at me with eyes that anticipated a speech of disappointment. He seemed like he was bracing himself for a bigger reaction. In fact, that's why he decided to bring me to a public place to tell me. I guess he figured my temper would be tamer in a public place. Honestly, however, I had no intention to make a scene. More than anything, I was flooded with thoughts of how this was going to affect the rest of his life. I had planned his life out from the moment I knew I was pregnant with him, and this wasn't what I had envisioned. I knew the type of job I wanted him to have, the type of opportunities I would make sure he was privy too, and even the type of wife that I wanted him to marry. I knew that having a baby as a high schooler would change his life forever. He was too young to see it, but I knew full well—from firsthand experience—what I was talking about.

In fact, seated right there at the restaurant table, I replayed the drama reel in my mind from being pregnant so young with his father. I didn't have a problem with them being young and in love—I had been there before. But because I had been there before, I knew that love could take a backseat when a baby came into the mix for teenagers. On top of that, Tyrone Jr. and Morgan were an interracial couple. That wasn't a problem for our family—but the world in which they lived, of course, wasn't always so understanding. I sighed. This was the last thing that I wanted for my baby. All these things and emotions began to play in my mind. It was going to be a rocky road, no matter where it was walked from. The remainder of the meal was pretty silent as we finished and went home. As soon as I got in, I phoned Kevin and told him the news. He was shocked and recalled my mentioning it weeks prior. We talked about it a bit more, and he told me that we'd discuss things further when he came home for the weekend. I went to bed that night with my mind racing. I had so much going on in my head already and now the reality that my baby was about to have a baby fast-forwarded to the top of the list. On top of wondering how he was going to be affected, I wondered about his girlfriend. She was only 16, and we didn't know how stable her family life was. I remembered my struggles becoming a teenage mom and knew that she was in for much more than she had bargained for.

The following week, I called a meeting for Kevin and I and Tabitha and Les—Morgan's mom and stepfather. Neither Morgan nor Tyrone Jr. was invited, as I felt this was meeting for the real adults. We gathered around the table at my home. Tabitha was around my age give or take a few years, and Les only looked about ten years or so older than Tyrone Jr. He was 25 at best. This was my first time officially meeting them. The only other time I had seen them was one day when Tyrone Jr. and Morgan were headed out for a date. I so happened to glance outside at his car before he left and saw a car full. "Who are those people in your car?" I asked Tyrone Jr.

"Oh, that's Morgan's mom and step-dad—we're going on a double date." He said. My forehead furrowed as I thought that strange. I couldn't see Kevin and I tagging along on a date with Tyrone Jr. and his girlfriend like we were friends, but to each its own. I got down to the gist of our meeting. I prefaced it by saying that we were of course here because Tyrone Jr. and Morgan were expecting a baby. I wanted to get things straight from a support standpoint of where each side of our families stood about how our lives were going to change.

"What it is that your family needs from ours?" I asked plainly, "We need food." Tabitha said. When she said it, there was this underlying interpretation that she meant for their entire family—not Morgan and the baby. I looked at Kevin, and Kevin looked at me. I leaned forward and decided to break this all down for her.

"I'm about to be real transparent with you," I said, prefacing all I was about to say. "Morgan and the baby are welcomed to any support whatsoever—she's even welcomed to move in our house if she needs to. However, what I'm not about to do is be pimped by you." She looked at me as if I had offended her. I continued. "I love my son, and I'm going to protect him at all costs. The plans I've made for him, I'm not about to change them because Morgan is pregnant. Tyrone Jr. is set to attend school in the summer, and he's going. It was your house where the two of them were laid up together—something that I would have never allowed—and now we're here." It's funny, the very moment I said that, took me back to the meeting with me Tyrone, my father, and his mother. "You knew they weren't over here, just holding hands," is what Lil Momma told my father. Now granted in my case, I did a lot of lying about where I was most of the time, but still, my father should have known better—like Morgan's mother should have known better. But to be honest, I had responsibility to take in it as well. I too should have been more on top of my game as far as taking the time to have a sit-down with Tyrone Jr. about the possible scenarios that could have played out by all his spending time with Morgan. I should have painted a more vivid picture of the realities of teenage pregnancy since that was such a pivotal time in my own life. Now, I will say that Kevin and I weren't naïve, and when we first saw the serious interest that Tyrone Jr. was taking with Morgan, we made the attempt to get in front of the situation by purchasing him condoms. We discussed their proper use and sex in general. I wasn't about to act like I didn't know how teenage hormones were. But still, here we were now, getting ready to make room in our lives for a grandchild.

All in all, that night, I had accomplished my purpose of the meeting. Morgan's family didn't have much time to say a whole lot as it was primarily about establishing an understanding of where I stood. I didn't know how Tabitha felt on behalf of her motherhood to Morgan, but the whole ordeal made me personally feel like I had failed Tyrone Jr. I also knew this wasn't a healthy mind frame to stay in. I resolved in my heart that no matter what, I would be present and engulfed in the life of this child. It was after all a part of me—it was the next generation of legacy for my family and the gift of life, of course, comes from God. That alone was something to celebrate, no matter the circumstances.

By now, the renovations at our new building were finally nearing completion. We were doing final stage items like painting and putting in furniture. One of the final major requirements in order to open was a fire and safety inspection that required the installation of a fire and security system. On a Monday, I got a call from the owner of Security Solutions notifying me that they were indeed ready to come and make the installations.

"Is it okay if we come out this Friday to finalize the install?" He asked. I knew that the cost of this step was $15,000, and I didn't have it. "Yes," I replied. He set the appointment, told me a few other particulars, and we hung up. I immediately felt like I was on the chopping block. To have come this far with the purchase of the building, jumping through the city's hoops, doing the renovations, and now to be almost ready to open the doors and have $15,000 stand in our way was nerve-wracking. Not to mention, I still had to figure out payroll. With employees now, the faith to make ends meet wasn't just for my livelihood but the livelihood of my staff as well.

That Wednesday morning, I decided to go to the weekly Morning Prayer at my church as I regularly did. I remember sitting in the back of the church, praying in a plum state of panic. I needed $15,000 before the week was out and didn't know how I was going to get it. I sat there praying and rocking, rocking and praying. That's the position I was in for the entire hour. Towards the end of the prayer service, I remember feeling a sense of peace come upon me. When the prayer service was over, a sister in my church who owned a coffee shop came to me and said that God told her to ask me for $1,000 for *her* payroll. Now, mind you, that's all I had towards the fire alarm installation. I just looked at her. As I had allowed myself to grow more in my faith, I was more sensitive to God's voice. I heard Him say, "If the finances you have don't meet your need, then they must be your seed." In other words, if the money you have doesn't even add up to the reason you need it for, then sow it for a return! Looking back over my life, I saw a reoccurring theme of this principle to be true. That as long as I kept my eyes on God, I was good, and as soon as I took them off Him, I felt like I was drowning. I wrote the woman a check for the $1,000 and put my faith in God for my return. The odds of this lady even asking me for the $1,000 that I needed seemed too coincidental not to be a test, so I made up in my mind that I would pass it.

A few days later, I was driving to Topeka, KS, with Momma Mary riding along with me. Momma Mary was an older woman at my church whom I connected with in 1999. She was wise, sweet, and was one of the closest semblances of having an ideal mother-daughter relationship that I can recall in my life. Her life was fairly simple and routine. She'd go to work, go to church, on Sundays we'd go to dinner and then she'd go back home. She worked for the school district for years, as well as with Head Start Program in both the kitchen and the classroom. As we rode along, a potential client of mine called me on my cell phone. I was surprised, as the client in particular and I hadn't spoken to in over a year. He initiated our conversation with greetings and a brief catch up. He refreshed me on our initial conversation and told me that he was still interested in soliciting my services for a variety of training that he needed for his company as we had previously discussed a while back. "Are you still available to do the training that we previously discussed?" He asked. I told him yes and would just need to provide him the necessary contracts. In all honesty, when we first talked, things were dramatically different than they were at present. I was spread way thinner now than the time when we first were in talks to do the work. But, I didn't want to appear flaky as far as business was concerned, so I agreed. "Okay, great, wherever you are, I'll meet you now and give you the money to get everything in motion, so my spot is solidified." He said insistently. I told him that I was driving along at the moment, headed towards Topeka. That seemed to be of no consequence to him as he so happened to be in the area. He told me that he would meet me off an upcoming exit at a gas station. I met him at the agreed upon exit, and when I got there, he handed me a folded check. We had talked about a variety of training sessions in a set series, so I didn't know if the check he was handing me was a deposit or for a certain amount of training to get started. I placed it immediately in my pocket as we exchanged information again and he brought me up to speed with the timeframes he needed. I told him that I would be in touch within the next three business days and send over the official paperwork. We said our goodbyes and both got back in our cars. I got back on the highway with Momma Marry. As we drove off, I began to wonder just how much the check was for. As I drove along, I reached inside my pocket and pulled it out. I unfolded it and saw that the check was for the exact amount of the fire installation—$15,000! I was in absolute awe. Tears welled in my eyes and started rolling down my cheeks. I knew God was real long before that incident, but it was just another reminder of His might on behalf of my financial concerns. I was reminded that day of how good of a Father God is and how He's concerned with every area of our lives. I knew immediately that the $1,000 I had given the lady at my church was the seed that made my $15,000 possible. I gave it willingly and without expecting her to pay me back. It wasn't about the money that I had given to her but rather the act of obedience and the act of faith. I was shocked, and none of it made sense. I don't think it's an accident that Momma Mary was riding in the car with me that day when I received that check. She rejoiced with me and reminded me in a calm, almost unsurprised way that God is faithful. "I might not be here when God brings this to full fruition," she said, "but you're going to walk in millions. All because you trust Him." I received that when she said it and held on to it even after. This doesn't mean I don't have questions from time to time, but above all else, I trust God.

We opened the renovated building in the summer of 2005. I sent out invitations for an open house and set up a ribbon-cutting ceremony through the local chamber of commerce association that I had joined. I invited church members, the city, community and political figureheads, and other businesses in the community to celebrate our grand opening. People entered and seemed to be taken aback by the excellence that they saw. They exclaimed aloud phrases like, "Wow, it's nice!" in a tone that seemed to convey that what they saw was in stark contrast with what they expected. Maybe it was my outspoken and boisterous personality that made them assume that I would put together some junk. Or maybe that's just what I felt; but more often than not, what you feel via intuition isn't too far from the truth. This was the biggest professional milestone that I had ever accomplished in my life. I felt a sense of satisfaction that God was able to use me to get it done. I knew it was going to make an impact on my community. Reflecting back on my mother's death, part of me would look back from time to time and wonder if I would have been willing to put my life on the line for one of my children—especially not yet knowing who they were or who they would grow up to become. So, knowing that my mother put her life on the line for me, I always felt like I owed it to her to become successful at something. With childcare, if I touched the life of a child, in my mind, my mother's death wouldn't have been in vain. And now, here I was, touching the lives of many. I was proud of that and believe that she would have been too.

On our first day being opened for official business, the center buzzed with excitement from teachers getting their rooms ready to receive the students, parents getting acclimated to the new sign-in system and the joyous noise from having the building occupied. In the middle of the day, one of the teachers noticed that the floor drain of the bottom level preschool bathroom area started to ooze with sewage. Come to find out, the entire sewer system collapsed underground. The buildup started to overflow in such a way that it covered the bathroom floor and was about to creep out into the classroom. Once it was brought to my attention, I couldn't believe it. This was a brand spanking new building, and it was our first day. How come this couldn't have happened during all of our walkthroughs and inspections? My sewage lines were 250 feet from the mainlines, and outside there was dirt piled up nearly 30 feet from where the collapse had happened. I called the city, and they sent someone out before the day was over to assess what the issue could possibly be. They told me the issue that I was having was not city-related and that I would have to contact a plumbing company. I contacted a plumbing company the next day, and they came out to take a look. The first thing they did was provide a temporary fix for the inside as I had a facility with 15 staff members and 60 plus students. Plumbing is a make or break requirement for running a childcare, so that was key.

Next, in order to assess the state of the sewage line, they had to dig around where the line was to get a clear understanding of the problem. Doing so left a pile of dirt in the front entryway of my building what was at least 30 feet high. It was covered with orange cones and in my opinion, was so unsightly. After figuring out the problem, the plumbing company told me that a full fix of the issue would cost me a whopping $50,000, which would include the new installation of a commercial sump pump. My countenance sunk. Where was I about to find $50,000? I thanked them for the quick fix and considered their bid as I wondered what I was going to do.

I took it upon myself to get a few other bids from plumbing companies, and all in all, the price range was about the same as what the first company had told me. Around this same time, my other building was trying to hold on to my $900 security deposit, and I had left the building in way better condition than when I had gotten there. I had done painting and had even put in a kitchen, which of course increased its value. Now, in addition to that hassle, I had to come up with $50,000 to repair my new building's entire sewer line. I decided to go to the church to see Bishop unannounced, which was out of the norm for me. Due to the nature of his schedule, he was primarily seen on an appointment basis. This day, however, he happened to be available.

Faith to Go Further

"Hi, LaFarris." His assistant said, greeting me as I entered the church office. I greeted her back. "Is Bishop available today?" I asked. She looked over his schedule and got up to see if he was in his office. She came back. "He is, actually, go right in." She said. I walked back into his office and greeted him. He was a bit surprised to see me without an appointment but was warm all the same. Seeing that I was a bit distraught, he asked me what was wrong. I told him the recent fiasco of what had just happened in light of my recent opening. He listened and was ready to provide help. "Is there something that the church can do? Are you in need of financial assistance?" He asked. "No, sir," I told him. "All I really want is some guidance and prayer. A prayer that God will give me a plan and the wisdom to know what to do."

"Ok." He said as he let me talk out the plan I was leaning towards and weigh out the pros and cons of how to go about getting the money. I didn't know of anyone else I could talk to for immediate guidance. Kevin was gone, and I didn't want to stress him out. Military personnel deal with so many other stressful situations from a professional standpoint that problems at home on top of those could cost them their lives—especially on active or deployed duty. There was no point in adding stress to him that he couldn't be home to help address. As far as family went, my father was dead, my other family members were too far away to even know what was going on, and as far as my children went, I didn't want to lose their faith. I had poured so much into this new location and expansion, and I couldn't let them see it fail at the beginning. Bishop, however, was the perfect person. I felt like I could vent and be totally transparent about my worries, the pressure of expectations, and even my feelings of despair that were trying to set in. After I was done, he prayed for me, and I left. All in all, it was about 30 minutes, but it was definitely well-spent. I left feeling encouraged and ready to face what it was that I had to do, with the faith that God would make a way; as He had done so many times before.

After praying and having peace and clarity of thought, I decided to tackle this new repair with a credit card. I didn't want to take out a second mortgage — my $60,000 Home Depot credit cards I had already paid off, so that looked good. I checked out interest rates and cards and was looking for one with 0% interest for 12 months. I found one that was actually 0% for 18 months. I applied for it, got approved, and it came within 10 days. As soon as it arrived, I called the plumbing company out to begin the installation. The project was so major that it would take about six months and had to be broken down into phases. That was perfect for me to be able to pay back on the credit card, little by little.

CHAPTER 13

Life's New Season

My first grandson, Tavon, was born July 10, 2005, and my world was rocked. I had accepted the fact that the baby was on the way, but when it was time for him to officially come, I couldn't help but revert back to my original stance of motherly woe. Just moments before he was born, I was at home in a silent protest to keep my distance from the crowd of visitors at the hospital until the absolute last minute. I didn't feel up to putting on a front with Morgan's side of the family, whom I barely knew, or anyone for that matter. I was a mother whose baby was about to have a baby, and it was one of the hardest pills for me to swallow. Tyronica called me from the hospital. "Momma, Tyrone wants to know, when are you coming up here?" She asked.

"It's enough people already up there, I know," I said.

"Momma, you need to come on." She insisted as I finally decided to give in and told her I would be there soon. I hung up and pulled myself together to head towards the hospital. I arrived, and sure enough, the room was packed out. I fell in and found a spot to occupy in the room as people tried to engage me in chitchat. I, however, wasn't interested in making any friends. All I could think as I looked around the room was how they had no idea what this pregnancy would mean for Morgan and Tyrone Jr.'s lives. Everyone was at the hospital oohing and ahhing over a 16-year old becoming a mother like it was something to be proud of. Don't get me wrong, my grandson was a gorgeous baby, and upon seeing him, I fell in love immediately. In that moment of joy, however, I knew the full scale of what came along with it. I knew firsthand what being a teen parent was truly like. Actually, Morgan's mom also knew, which was also why I couldn't understand why she too wasn't sharing my sentiment of parental concern. With the exception of Tyrone Jr., Tyronica, and myself, most of the visitors in the hospital room were Morgan's friends and family. All I could think about was how none of the people standing around with their congratulations would be the ones to buy pampers, formula, or needs for the baby. Those duties would fall on my family and me. I knew one way or the other I would have to help Tyrone Jr. and Morgan raise this baby. Tyrone Jr. couldn't do it by himself at the age of 17 and Morgan was 16. What did either one of them know about parenting? Nothing! Absolutely nothing. I knew that I knew nothing at 15. In fact, at that moment in my late 30s, I still was learning about parenting. There was no manual, and it was all on the job training.

I came back home and laid in bed and cried all night long. Kevin finally arrived home from Wichita, and when he did, he found me in our bed, bawling uncontrollably. "What's wrong?" He asked concernedly as he came swiftly to my side. "He'll never be my little boy ever again." I mustered through tears. "He'll never be my little boy again," I repeated as I began to cry even harder. He held me in his arms, and I cried and cried. That phrase was all I could keep repeating. My son was someone's father now and all the experiences that I wanted him to encounter in his youth—going to college, making lifelong friends, playing sports, maybe even joining a fraternity—would be hindered now. I didn't have those memories of my own, and now I wept at the fact that he may miss out on them too. All I knew was, what I wanted for my son was not going to turn out how I had hoped. Tyrone Jr. was set to leave for his college football camp on July 12th. As far as I was concerned, he was going to do just that. He had received a two-year scholarship to play for Highland Community College, and he needed to go. Tyrone Jr. approached Kevin on the side and asked him to convince me to let up on insisting that he keep his July 12th departure date. "The answer is no," I told Kevin. Morgan's mom even tried to talk to me. "Do you think it's a good idea for Tyrone Jr. to go to football camp and leave Morgan here alone with the baby?" She asked. My facial expression alone could have stabbed her. Who was she to question me about what was best for my son? "Morgan isn't alone—she has you, and she has me." I retorted. She looked at me and walked away in seeming disgust. But once again, I didn't care. Even though if I was Morgan, I would have wanted Tyrone Jr. to stay too. I wanted her to see the bigger picture. I felt that if he didn't leave now, he would never leave. And if he never left, I feared he wouldn't be able to learn how to provide for his son. It was funny, I was in a similar situation when I was 15, but my wisdom gave me a different vantage point now. I didn't have my mother around to help me navigate my way as a young parent, so it was important to me to be active in helping guide my son on what was best for him. Once I knew that he and Morgan were expecting, I bought him a brand-new car as a graduation gift. The 12th came, and he packed it up and was ready to go. Morgan was still in the hospital, and though I hadn't spoken to her directly about Tyrone Jr.'s leaving, I knew from her mother's attempt to talk me out of making him go, where she stood. It was a beautiful day when he prepared to leave, and I remember him stopping by the center before leaving. I hugged him and felt his stiffness from my insisting that he leaves. I felt that he didn't want to go, and my heart broke at the thought. However, my heart would break even more if he stayed in Junction City and didn't go and take advantage of this great opportunity that awaited him. He never was the type of child to talk back or be argumentative with me. He respected me, even when it was hard for him to do. As I hugged him, I prayed a prayer in my heart, "Lord, don't let him be resentful of me." I kissed him and told him not to worry. "Anything that Morgan and the baby need, I've got it handled."

Over the next year, I kept my head focused on my business amidst a variety of changes in my family. For one, my sister Trish Ann had a stroke. She was still living in Junction City but had moved out of our house into her own apartment. Actually, it was her second apartment, as the first one I helped her get, I fully furnished it with brand-new items, only for her to get behind on her rent and get put out. The landlord padlocked the place with all of the furniture inside. The next apartment, she was on her own! After her stroke, she decided that she wanted to be nearer to home and moved back to Arkansas with Carla, who would also be able to help with her recovery. As for my immediate family, Tyronica had fallen in love with her longtime friend and he had proposed. The two were wed in Atlanta, Georgia in the summer and Kevin and I put a great deal of money into it. Tyronica was to graduate the coming December, and after doing so, the two planned to relocate to Augusta, Georgia where her husband had been stationed. He was getting ready to get deployed to Iraq, and they wanted to get married before that occurred. While he was away, she spent a lot of time back and forth between Georgia and Kansas to contribute and help out with the childcare, as well as get her business, "The Learning Cupboard," off the ground. At one point, she moved back home temporarily as she knew no one in Augusta, Georgia. He was over there for about a year. His mother didn't care much for Tyronica, and that created a base for problems in their relationship. Tyronica, of course, wasn't going to be treated any kind of a way. In my opinion, they were young, inexperienced, and living in a fantasy world about what marriage took to sustain.

Tyrone left Highland Community College after a year and told me his plans to transfer to Coffeyville Community College, which was still in Kansas, but further than Highland was. He told me he had already applied and been accepted, and his decision was more conducive for his football career and especially keeping his family intact. He was traveling home practically every weekend to see Tavon and spend time with Morgan. After his first semester at Coffeyville, just before school was to get back in session, Tyrone Jr. told me that he had decided *not* to return to school. He mentioned that things with Morgan's at-home living situation had become strained and that it was his responsibility to be there to take care of her and the baby. The news of his decision shattered me. It brought me back to the decision that his father had to make with his own opportunity to attend college and play football. I knew how that story ended up. Tyrone Sr. focused on providing for his family and never revisited his dreams of playing ball again. I couldn't help but think that our son now had to walk out those same decisions that his father had to years prior.

Upon returning home, Tyrone Jr. began his first official role working at the childcare center as a Deputy Director. He was third in command as far as leadership went and his duties had significantly increased from his days of janitorial work. Right out the gate, Tyrone Jr. seemed to think that being the owner's son meant he was immune to professional protocol. He struggled with getting to work on time and would fraternize with the staff after hours.

One morning, he had a worker call in sick, who was actually just hung over from the night before. He knew this because he was in the same place. Upon learning this, I told him that his being a supervisor and hanging with his staff demeaned his authority. I also told him that because he was my son that people would be watching his every move closely as either a standard or a loophole. It was important to me that my staff knew that principles took precedence over proximity. In other words, it didn't matter if a worker was related to me or not, right was going to be enforced. On his second time being late, I warned him that a third time would mean that he would be fired. A few weeks later, he was late again. So, I fired him. I wasn't bluffing whatsoever, but I guess he thought I was.

"Is Momma serious?!" He asked Tyronica.

"Yep. She is." She told him.

This was *my* business, and he didn't have any privileged buy-in just because he was my son. I was passionate about my business, and being a good steward of what God had blessed me with, no one was going to thwart that.

After he was fired, Tyrone Jr. took on a few odd and end jobs but realized that he needed something that was more stable and career-based so that he could build a life for himself and his family. Though he was fired from the center, as my son, he was still obligated to the family business—whether willingly or unwillingly. If the grass needed to be mowed—practically an all-day job on 4.5 acres of land—Tyrone Jr. was whom I was calling. If someone called in sick and we needed a stand-in teacher for the day, or I needed some furniture to be moved, I was calling him. That was the nature of a family business, whether he was on the payroll or not.

One day while at the center, a man came in the main entrance and Tyronica greeted him. He mentioned that he was there to speak with Tyrone Jr. and so she led him upstairs to the office area and went to get her brother who was downstairs.

"Your recruiter is here to see you." She said to him.

"My recruiter?" He said in shock. "What the hell is he doing here?" He asked. Tyronica looked confused. "Wait a minute; you haven't told Momma that you're going into the Air force?" She asked.

Apparently, I was the only one late to the party. "Look, keep Momma occupied and don't let her see this man here," Tyrone Jr. told his sister. As the owner, I always made it my business to be aware of who was coming in and out of my facility. I was seated in my office when Tyronica first walked the man upstairs and therefore was already alerted to his presence. I got up from my desk and stepped in the hallway where the man was waiting on Tyrone Jr.

"Hello," I said to him.

"Hi." He replied politely.

"Is there something I can help you with?" I asked him as I looked him over, trying to determine who he might have been or what he might have wanted. The man introduced himself formally as Sgt. Terry and told me that he was there to talk with Tyrone Jr. I introduced myself and told him that I was Tyrone Jr.'s mother. He told me that it was nice to make my acquaintance and said that he was there to talk with Tyrone Jr. about final enlistment details. "Enlistment?" I repeated back to him. The man looked somewhat surprised that the sentence he uttered was news to me.

"Yes, ma'am." He affirmed. He went on to bring me up to speed about how Tyrone Jr. had begun the preliminary sign up for Air Force back in January. It was now April, and things were just about solidified for him to join. My reception to the man's news was anything but warm. Rightfully sensing my objection to the news, he began trying to tell me about all of the pros of Tyrone Jr. enlisting. How it was great for financial security, college tuition, and so on. I was unimpressed. I myself had solidified Tyrone Jr.'s college finances, so the military didn't mean anything as far as that was concerned. Tyrone Jr. walked up in time to see that the two of us had already made an acquaintance. He looked like a deer in headlights.

"Hi, Tyrone," Sgt. Terry greeted him. I looked at Tyrone Jr. with a face that demanded answers. He greeted Sgt. Terry and I decided to leave the two of them to talk privately for a moment. After a while, I stepped back into where they were meeting and sat down to listen to the recruiter go into more details about Tyrone Jr.'s decision. The truth was that he was a grown man, and my choices were to either get on board or get over it. After the recruiter's final attempt to further persuade me, he thanked us for our time and left.

"So you were just gon' up and leave, huh?" I said to him, still somewhat irritated at my son's decision of secrecy. "I was going to tell you." He said. "I was just waiting on the right time." I nodded and returned to work. Once again, my son was living his life in a way that *I* hadn't planned.

The very next month, Morgan and Tyrone Jr. got married in May 2008. Right after that in June, Tyrone Jr. was scheduled to depart for basic training for 8 weeks in Texas. After basic, he would have to go to Tech School to learn the ins and outs of his job in the Air Force. I was so distraught, that, truth be told, I was glad that a conference that Tyronica and I had previously scheduled to attend coincided with his departure. I knew I couldn't handle being there on the actual day that he left. Morgan and Tavon stayed behind in Kansas for the duration of his being in Texas.

When he returned home, it was the early fall, and he had his orders for his first duty station at McDill Airforce Base in Tampa, Florida. This time, of course, his family would join him. That was also hard for me—having to be so far away from my grandson, whom I adored. I had always been a person who liked to be in control of what was going on in my world. Having to accept the fact that my son was a man now with his own family was a major adjustment for me, especially since he had opted to journey down paths that I never envisioned for him.

I remember shortly before it was time for him to leave for basic training, God telling me to, "let your Issac go, I'll bring him back."

He told me this as far as worrying and trying to control things in my son's life. Hesitantly, but obedient nonetheless, I "let go." Tyrone Jr. would have never become a real man if he had remained in Junction City. He would never have taken the steps towards true growth if he didn't enlist into the service. I had done all that I knew to do as far as raising him to be a productive adult in society, and it was time to let those seeds flourish. Mothers need to know that their labor of love will produce fruit. God will return on your investment.

In 2007, my family learned that my sister, Trish Ann, had cancer. She was a longtime smoker like my dad was. When my dad died from lung cancer, she kept right on smoking. I couldn't understand why she would do such a thing knowing it had snatched the life of our father. Then again, all her life, she had this sort of nonchalance about anything to do with conformity. She was the kind of person who kept you on your Ps and Qs when you had to deal with her. Only God would know what she would indirectly get you dragged into. She never had any children, so she would find herself in these random, irresponsible situations without real consequence. She wouldn't pay her bills, would hardly ever have groceries, and would do haphazard things like going to get her hair done, knowing she didn't have any money. She did this once, and I had to stop what I was doing and come and pay her beautician. When she lived in Kansas, she even ran off to South Dakota with her boyfriend for a few months, and when things didn't pan out, I had to get a U-Haul and bring him and her home. I guess you could say she was a bit of a free spirit. In 2008, she lost her fight to lung cancer and died at age 56.

In 2009 Tyrone Jr. and Morgan gave me my second grandchild, Alani, and by then, they were much more established. They had overcome the hurdles that young love brought, like mastering their finances and relocating to a new city. 2009 also marks the timeframe that I started thinking about the childcare center on a bigger scale. I didn't want it to be a "mom and pop" shop where everything depended on my being there. I had been thinking about preparing the business for transition for quite some time but had never put anything into play. Tyronica had moved back home as her marriage was coming to an end. Though bittersweet, now that she was home again, she fell right back into her role of assisting with the day-to-day operations of the center. It was good to have her home as she embarked upon a journey of reinventing herself personally, as well as got back to her creativity and gifting professionally. Her being home also coincided with the transitioning process that I was trying to prepare the center for. The first thing I did was hire my first director that was outside of my family. I began to train her on the day-to-day operations of effectively running the business. It was hard at first as Loving Arms was my baby and my livelihood.

I had invested my time and life in this business for nearly twenty years. However, unless I wanted to be obligated to another twenty, I had to be okay with phasing my mandatory presence out so that I could move us forward for long-term and strategic growth. I needed the ability to be mobile in my productivity and pull myself out of the day-to-day mix. I had two grandbabies now, and I longed to enrich my role as a grandmother. With Morgan and Tyrone Jr. so far away in Florida, I wanted to be near my grandchildren every chance I got. I wanted to be an active part of their lives and for them to know me. I always felt saddened by the fact that my children only heard stories about my mother instead of being able to have a rich relationship with her.

My travels to Florida became a frequent event. And when I went, it wasn't a fly by night weekend sort of a thing—I'd go for a minimum of two weeks at a time. In fact, two weeks was the shortest duration I can remember. Most times, I'd go for up to six to eight weeks at a time. At this point in my life, living the married but single life had its perks. Kevin had taken a recruiter position in Iowa, which meant we had to spend time with each other on rotational weekends between there and Kansas. I'd stay with him in Iowa for a couple of weeks; then he'd come to Junction the next week or so if his schedule permitted. After spending time in Florida or Iowa, I'd always check back in with the business at home and then assess my schedule for where I was off to next. Also, around this time, I began to take advantage of putting my certifications to work to conduct training for various businesses in need. In addition to the regular word of mouth and interactive networking I would get from conferences and working generally in my field, I would let the national network that I belonged to know in advance if I would be traveling to a certain state or area. This would aid in my being able to take advantage of businesses that needed specific training while I traveled. The next tier of expanding the business would focus on assisting other childcare providers in growing their businesses. Other than a few topical courses in college, I had been in business for nearly twenty years without formal education on business processes or even a business certification.

In 2010, while at church one day, my Bishop announced the opportunity for members to join a chapter of a Christian-based Business School that originated at a popular church in Chicago and would be annexed at another ministry in Kansas City, Missouri. My Bishop and the Pastor of that church were dear friends, and as such, frequently partnered together and supported one another's endeavors. I thought this would be the perfect opportunity to go back and learn the formal steps of business that could possibly enrich the future endeavors of the childcare, as well as whatever personal endeavors I might venture out to do. The program was about nine months, and I traveled weekly on Saturdays from Junction City, Kansas to Kansas City, Missouri, for the all-day sessions. Taking these business courses was a pivotal point for me professionally. With each class, I learned so much about the formal background of how to run a business to maximum effectiveness. I learned the full ramification about practices that I had been implementing all along in my business, like accounting, hiring (human resources), and pricing of products and services. These were concepts that I realized I had been led by God to address. Class by class, I was in awe with the various ways He had guided me on the path of entrepreneurship, even when I didn't fully have the background knowledge for what all it entailed. Then, of course, my eyes began to open to the different systems of knowledge that were either totally absent or not very prevalent in my business. Topics like writing a Business Plan, Marketing Analysis, Outsourcing, Leadership & Organization, and so much more. Around this time, I realized that there was a difference between being an entrepreneur and a business owner. A business owner has a limited scope of mobility and works within their business without an opportunity to work outside of it. They function mainly as an employee, even though they are the employer. They never learn how to automate themselves. An entrepreneur solves problems. They automate processes so that the business' success isn't dependent on them alone. This usually frees them up to move on to the next venture, or at least manage it from a distance.

My class schedule inhibited my ability to travel and see my grandkids like I had been accustomed to, but I kept my focus and told myself that I was doing it in part for them. Legacy was important to me, and getting the background knowledge on how to nurture the business I had worked so hard to create was a branch of my family's legacy as well. I graduated Joseph Business in 2012 at the top of my class and felt like the information I had learned had equipped me with knowledge for making my business better for this phase of transition. I immediately adopted the automation of my payroll system and outsourced it to a third-party company owned by one of the instructors in JBS. She owned an accounting and small business firm and helped me revisit crucial accounting principles for my business operation. I phased out the use of checks, cash, and money orders as forms of payment and moved to electronic transactions. As far as my payroll went, before outsourcing, I had been using a computer software program specifically designed for childcare companies. It was fairly simple and worked well; however, still required my presence. If it was outsourced, I wasn't required to physically be on-site to sign checks for employees. I also beefed up our marketing presence by using our website more purposely and interactively. We started to take applications online and created portals of communication for the staff to be able to access information and data. I began to write and publish brown bag parenting articles and tips, as well and advertise various parenting classes that we were offering. My evolution from being a mere business owner to a forward-thinking entrepreneur was taking place, step by step.

CHAPTER 14

Lessons from Loss

Beginning in 2014, right after another, it seemed, sickness showed up at my family's door. Momma Mary, the church mother whom I had come to love and adore, lost her battle to cancer in August. Around 2006, she had moved back to Virginia, where she was from, to be closer to her two daughters and other family members. Even though she had moved, we talked every Saturday morning right after prayer, no matter what.

Once she was gone, it seemed like I suffered the loss of my very own mother all over again. After she passed, I would find myself longing to pick up the phone and talk to her per our usual. Her daughters knew of me and our close relationship, and one day, one of them called me. "I wanted to talk to momma, so I called and talked to you." She said. Momma Mary used to tell me that once she was gone, I'd have to help her daughters oversee that her last wishes were in place. When she was alive, it seemed so far off that I, of course, agreed without a thought. Never in a million years, however, did I think I'd have to walk that promise out, much less that she'd be gone. For instance, one of her wishes was to be cremated and to have her ashes buried back in Fort Riley, alongside her late husband. So, I did my part to make sure her extended family in Junction City—mainly her church family and old co-workers—were present for a quaint memorial service. From time to time, I still go and visit her gravesite. Although I know she's not there, I still find comfort in visiting.

In November, during our big Thanksgiving family gathering, Carla told us she had cancer in her lymph nodes, and I felt as if someone had kicked me in my chest. Her being her, though, she told us nonchalantly and had things already planned ahead about how her treatment was going to go. Robin, who was in Oklahoma, Tammy, who was in Maryland, along with my brother and myself in Kansas, took turns going to stay with her in Arkansas as she began her chemotherapy treatments. It wasn't necessarily that she needed it because she was strong; but more so, just to be there with her. We didn't know what was going to happen, but I'm the type of person who doesn't like to live my life in regret. I was going to be there for my sister while I still had the chance. Her doctors put her under a form of at home quarantine, as her system was susceptible to germs that her immune system was too weak to fight off. She would take a shot on Monday and be quarantined for the remainder of the week. That was the hardest part, not only for her, but also to witness. Carla's life is a lot like mine. She's very busy, active in the community and church, plays piano, and is even a justice of the peace. Having to keep her in the house was a challenge, indeed. When Mother's day came, we found out that the chemo treatments she was undergoing were working and that she was cleared.

Aunt Athalean was now my last living Aunt on my mother's side, and I hadn't seen her in years. In fact, the only time I had seen her since I moved away back in 1981 was when I was in Pittsburgh for a conference in 2008. Cleveland was only a few hours away by drive, so I decided to go and see her, as I knew she was getting up in age. Her house looked the exact same as it did in 1979 when I lived with her. Right down to the furniture, there were no changes or signs of redecorating. It was like a frozen moment in time. I told her that I would love to invite her to Kansas to spend some time with my family. I told her I would be more than happy to come back and get her and show her a great time and a change of scenery. However, she was the same Aunt Athalean, polite but content with her status quo of things—having no real desire to leave her world or be inconvenienced in such a way. She, unfortunately, seemed to have never got past the place of Uncle Bill's death in her life. She never chose to be a survivor after all of those years that passed, and a lot of people have a similar story. Whether it's the death of a loved one, the end of a relationship, the loss of a job or home, a rape, or any other difficult aspect of life, some people, unfortunately, choose to remain victims when the power to become a survivor is solely up to them.

After that visit, I would periodically call and check on Aunt Athalean as she had no other family left in Cleveland, and the nearest family to her was in Michigan. I had made some attempts in March and April of 2015 to get in contact with her to no avail. The phone just rang and rang. I called my cousin Jean who lived in Michigan.

"Is there something wrong with Aunt Athalean? Is everything okay?" I asked. Jean wrote it off to Aunt Athalean's usual reclusive, stand-offish nature.

"You know how Athalean is, she's fine. I'm sure." I heard her, but my spirit still didn't sit right. I called Carla and asked her the same thing I had asked Jean.

Her response was similar. "You're paranoid, leave it alone, it's ok," she said. My brother even said the same. I still refused to let it go. They acted as if I was being odd, and I thought it was odd that we weren't more so collectively bothered. It wasn't like Aunt Athalean was a spring chicken. She was old now, and no one saw any red flags that she couldn't be reached. She was a diehard homebody, so where else would she be that she couldn't answer the phone at least once out of all the times I had called? Not only that, I had purposefully switched up the mix of when I had called. Considering that she might sleep late, I'd call in the afternoon. Another time, I'd try at night. I even tried calling her once at 3 in the morning, and still, nothing. On August 17th, Kevin and I were in Michigan, visiting family for his birthday. I woke up in the middle of the night and said, "I want to go to Cleveland." He asked me what this was all about, and I told him I needed to go and check on my aunt at once. He obliged my urgency, and we got dressed and went. Something as simple as driving up to the house didn't look or feel right. At face value, it was the same four-level house that I had lived in with her all those years back. The exterior was the same color and all—only it looked more worn and aged now. I told Kevin to pull up in front of the house but not the driveway. I got out and rang the doorbell and looked around. It was quiet. I looked over and saw a trashcan near the side of the house and driveway, and there was fresh trash in it. That let me know someone had to be there, at least recently. I knocked again and still no answer. Kevin eventually got out of the truck and joined me on the porch.

"No one's here." He said.

I knew something wasn't right. "I'm not leaving here until we get inside," I said. I went next door to the neighbors' houses that I used to know, but all the former neighbors I knew had moved away. I saw a lady outside and asked her if she had seen my Aunt or any activity at her house, and she pointed me to the direction of a neighbor whom she knew interacted with her.

"Her caretaker hasn't been here, but she'll be back," she said. We got back in the car and sat and thought for a second when soon after, a car pulled up slowly in front of the house. They drove slowly, seemingly spotted our truck, and then sped off. Our truck deterred whomever it was from stopping, and I was officially determined to get some answers. I described to the neighbor what had just taken place and inquired as to whether my description of the vehicle sounded familiar with what she had observed at my Aunt's house. The neighbor confirmed for me that the car I described belonged to my Aunt's caretaker. At this point, I began to become uneasy about the whole scenario. My Aunt's house didn't have air conditioning. She could have been in there, dead or anything. I called my brother and sister, and they told me to do whatever I thought was best, so I called the police. It took them 3 hours to arrive, and for every one of them, I couldn't seem to sit down. I found myself pacing back and forth, growing more and more anxious and feeling more and more frustrated and helpless. We were wasting time, and only God knew how much time had already been wasted.

By now, the neighbor's grandson had come over to where we were and told Kevin and I that he had known the guy who had supposedly been living there. He said the guy was known for breaking into houses and that the caretaker had been saying that she was my Aunt's daughter. I became infuriated.

"Where does she live?" I asked. He told me that she lived not too far from where we were. After he gave us the details, I told Kevin to take me there. We pulled up in front of the house that the neighbor's grandson had given us directions to, and I got out and knocked on the door. After two or so knocks, a young woman finally answered.

"My name is LaFarris," I said. "You've been living at my Aunt's house, is that right?"

I got right to the point. She looked stunned.

I continued. "Yes, Athalean—you are her caretaker, right?"

She looked like she had seen a ghost and muttered a confirmation.

"That is my Aunt you've been caring for, and you need to let me in her house."

Uneasily and hesitantly, she responded, "No."

My eyebrows furrowed, and my forehead wrinkled in confusion. She must have misunderstood me. I wasn't asking. I wasn't requesting. I wasn't even suggesting—she was going to take me to that house! I told her quite sternly and quite adamantly that if she didn't take me to my aunt's house that we were going to have a real problem, real quick. She saw that I was unrelenting and properly consented. "Well, come in." She said.

I stepped inside and proceeded to ask her again. "Where's my Aunt?"

"Well, I didn't have a contact number for you or any of her family, so…she's dead. I had her cremated."

I had so many emotions rush upon me in that instance that I didn't know which one to address first. I *knew* something was wrong. I had just known it in my spirit. I was angry. I was saddened. I had questions. How did she die? Where were her ashes? Was she really murdered? How come me, my siblings or cousins didn't take better concern for her? The girl was still conducting herself in an odd sort of way, which made me even more angry. Kevin was still in the car. I got in the girl's face.

"This is what you're going to do," I said with a tone and demeanor so serious that she looked fearful and unsure of what I was going to resort to. "You're going to let me in her house, and I have the police on the way, so let's go." I was seeing red, fighting tears and taken aback all at once.

I started to walk towards the car when all of a sudden, the church administrator back in Junction City phoned me. I answered the phone out of sorts with all that was going on at present.

"Are you ready for the board meeting?" Ms. Benson said on the other end. "I'm busy right now, Ms. Benson, I'll have to call you back," I said. When I said that, she told me that was fine, but that she'd like for me to open up in prayer for the conference call. Funny how

Lessons from Loss

things work when they do. I agreed, and doing so calmed the rage that was stirring on the inside of me. After that, I passed the phone to Kevin, so he could talk further with Ms. Benson as I got right back to the girl. She was acting strange, and I was not in the mood for any more deviations or distractions from the issue at hand. She acted as if she didn't want to let us in, and I wasn't having it. As I was getting worked up all over again, I sensed the Holy Spirit telling me to calm down. I was reminded of the verse that says never to let your right hand know what the left is doing, and I decided to play her game. I convinced her that I needed to get inside the house for pictures that I needed for a memory book.

We went to the house, and she let us in. I frantically looked around and around as if I was going to find my Aunt. It all still didn't make sense to me, and the story was so farfetched. How does a stranger cremate a whole person without attempting to notify loved ones or family members at all? The police finally showed up and searched the house, and my Aunt's body indeed was nowhere to be found. There were only a few priceless possessions of my aunt's that remained now. You could tell that the house had been sifted through; at least the level for Aunt Athalean had always lived. The rooms were devoid of their former furniture, and even her massive wardrobe was now non-existent. The only things that remained were priceless odds and ends, like family photo albums. I grabbed those, and we left.

I didn't stay overnight, but I was so upset on the way home. All I could think was, *this was my mother's baby sister, and she died alone.* I got her death certificate and discovered that somehow, the girl's name had been placed on my aunt's house and possessions right before she died, so everything went to her. What I also discovered from the death certificate was that aunt had been diagnosed with dementia. This was all the more appalling that someone would have let her sign her belongings away in such an incapacitated mental state. I asked my family how we could have allowed this to happen. Everyone was so wrapped up in their own lives and day-to-day schedules and routines that we just let one of the eldest matriarchs of our family die with no real concern or inkling to see about her. It disturbed me so much. I couldn't shake it just knowing that this girl had done something sneaky or covert that perhaps might have played a role in my Aunt's death. My aunt didn't have a proper burial, and her ashes were at the girl's house for crying out loud! The girl knew she had family; she wasn't that "lost." We didn't get the opportunity to say goodbye to her or anything. We all knew my aunt was a loner, but still, on our part, I felt like we had failed her in her final days. It still bothers me that my family is so nonchalant about it. We make everything else so much more important, but at the end of the day, isn't family the most important thing? Aunt Athalean's death held me accountable to being better about my family. For me, it was a wakeup call to make family—even extended—a priority over all.

After dealing with the drama surrounding Aunt Athalean's death, I had to prepare my heart for another swing from life. For about six months, I had taken notice to particular changes in Kevin's body that were showing up in the bedroom, as well as his frequent late-night trips to the restroom. I was noticing it, but he didn't seem to be. I kept saying to him, "You're different—something is going on with you." He'd, of course, downplay what I was saying.

"No, I'm just stressed and tired, everything is fine," He'd say. Stress and needing rest were one thing, but ongoing changes in weight and appearance were another. One day, I just got up and snapped. "I'm not hearing any more about this; we're going to the doctor!"

We made the appointment and sure enough, it was much more than stress. The doctor uttered the words that as of late, I had become accustomed to hearing, it seemed, when it came to those who were closest to me—cancer. That's what it was. I'm not sure if it was my intuition as a wife or what, but I knew that Saturday prior to his appointment what the diagnosis would be. I knew it, and I sensed God telling me that it would NOT be unto death.

When it was confirmed that following week, I felt a strange peace. It was almost like God confirmed His voice and affirmed His promise of healing all at once. Kevin's cancer was in his prostate, and the doctors told him that the severity was a 7 on a scale of 1 to 10. We initially decided that we were not going to tell the kids. We began researching and educating ourselves about what exactly his diagnosis meant, what prostate cancer was, and the likes. We needed time to process all that was happening so that when we did decide to tell Tyrone Jr. and Tyronica, we'd do so eloquently and with as little fear or upset as possible.

When we initially went in, the doctor told us a very humbling truth. He said, compared to their white counterparts, black men died from prostate cancer at a much higher rate because they refuse to get checked. He went on to further tell Kevin that he was glad that I had stayed on him. I am, too. Ladies, don't let up on the men in your lives. In many ways, they're little boys who grow up and out of "momma's" house, but never out of needing that type of care. Be an advocate for their health, even when they won't do the same for themselves!

We discussed our options. We could wait and see how it was advancing, opt for chemo and radiation, or surgically remove it. Initially, it was a lot to think and pray on. We weighed the pros and cons of every option presented and agreed that we would have it surgically removed. I thoroughly read up on the procedure so that I had a peace and understanding about what was about to happen. The procedure would be similar to that which a woman experiences for a hysterectomy. I had undergone one myself as well as friends of mine, so I knew all too well how his recovery would be post-procedure and tried to prepare accordingly. He, on the other hand, didn't quite grasp the limitations that would be incurred. For the first few weeks that he was home, Kevin had to get used to not being able to do mundane tasks on his own. He couldn't lift anything over ten pounds, couldn't drive, and had to wear a colonoscopy bag. At the time of my hysterectomy procedure in 2013, Kevin couldn't understand the emotional rollercoaster that a surgery relevant to your reproductive organs could cause. You're literally losing a portion of your body that is greatly responsible for hormonal balance. So after you do, things are a little hard to deal with. After he underwent his operation, he was able to empathize. He didn't realize that it would alter his life physically and even intimately in such a way. With the magnitude of the operation, it seemed obvious, but men don't function that way. The more time went on, the more he got bent out of shape. He tended to be a bit more impatient and irritated about things that didn't bother him before. He grew impatient waiting in the line at the grocery store for instance or irritable at my asking him to stop by Sonic to get me a cup of crushed ice to combat my hot flashes. Pre-procedure, he would sometimes make multiple trips to a Sonic to appease my craving. It seems insignificant—but I could notice his meter for irritability was more quickly set off now.

"You're not six feet under so, therefore, you CAN deal with it." I would remind him. It was a day-to-day fight, but we fought it—together, like we did with any other occurrence that so happened to arise in our lives. After his follow-up, the doctor reported that there was no other cancer in his body, and the Word that God spoke to me was confirmed. God is awesome.

Marriage teaches you so much and stretches you in ways not nearly possible if you were single. Don't get me wrong. I'm not saying that the triumphs and lessons for singles are "easy" or not as revelatory; I'm simply saying that the institution of marriage—with the intended help and guidance of God, develops you in so many ways.

Lessons from Loss

You learn about trust, sacrificing someone's needs above your own, and how to love in spite of situations that challenge your full commitment to one another. When tests and trials come to a marriage, that's an opportunity to grow together, stronger as one. All the other stuff we encounter, we simply need to learn how to deal with. It's all about communication. At that moment when I found out Kevin had cancer, he became my priority—our priority. Quite frankly, for the first time in our marriage, he became of center stage importance. I didn't care about anything else. All I knew was, "that's my husband; that's my priority." You're probably reading this and thinking, *wow, your husband wasn't a priority for you before?* Well, to be honest, and that's one of the great endeavors of this book, no. I've always loved him, and he has always been important, but I don't think prior to enduring this cancer diagnosis could I truly have said that he was the number one priority in my life. That fact alone is hope for all marriages and for anyone reading this book. There's always room to improve, room to correct and modify and make more perfect the covenant relationship that God blessed you to have with your spouse. His diagnosis snatched me. It made me realize that there was a level that I was taking him for granted on, and it made me realize that if circumstances be permitted to change, he could be gone. I realized for the first time, and with all of our years of marriage, that I became a better wife in that instant. I'm strong-willed, and Kevin gives a lot. He lets me have my way, and the truth of the matter is he's strong enough to be ok with it. If there's something that he really is adamant about, he will, of course, put his foot down, but everything else, he freely gives to me. Kevin's bout with cancer strengthened our marriage. It gave me an appreciation for him on a newer level. I've always loved him, but this trial, this test, this season, gave me an appreciation for him, my marriage, and what he brings to our oneness. He is my leveler in life. Everything can be changing, but he is a constant.

When Tyrone Jr. and Morgan first moved to Florida, I prayed to God and boldly told Him that I wanted them to be within a 12-hour driving radius from where I was. They had been in Florida for six years, and I was still in patient faith for my prayer to be answered as I traveled back and forth to Florida to visit. Tyrone Jr. was open to being closer to home, and upon reenlistment, made the attempt to request a duty station that was closer to home. Sometime after that prayer, Tyrone Jr. was stationed in Las Vegas in 2014. "Ugh!" I thought. "Lord, I thought I asked you to move them closer?" I lamented. Vegas was just as far as Florida. It wasn't until Kevin was diagnosed with cancer, however, that I think it finally registered for Tyrone Jr. that as far as family was concerned, being nearby was a factor that needed to be seriously considered. For starters, he was upset that Kevin and I had delayed telling him and Tyronica about Kevin's cancer. He also felt a great deal of frustration that he wasn't able to be home during the time of Kevin's surgery. Making frequent visits to Vegas wouldn't be so easy now with Kevin's long-term recovery ahead. That and, I had to face the fact that as I was getting older, I wouldn't want to put my body through the exertion of frequent travel via car. I felt a new dilemma emerging as far as spending frequent time with my grandchildren, and no amount of distance or a convoluted schedule would stand in the way of that. To my surprise, with all that was going on, Tyrone Jr. told us that he was considering getting out of the military.

Shortly after Kevin's surgery, during a Monday night prayer meeting at our sister church in Kansas City, a woman approached me after a powerful prayer session had taken place and said, "Stop worrying, God told me to tell you that he'll be home before he's supposed to. Take time to relax and enjoy your trip."

During that meeting, I had just been praying about Tyrone Jr. making an emotional decision to get out of the military. Emotions were one thing, but livelihood was another. Though I wanted him home, I didn't want him to make a decision that was hasty or that he would later regret. This woman didn't know me all that well to have any background information on my life, yet alone to know about my son. When she gave me that confirming word, somehow, I had a sort of confirming peace.

The next month, Kevin and I visited the kids in Vegas. While there, Tyrone Jr. got the idea for us to take a trip driving up the coast like he and Morgan had done the summer prior. It was an on the whim decision, but we were game. After Kevin's surgery and everything else that the year had brought, we were all kind of stressed and needed some unwind. I had the time of my life as we ate, visited the beach, looked at whales, took pictures, shopped on Rodeo drive, and rested. To this day, it is one of the best trips that I have ever taken. It wasn't until after returning home that I remembered the words of the woman during the prayer meeting in Kansas City. "…enjoy your trip." She said. *Wow.* I thought in amazement of God's revelation. When March 2016 came around, Tyrone Jr. made a trip home to Kansas to begin the process of building a home for his family.

On the 5th of June 2016, I got a jarring call while visiting Morgan, Tyrone Jr., and the kids in Vegas. Tyrone Sr.'s sister-in-law told me that Tyrone Sr. had taken his last breath, suffering a massive heart attack. The father of my children and one of the people I had known the longest in life, was gone. The news was beyond unreal to me. I spoke with him on Saturday, and on Sunday, he was gone. We had talked about family plans for Christmas and more upcoming than that, what the plan for the Fourth of July would be. When I first received the news, there was another layer of panic that set in as I immediately heard the name Tyrone and thought of my son. That really didn't make sense, however, as I was at Tyrone Jr.'s house and I knew that he was upstairs sleeping. "What?" Was all I could muster on the other end of the phone. Past that my other response was, "No… you know what, let me call you back." When I got off of the phone, it finally dawned on me who had phoned me. It was Tyrone Sr.'s sister-in-law, Gayle. It was then that I was certain that the news was about Tyrone Sr., my ex-husband, and not my son. I was still. Almost in a daze as my mind calculated this new reality.

"Ok," I said to myself, almost needing someone to affirm what was happening; even if that someone was me. I called Kevin and broke the news to him. My next concern was Tyronica. I asked him to go over to her house so that he could be with her when I told her. I didn't want her to catch the news via Facebook or some other source first. I knew that Tyrone Jr. and Tyronica's relationship was strong. She had in fact just come from visiting him in Georgia for his birthday celebration. Both Kevin and I tried to call her, but neither of us got an answer. The news was so fresh and so stunning. I was in a daze. I had *just* spoken to him, and now he was dead? It was 9 in the am and I was barely fully awake in the first place, only to now be numb. I had to collect myself as I prepared to go and tell my son. He was still asleep in his bed, and here I was about to have to wake him up and tell him that his father was dead. It didn't make sense, and I didn't know how to feel. I climbed the stairs and knocked on his bedroom door. He was actually awake. He answered the door. "Hey." He said.

"I have something to tell you," I told him. The look on my face must have given him concern. "What's wrong, Momma? What is it?" He asked attentively.

"I, uh, I just got a call from your Aunt Gayle," I said, trying to get the words out as if my brain still didn't understand them. "She said your father passed." I let the words go as if my lips were a forklift dropping a heavy load. He processed what I said but showed no external sign of being unhinged—only blinked and shifted his eyes from side to side as if his head was computing. He looked at me again.

"Are you okay?" He asked me.

Lessons from Loss

"I think I am…" I said back.

I don't know what reaction I expected him to have, but I was comforted somehow in his calmness. Lord knows I was out of sorts enough for the both of us.

Tyrone Sr. had been talking about moving back to Arkansas and not long before his death, Kevin was supposed to help him sort through some old VA paperwork so that he could redo some claims. In retrospect now, I think that he knew all along that his time was coming. The coming week before his death, he was scheduled to go to the doctor but of course, never made it. He had gone to the doctor prior and said that the report was nothing more than a serious case of acid reflux. Now that my mind has had a chance to settle *and* analyze *and* ponder *and* think on details over and over again, I'm almost certain he knew. You don't die from acid reflux, and you don't die from something ailing your health that has not given you signs prior to.

I cut my trip short and returned home to Kansas. I was concerned about coming back and dealing with Tyronica's reactions from the news. I spent the next few days trying to get myself together. I was invited to a women's entrepreneurial and empowerment event that was the same day that Tyrone Sr.'s funeral was scheduled to be on. Part of me wanted closure, but I couldn't do it on *that* Saturday. I was terribly torn. With the funeral approaching, there were so many ends to tie up and so much paperwork and forms to finalize and find for Tyrone Sr.'s services. No one could find his DD form 214, the official military discharge document that was necessary to iron out benefits and life insurance details. I had to start thinking like my ex-husband. He wasn't very technological and was still adamant about receiving paper checks.

Kevin got an idea to call around to a local storage company to see if Tyrone Sr. had a unit and if some of his important info might be there. Sure enough, Kevin called, and there was a Storage Shed Unit that belonged to my ex-husband. Tyrone Sr.'s family went to the facility, searched it and of course found the paperwork we were looking for. I'm blessed to have a husband like Kevin. He's supportive, secure in himself, and has character traits like no one I've ever known. He helped out with the details and planning of Tyrone Sr.'s funeral down to the details of the tombstone. He was there every step of the way, working alongside the kids to make sure things were in order as they laid their father to rest.

I recall on the Wednesday before the funeral, I was in the bed sound asleep when I had the strangest spiritual experience. It sounds totally crazy, but I was awake, yet unable to move. I woke up around 4:15 and could sense a presence. I cannot articulate it in terms that would make sense to anyone else, but I *knew* Tyrone Sr. was there. I had a vision or dream that Tyrone Sr. and I were in a park. I was seated at the bench of a picnic table, and he was seated on top of the table. He told me to tell Tyronica that her visiting him for his birthday was the best birthday that he had ever had. He told me to tell Tyrone Jr. to put God first and his family. He told me that Kevin was a good man and that he was grateful that Kevin was there to pick up the slack that he didn't—not only pertaining to our marriage but even with our children. Whenever we would talk about the kids, he would always speak with the mind frame as if they were still children. When he talked about Tyronica, it was like he was referring to her as a 12-year-old. I guess all parents at times do. He went on to say that he himself was okay and talked about how he had been unhappy for so long. Tyrone Sr. lived a lot of his life stuck in the regrets from 1994 when we divorced, and our family's dynamic changed. He always basked in his "shoulda, coulda, wouldas," and in this dream-like vision, he apologized for all of that and told me that he would always love me. He apologized for leaving so many things undone. "I won't be there with you all anymore, but I'll be your guardian angel." He said. With that statement, the vision was over, and my consciousness brought me back to my bed. It felt seemingly like hours, but I knew it wasn't that long. When I finally officially woke up around 5 a.m., I went to the restroom and was still stunned. I wasn't going to say anything about the experience with anyone, but when Kevin woke up, I had to tell him.

By Wednesday, I still felt a tremendous weight on my shoulders as to whether or not I should attend Tyrone Sr.'s funeral or go ahead with my scheduled trip. My colleague who I was traveling with even emailed me and told me, *"If you attend, we would love to have you, and if you don't, we totally understand."* I was so torn. I finally couldn't take the vacillating anymore and mentioned my dilemma to my son. He's so matter-of-fact like me. "Mom," he said, "If you attend his funeral, that's fine, and if you don't, that's also fine. Either way, I understand." Knowing my son and the gauge of his sincerity and straightforwardness, I felt like I had the green light to go on to my event as planned. I felt a little relief from his words and appreciated his resolve. The next day, however, was something entirely different. I started having chest pains that Thursday and drove myself to the emergency room. The sensation put me in the mind frame of a heart attack, and I was very concerned. Once there, the doctor told me that she didn't think that I was having a heart attack but rather an anxiety attack. Between finding out about Momma Mary, dealing with my sister and her cancer diagnosis, Aunt Athalean's unsolved death, Kevin's cancer, and Tyrone Sr.'s death, I felt like my world and the worlds around me were caving in. Although they all happened at different times, it seemed like before I could get a chance to process one event, another happened. I realized that even with Tyrone Jr.'s "blessing" for me to go ahead and make my decision on whether or not I attended the funeral or went on to Indianapolis, that I still had yet to solidify what that decision would be. I came back home from the hospital, sat down and prayed, saying, "Lord, I need a release." I called Tyrone Jr. and talked to him. "I'll go to the funeral with Tyronica." He said. Dealing with Tyrone Sr.'s death brought about a new realization of viewing my son as an adult. I mean, of course, I had known that he was an adult for quite some time, but his response to me was so stern and so parent-like that I saw him in a way that I had not realized before.

"Mom, there's nothing you can do about this," he said. "You need to focus on you and go make it rain. Go get what you need to get to move your brand and our company forward. Tyrone is your past, and your scheduled engagement is part of your future."

When he said that, I realized that my baby boy was a man. He was a man of wisdom. The same young man that I had to fire after I hired because he refused to come to work on time was pouring simple life lessons into me—and I needed it so at that very moment.

Once I officially decided that I was going to proceed with the trip, the weight and anxiety were lifted for real this time. On the morning of the funeral, however, I literally couldn't concentrate. I received a text that something had happened and a problem had surfaced with the finalization of the funeral arrangements due to finances. The funeral home called and said that they needed additional money to finish the burial as the life insurance payout was still being processed. I didn't second think it. I sent the money. Any time that Tyrone Jr. would call me, and I needed him or vice versa, we were there for one another. I gave them the credit card number, and that was that. Why? Because it was my children's father. That's what he would have expected me to do, and that's what my children deserved; to lay their father to rest in peace. The funeral went off without a hitch, and that chapter was ready to be closed, or so I thought. I admittedly felt sad that I wasn't going to be present to say an actual "goodbye," but later, my son and my daughter told me that my decision worked out for the best and that I wouldn't have been able to handle it. I recall my sister Carla trying to ease my mind about not attending the funeral. She assured me that she would be there to help the kids get through the day and insisted that I stay focused on where I was and what I had to do. "You and Tyrone Sr. haven't even been together in over 20 years, what's the difference whether you attend his funeral or not?" She said attempting to offer me sound rationalization. I guess she had a point, but still it was the principle. "His family is my family. He's my children's father, and we were in one another's lives—that's the difference." I replied. Tyrone Sr. and I grew up together. We had an intermingled past that connects our families and lives. After he and Terri divorced, it seemed that our friendship started to bud again.

I remember after our divorce praying to God and asking Him to give me a love for Tyrone Sr. that wasn't tainted in the midst of all the hurt we had caused one another and all that we had been through. I believe God answered that prayer. Though Tyrone Sr. and I had a rough and dramatic history starting out, we eventually managed to cultivate a good friendship as the years went on. Aside from our own relationship, we, of course, had children and intertwined connections with each other's family that guaranteed our having to remain in one another's lives, one way or the other. During the last few years of his life, we seemed to talk more on the telephone; whether we were synchronizing a family vacation, exchanging updates about each other's family, or sometimes even, he would be shooting the breeze with Kevin. Tyrone Jr.'s on and off girlfriend of many years even came to accept the fact that Tyrone Sr. and I were going to remain good friends. I know it seems awkward or unusual to some people that I had such a unique friendship with my ex-husband, but that's the nature of what our overlapped lives always were. It's realities like these that make me grateful for the husband that God blessed me with in Kevin. In all of our years of marriage, he's never once told me that

I couldn't do this or that in regards to my dealings with my ex-husband. I found myself calling Kevin on his lunch break and him being so willing to help me iron out Tyrone Sr.'s funeral arrangements and etc. He never once uttered the words, "Hey, that's your *ex*-husband," with disdain or a feeling of slight. He only said, "That's Tyrone Jr. and Tyronica's father; they need to see about the proper burial for him, even if I have to tell that to them myself."

CHAPTER 15

Cutting Your Losses

Though Kevin's bout with cancer was the initial inspiration for Tyrone Jr. seeing the benefit of being closer to home, it was his father's death that solidified the decision. He went on terminal leave in December 2016 and moved back to Kansas just as the building of his family's home was completed 25 to 30 miles from my own. God answered my prayer, and I was thankful. In all honesty, as far as preference went, neither Tyrone Jr. nor Morgan had a desire to relocate to Kansas again. It was a decision prompted solely on family. While in the service, Tyrone Jr. always mentioned making more time for his kids to get close to Tyrone Sr. so that they could get the chance to know who he was. After he died, he had a wake-up call that time was not something to be taken lightly. He stated that he had a revelation that I wouldn't always be around, at not being close when he had the opportunity, was a gamble. I appreciated their decision to make the sacrifice to move back. Upon first hearing the official news of their move, I was prompted to think a lot along the lines of building an empire and the legacy of our family and business. It was time for me to think seriously about what was next, stemming from my years and time sowed in childcare.

Dare to Dream

An opportunity of a lifetime presented itself for the expansion and citywide growth of my childcare career. The We Care program in my county had been in existence for over half a century and was a supplemental family education program for low-income families. In 2014, the organization that sponsored the program announced that they would be closing the program, and therefore no longer competing for the grant to fund its operation. This announcement created lots of anguish and angst amongst the locals who depended on the program for early childhood education and other community resources. The regional director of the program traveled to Junction City to speak with all of the employees and managers with respect as to why the program was being terminated. The program had received several unfavorable marks over the course of 4 to 5 years that they were to correct and improve. In that course of time, however, the local director was not consistently monitoring that the implementation of these changes was taking place. The regional office warned that a failure to comply with these corrections would put the local program in a state of withdrawal. During this same time, a chief education officer of the county had been trying to secure federal aid dollars in excess of 10 million dollars to fund educational initiatives for young children. He had been working diligently for over a decade to do so. When he was finally successful in securing the funds, the county knew they would receive that money, and chose to no longer compete for the grant that funded the We Care Program. In other words, longtime employees who had been working in the program for ten to fifteen years or more, along with families who were patrons of the We Care program, were suddenly kicked to the curb, creating resentment and hardship. A local public official in the county, Sam Barnes, felt led to do something. He reached out to the regional director and inquired what was required to make an effort to keep the program in the county, as it was needed. After a long talk and many trips back and forth between the county and the regional office, Barnes was provided the info that he needed. The regional director told him that it was a federal program that had its challenges. He told him that it was extremely regulated and had lots of bureaucracy tied into it. Adamant about not seeing the program absolved, Barnes stated that he would do whatever was needed to try and get it back. The regional office told him to identify someone who had the ability to run the program. Barnes began the process of searching for someone in the county who could meet the demands that were required to keep the program running. After about a year, he met me. After the observation of how I ran my business, management skills, personal tenacity, and commitment to children and families, he approached me about the terms of bringing the program back. There was a $2M grant available to operate the program, and if I pursued it, I would be the first African-American and female not affiliated with the school district, to run the program on their own accord. I told him I would have to pray about it. He understood. I prayed for a while, and two to three weeks later, finally arrived at the decision to say yes. We sat down and had further talks about putting a team together to compete for the grant.

We proceeded to try and identify local personalities who might be helpful in structuring the outline for the grant. Barnes had some suggestions. One, Dr. Evans, an executive board member at a prominent university in Kansas and had a background with the education system in New York. She was helpful. Another woman, Leslie, came from the Health Department, and her husband too worked for the university, so he also came on board. The three of them, Sam Barnes and myself worked diligently on the structuring. We had a deadline to meet for submission. The woman from the Health Department was very helpful with the structure but wanted a salary that was going to be more than mine's. We had to have the grant submitted by midnight, and because of a computer glitch, we didn't make the first turnaround. The next submission date would come around three to four months later.

During the first submission, we were the only group who responded to the grant. We had no competition from churches, educational or social organizations. The second time around, Dr. Evans was not able to work with us. Also, Leslie didn't return either—her reason more so dealing with a salary discrepancy as she mentioned wanting to receive compensation that was going to be even more than mine. Barnes began the search for replacements. He knew of a young woman who had just graduated from college. Barnes knew of her family and her business endeavors. She was doing some grants with small agencies and had developed a team with two other ladies her age. He spoke highly of their enthusiasm and professionalism after several talks and briefings about what the purpose was about. I had some reservations about the young ladies as they kept trying to restructure requirements that I knew were important. I had skepticism. Their approach seemed at odds with the point system that the regional office gave us. The point system was 150, and after we submitted the grant with their help, our score was 75. The regional director took notice and even called Barnes to inquire about what was going on. As we were writing the grant, I kept insisting that we were not meeting all of the guidelines that the regional office wanted to see, but her team didn't see it that way. If the truth be told, she was using her work with us to market herself for other opportunities that were coming along. When Barnes approached her about the score, she wasn't too enthused to take responsibility for the outcome. "Maybe you all should just wait." She kept alluding. I didn't understand that response as time was of the essence and Barnes tried to explain the same. "These opportunities come once in a lifetime, LaFarris has invested time and money in this, and she doesn't want to wait." He told her. The only role that remained for her would be to facilitate a rewrite—which she didn't want to do without a new installment of payment. That was something I was not about to do. So, we were now approaching round three of applying for this grant, once again forced to find other resources. We were on a time crunch, so I found two replacements, met with them, and reported back to Barnes. They specialized in grant writing for We Care programs. They had a 97 percent success rate and agreed to a free rewrite if for some reason their grant was not approved. That alone let me know they were confident in their project. We had less than 4 weeks to be able to put everything together. We came in up under the deadline and submitted our grant in May of 2016.

We Care was going to be an extension of what I was already doing. I felt like it could become an educational place for families, as well as childcare providers who needed resources. Those same children in We Care would be in centers, homes, especially if they participated in part-day programs versus full-day. So, part of the initial goal was to be a hub of resources for all those parties to benefit from.

The members of the management team I was working with at We Care weren't working with me. I knew that, eventually, it wasn't going to work. It also opened up the door for my legacy to work together. I was so consumed with this program that my children had to learn how to work together as a team. I had no time for my health, no time for my family, no time to give input into my business--I didn't have time for anything. I was getting up around 2 and 3 in the morning and sometimes wouldn't get to bed until midnight, trying to get things together, research regulations, catch up on things and the like because my original team that I was given from the organization gave me less than minimal support. It was almost like they set out for me to fail. In fact, four or five of the teachers up under me were former

Dare to Dream

employees that I had fired from Loving Arms Childcare & Preschool. You can imagine how eager they were to support me in my new role.

As far as the regional team over the program was concerned, I never received positive feedback—only areas that I was lacking in. I felt that as developers of a new program, there should have been some type of guidance in place or mentorship. I had to seek out my own mentor. I received the grant in Nov 2016, and the first time I met my Program Advisor was in March of 2017. By then, I had made plenty of mistakes. There are 15 regions in the U.S., and from talking to other people in other regions, most steer from working within the region that I was assigned to. I talked to another mentor at UCLA, who held the same title as I did in another region, and she had never heard some of the hoops that I had to jump through. My experience seemed to be about exuding control. As the founder of my preschool, I believe their belief was that I wouldn't be committed to the program with my business in the picture. This, however, wasn't the case as I hadn't been involved in the day-to-day workflow for quite some time. I had long before hired a director, not to mention that both Tyronica and Tyrone Jr. were also heavily involved. Having already had an office headquarters where I was paying a mortgage, I was requested to move my office to another side of town, away from where my childcare center and my non-for-profit were located. The building that I was to relocate to was the headquarters for the We Care program. This was strange, as there were other executive directors that I knew of who weren't obligated to work in the buildings where their programs were located. But I obliged.

One day in October, while attending a We Care Leadership conference, I was called to an impromptu meeting with a few of my board members and regional reps. During the meeting, my Program Advisor mentioned to me that she had noticed an event on my personal Facebook page from August. The event that she spoke of was a business seminar that I hosted under my LaFarris, Inc. brand—an entity having zero to do with my role as the We Care executive director. She went on to express her concern that it was something that I shouldn't have been doing as she felt that I wasn't giving the amount of time to We Care that I should have been. I told her that the event was at 7 p.m. on a Friday, and that was my personal time. During this meeting, Barnes took a moment to applaud me on a recent honor of being selected to be a session speaker at the annual National Association for the Education of Young Children (NAEYC) conference, which was taking place the very next month in November. In the field of early childhood education, to be affiliated, let alone selected as a conference session speaker, was a remarkable honor. It's one of the biggest organizations for early childhood. Upon hearing this, my Program Advisor said that she thought it was a bad idea because it didn't have anything to do with We Care. In actuality, many of the attendees of the conference have some sort of affiliation with We Care. This speaking opportunity was something that I had already established before I took on the grant. A few of my board members, as well as Barnes, challenged the rationale of my Program Advisor.

"LaFarris has been working on this for quite a while—long before the development of the grant came to be. It's an event that's relevant to what she's doing with the program." Barnes offered. But it was of no consequence. Even after he and other of my board of directors chimed in, my Program Advisor seemed unmoved. She made it be known that her final advice was for me not to attend; she did so in such a way that I knew if I chose to go anyway, that some sort of backlash or unforeseen consequence would be waiting on me when I returned. So, I didn't go. The following year, NAEYC didn't select me to go, and that was a lost opportunity that I would have to work again to nourish in the future. It was at that point, that day, that I decided, as soon as I saw an opening for an out, I was taking it. I would, of course, do my best for as long as I was in the position, but I knew it was time for me to be done. I wasn't willing to be bought for $7.5M. There wasn't a price tag high enough for me to forfeit my dreams. The regional team didn't want me to attend events that benefitted me professionally for the We Care program, nor personally. I loved the program at heart, but the structure presented a challenge for me from day one.

When I initially wrote the grant, being an executive director involved in day-to-day operations was not the goal. I was told later down the road after we got the grant that it was going to be expected. Originally, the grant allotted for a director and assistant director. As it turned out, I was going to have to be an employee instead of the Board Chair as I had planned. My attorney even commented, "I've sat on We Care boards, and I've never seen anything like this." My entire life stopped for this program. Every vacation that my husband and I had planned always seemed to coincide with a duty that I had to fulfill.

When I was on vacation, I was even working. It hindered my family business, my LaFarris Inc., my non-for-profit entity, my health, and almost my marriage. My husband was concerned, as many nights, I'd come home at 3 or 4 o'clock in the morning crying from working late on another side of town that wasn't the safest. It took a lot out of me, mentally and financially. I spent over $20,000 of my own money only to be told that I didn't really care about the program, or I didn't put enough time and energy into it. That was an absolute insult. We had a board meeting, and we had got written up on some things that were true and some that were not. The bottom line is that I never took anything that wasn't mine, and I gave 110 percent every day I walked through those doors. It was, after all, my name on the line. I took my own and sowed it into this program. I remember the

Cutting Your Losses

regional director even commenting, "You sure are concerned about your name."

"Hell yes, I'm concerned about my name. Just like you're concerned about We Care's name, I'm concerned about mine." I retorted to him. It took me twenty years to build my name professionally, and here they were, trying to tear down my credibility. Who the hell did he think he was? I built my name from the bottom with $50 to my name, diligence, sweat, tears, sacrifice for my family, and God's guidance. I told him that his insinuations were an insult to me, my character, what I stood for, and I wasn't about to let him or anyone else destroy it, based on what they "thought." I'm the type of person who does what she believes. I'm very direct.

My Program Advisor asked, "Why didn't you tell us that you wanted out?" I replied, "The same reason why you didn't tell me you weren't helping me." That's the reason; because a lack of trust existed. This was a relationship, and it couldn't be one-sided. They hadn't proven themselves to be trustworthy. In fact, with the exception of two or three people, most of the people I worked with, I couldn't trust either. I had members on my team frequently calling regional every other day with something they didn't like or something I did or didn't do. My Program Advisor was even a reference of one of the girls I had to fire. They wanted my children off the board of directors and wanted me to be an employee. Well, it was actually the best decision they could have made for me. If the board operated everything and what they said was law, when I decided to leave, then they would be left to sort through whatever mess there was. I couldn't be both the chairperson and the executive director, so I became an employee. My daughter was a certified family life educator and put in an application with We Care. The family advocate manager hired her, and I made it clear that I didn't want to sit on the process or have any involvement with that piece. My daughter was the most qualified candidate, if not overqualified. So she was hired. When my Program Advisor came for a December visit, she told me that I had to fire her. "I hope this doesn't cause any confusion between you and your daughter." She said. I replied, "We operate a business and know how to separate business matters from personal ones. This is a business decision, and I don't have a problem with it, and neither will she." The funny thing was, there were family ties amongst other members of my team. There existed sisters and even a husband and wife. I wondered why they weren't moved to fire them also. But it didn't matter; I was aware of how they moved by now. So, I fired her and knew all the while that the day of my departure was coming. I was buying my time. From stalking me on Facebook and monitoring my travel, I knew this was not the norm for other executive directors. I had a social media manager for my brand who constantly pushed for me to post things that amplified my image, and because of my employment within the program, I kept it to a minimum. I was even selected as a Goldman Sachs 10,000 small businesses participant on behalf of Loving Arms Childcare & Preschool, and I hesitated posting the honor to the public. I shouldn't have had to feel like I had to hide a recognition that only reflected my integrity and God's goodness for my business. More than anything, I lost money. When the word got out that Loving Arms We Care was closing, many incorrectly associated the news with "Loving Arms Child Care and Preschool" closing. Prospective parents stopped inquiring about enrollment, and our numbers took a hit. For the last half of 2018, my company was in the red—something that had never before happened in the history of my being in business. Luckily, I had to use my savings to plug back into the Childcare Center. The only thing was, that meant I didn't have money available for my personal emergency fund. Not to mention, for the first time, it seemed since I founded it, I couldn't take income from the preschool because now, my children were taking that income. My board of directors called me and advised me to file for unemployment. That would at least help me for the next couple of months. That would at least act as a cushion as I prepared to get things back in motion. My lawyer advised me to shut down Loving Arms Learning Center in its entirety. That was hard since that was something that I had built independent of even the childcare and long before entering the We Care program. He advised me that later down the line, I could pursue opening another 501c3 venture. The important thing now was to distance my association from the We Care program and focus on rebuilding my own brand.

The bottom line is that you have to know when to let something go. The We Care fiasco taught me a lot about what I didn't want, the types of people I didn't want to work with, it taught me more about a team than ever before. It also helped me to recognize and appreciate the team I have at Loving Arms Childcare & Preschool to a greater degree. It taught me that a house divided against itself cannot stand. There was a point that all of this had me second-guessing if I was capable of doing what God created and called me to do. I went through the stages of death with We Care, even. I had to come back to myself and lean on the realization that everything I needed was within me.

What I learned in all of this was a new chapter of daring to dream. It's so fitting even in writing this book. Time elapsed between writing this chapter. At the beginning, it seemed to be a blessing. In the midst of writing, and even having to stop writing because of the demand of the program, this chapter itself has even transformed into a lesson. I had three kidney stones in the same year. I got discharged from the hospital and went to work the next morning. I felt like I had to. I constantly needed to prove myself and worthiness of the position. I even think cancer would have built up in my body from the stress eventually. I had never had a bad breast exam, but my most concerning breast exam came during the time period of the We Care saga. The doctor discovered cysts, and I was called back to do two follow-ups. But even still, all of these factors weren't enough on their own to convince me that this was adversarial to my growth.

After the dust from dealing with We Care settled, I saw that it was indeed necessary. What the enemy thought would be my demise, would only be the groundwork for God rerouting me. Tyrone Jr. and Tyronica began working together like never before, and it was remarkable to me. When my director Melba moved away, Tyronica fell into the role for some time. Though dedicated, being in the position of director was a far cry from her true passion for preparing lesson plans and curriculums. When she first returned home, it was the perfect time for her to finally resume her plans for curriculum writing for "The Learning Cupboard." In fact, we replaced popular industry curriculums that we were using for the original ones that she wrote.

When Tyrone Jr. came home, she was all too happy to relinquish the role of director to her little brother's hand, even though she bucked his lead at times. For one as the older sibling, Tyronica had been intricately involved with the childcare far longer than Tyrone Jr. had and secondly, her background was directly correlated to working with children in education, whereas his involved working with adults in leadership. It's a dance that the two of them have learned to adjust to. Tyrone Jr.'s role as director and CEO has brought about new changes in operational efficiency and processes. I remember coming in one day and not recognizing some folk.

"What happened to you not hiring anyone without going through me?" I asked him. "You made me CEO—the CEO doesn't go through you. Either you're going to run it, or I am." The young man that I once fired from the same company was now running it and doing an amazing job. My son chose to get out of the military for that very reason. He reminded me that this was important to him. After my husband got cancer, and his father passed away, he realized that he needed to come home. He went on to say that honestly while it wasn't his first choice for employment, it made no sense to go work like a dog for someone else when there was a legacy already established to build. My son took the keys from me. He told me my job title was the founder and as such would be called upon for counsel and major decisions but that my role had changed. He set me straight about the hierarchy of employees talking to him instead of me, and so on. "You're awesome." He said. "I didn't realize how awesome because you're my mom—but you are. But it's time for you to go make it rain." Be careful what you pray for is all I can say. Though I always wanted my children to work for the family business one day, I had never taken the time to fully prepare myself for what all that transition would involve. My babies were now nurturing my "other baby," and it was time for me to set my faith on new horizons.

CHAPTER 16

Coming Full Circle

Looking back on the drawn-out history between my ex-husband and me, I looked up, and a year and a half had passed since his death, and there was still a major lingering loose end hanging in the balance. His tombstone was still lost somewhere in limbo. The funeral home that the Veteran Administration had originally sent his tombstone to had supposedly never received it. About six months after Tyrone's funeral, I attempted to call the funeral home to check on the status of Tyrone's headstone being placed. After a few failed attempts to call the disconnected number, I looked them up on Facebook, only to discover that they had gone out of business. I then took my call to Marsha, the VA representative in Junction City, KS, and asked her to look into the status of the tombstone. She told me that the tombstone had indeed been mailed out. Since it had yet to arrive still, we applied for another tombstone. We went through another funeral home where the delivery was 4-6 weeks. Turns out, the original stone was sitting in the warehouse of another local funeral home for at least 6 months, waiting for someone to give some clarity on what to do with it. My best guess is that the funeral home that went out of business transferred their clientele to this other funeral home. All that to say, it was now the summer of 2018, two years after this man's death, and there was still no headstone.

Though my son had given me comfort and permission to finish out my business trip in lieu of attending Tyrone Sr.'s funeral, the fact remained that I had no closure of my own. I would get my opportunity to finally close the chapter of Tyrone being in my life when Tyrone Sr.'s sister-in-law invited my family and I to attend the 60th surprise birthday celebration of his oldest brother, Dennis. Months in advance, Dennis's wife had invited our family to the birthday party, and I knew then that a potential opportunity to finally get my closure without hassle or awkwardness had presented itself. I really didn't want to try and make the trip outside of an event as I'm sure my children or Kevin would have insisted on accompanying me, and this, I knew I had to do on my own. I didn't know the range of emotions that might come about as a result of my visiting Tyrone's burial site, and the last thing I wanted was to hurt my husband in any way. Tyrone and I had married in 1986 and divorced in 1994 for crying out loud. Kevin and I had been married since 1997. I didn't want the possibility of emotions to offend him or give him a reason to question my love or loyalty to him. A trip where the visit wasn't based on the closure seemed right on time.

Other than to visit my sister and Tyrone Sr.'s family, I hadn't been back to Warren since around 2015. Tyrone Jr. and I had just come from the global diversity conference in Atlanta and drove there, arriving around 3 o'clock in the early evening on a Friday. To my surprise, Kevin and my brother drove from Kansas to Warren and arrived on Friday shortly after we did. This honestly threw me off a bit as I now had to figure out when I would have a moment of alone time to go and visit Tyrone's burial site. Just like any other visit to Warren, my family and I stayed with my sister Carla that weekend. The next day on Saturday while sitting at Carla's house, we had a memorable time visiting with a house full of family, including myself, Kevin, Tyrone Jr., my nephew Darion, my brother, and Carla's ex-husband. We caught up and spent a great deal of time laughing at my nephew's comedic recounts of his time serving in the military, as well as catching up in general.

As we sat around laughing, I couldn't help but think, "*if I'm going to go and make this trip, I had better make a break for it while the attention isn't on me.*" I knew that if I didn't do it then, that I might never do it. I might have backed out, or more probably, never get the opportunity to do so, unsuspectingly. I got up.

"I'll be back in a little bit," I said nonchalantly while the laughter was at a bit of high. My son being the keen observer that he is, asked, "You need me to go with you?"

"No, I'm fine," I said, "I'll be right back." I answered coolly and quickly, hoping to steer him from any insistence of "chaperoning" me. I wanted to give off the casual air of running to the store or gas station—something that wouldn't cause an inquisition. Still in tune with the likelihood of my real mission, he asked again, "You sure you don't need me to go with you?" Just as coolly as I replied the first time, I again said, "No, I'll be right back," headed out of the door, and got into my truck.

On the way to the gravesite, I rehearsed what I would say while there as if I would be talking to him face-to-face. I felt solemn, happy, depressed, lonely, upset—just all these different emotions at once. I struggled with why I was still needing this closure at all. Tyrone was buried in his family burial site in New Edinburg, Arkansas, about 19 or 20 miles outside of Warren. It was a cool brisk September Saturday. I drove off the highway onto a dirt path that was about 500 feet from the highway itself. There was an old silver schoolyard-style fence that surrounded the property and two gated entrances. One entrance for the hearses was locked, and the other entrance was closed but not locked. I backed my truck in front of the hearse entrance, parked it, left it running, and got out to open the gate to walk in. The cemetery was deep in the woods. And I mean deep. I was surrounded by a thick marsh of weeds. The weeds were tall, and many of the tombstones had sunken in. Tyrone was buried near his mom. I stopped briefly at Lil Momma's grave. She had died of cancer in the year 2000.

Ever since the moment I sat in her living room confessing my pregnancy with her, my father and Tyrone, she had always been a support in my life. In the midst of all that Tyrone and I went through, she always managed to remain neutral and honest. If he was wrong, she would say so, and if I was wrong, she'd say so. I appreciated that. In fact, it influences how I conduct my input when solicited, for my son and his wife. She was a loving mother-in-law and grandmother to my children and even loved Kevin without bias. Though I had never visited his burial place before, I had attended his mother's funeral and knew at the minimum that he was buried near her. I thought back to the night when I had the dream about talking to Tyrone one final time. As far as his death was concerned, I believe he knew that he was sick and didn't tell anybody. With the headstone fiasco still unresolved, next to his burial plot was a marker with his name and information on it. I looked down at it. *Is this really happening?* I asked myself. I stood there, struggling to put things in perspective. For a while, I had the luxury of occupying my mind with so many other things that I hadn't taken the time to really stew on experiencing closure. It was sort of like an out of sight, out of mind thing. Now that I was there undistracted and very much present in the moment, I felt alone for some reason—in a hopeless sort of way.

"*Why didn't you tell me?*" I thought in my head.

Perhaps if I had known about his being sick, I could have at least offered support or guidance on maximizing his health. I sat down directly on the soil and grass with my legs folded like a child at circle time. The spot where I sat was warmed by the sunlight from above as the breeze made its way lightly through the trees of the woods. "If I had known you had this much stuff to do, I would have choked the life out of you," I said aloud as if he could hear me. I let an effortless chuckle escape my chest at the thought to be sitting there talking to a gravesite. I sat there in deep thought. I analyzed various portions of my life and how Tyrone was somehow present in all facets of my past, present, and future. I thought, of course, of our drama and the hurt. Now that time had passed, and I had moved on from loving him in that old way, I could see the positive in all of it.

All of the pain ultimately pushed me into my destiny. I also thought of the good times and how our wonderful children, and now grandchildren, were his living legacy in the earth. In fact, right after his death, his sister sent me his last paycheck from his job. Immediately, I got the idea to split the check and place the money in 529 educational savings plans that I had started for our grandchildren. In doing so, I felt that his legacy would continue to live on through whatever educational opportunities they took advantage of. I sat there for what must have been at least an hour, just reflecting. Before I left, I told him, "I don't think I'll have the strength to come back and so, you'll always be a part of me, and I'll always be a part of you."

I appreciated him for helping me grow up and the role he played in my becoming the woman that I am today. I told him that I always loved him and that I knew, deep down, he always loved me. With that, I got up, dusted myself off, and walked back towards the truck—which was still running. I guess I left it running for my own safety, even though that didn't really make much sense. I was out in the middle of the woods, and even if something had happened, I wouldn't have been able to get back to the truck in time. Anyhow, I got inside and drove back the way I had come on the gravel drive until I got back on the highway and headed back to my family's home. From the occasion of the trip to the timing, everything worked out how it was supposed to. The birthday was a good reason for me to be able to handle my need for closure without having to make it an "event."

In many ways, my closure with Tyrone's death was like an official pardon from my past and a variety of negative things that I had formerly identified with. Looking back to my early need for validation and receiving any old kind of love despite the red flags, disrespect, and pain that came along with it, I was now able to see so clearly that the only reason I had ever tolerated any of it, pointed back to the void that I felt from my mother's death. As time went on and I embarked on a path to heal through legacy (my children), purpose (my business), and most importantly, faith (my salvation), I discovered the characteristics of real love versus the poor substitute that I had been settling for. That love began with God, but next, it dealt with loving myself. Some of the things I had put up with when it came to Tyrone would have never been possible if I had loved myself first. When I made the decision to love myself, I think that cleared the way for me to find life love in Kevin, and I'm grateful for that. Somehow, taking the time to gain closure from Tyrone's death paralleled with my getting closure with all the negative parts of my past that God still managed to use anyway. Overcoming my mother's death, surviving an abusive relationship, enduring teenage motherhood, and starting over—all the worst parts of life—had really made me into the best person that I could have ever been. It all seemed to come full circle now. Here I was, whole from my mother's death, stronger because of an abusive relationship and helping other young women navigate their way through similar situations, a proud and wise parent that managed to raise successful children and now grandchildren, and a vigilant business owner who had started from the bottom and now had more ahead on the horizon. And most of all, I was fulfilled in love. Kevin's love for me was so secure and so dedicated that even he mourned Tyrone's death. The dynamic is hard to articulate, but it all goes back to having an understanding husband who allowed me the space to move within our complex blended family situation. Kevin never questioned my love for him in all the years Tyrone and I had these complicated dealings. Whenever I felt myself drift to wallowing in the bad memories or even "what ifs" of me and Tyrone's past, I'd fast forward back to my present and realize that the peace and love that Kevin brought to my life were incomparable. The best that I could have ever gotten from Tyrone, I already did—in Tyronica, Tyrone Jr., Tavon, and Alani. With Kevin, however, my future happiness abounds and still includes my children and grandchildren seamlessly. Saying goodbye to Tyrone ended an era in my life and officially permitted a better one to begin.

CHAPTER 17

Reflections to the Reader

From Faith To Faith

In sharing my story, it was very important for me to start from the beginning so that you could clearly get a glimpse of God's faithfulness. If I had started out telling you about the success of my childcare, public speaking, or awards and accolades in business, you might have been enlightened, but sharing my failures and trials is more likely to leave you inspired!

Telling my full story shows a journey from faith to faith and faith is key. Whether you realize it or not, your life's experiences tell their own inspiring story. Look back over the things you've overcome; things at the time that you thought might break you and destroy your will. Look at the lessons you learned and the opportunities you had for developing your character. These are part of your life's "faith to faith" journey. I hope you have faith if you have nothing else. If you can't honestly agree with that right now, I want to encourage you to develop a lifestyle of faith. Specifically, I hope you have faith in God! But even if you don't, I want to assure you that you have faith in *something,* whether you believe it or not.

For instance, if you work at a job before receiving pay, the fact that you showed up to work for days before seeing your money, is an act of faith. You only continued to show up because you had faith that they would give you money in exchange for your days worked. Faith is a bonafide belief in things that you hope, for even when you can't see the way (Hebrews 11:1). Develop your faith in something fulfilling and don't waver from it.

Also, develop faith in your gifts and talents. Just like when I made that list before starting my childcare business, make your list! Write down the things that you're good at, the things you have a passion for, the things you have experience in, and even the things you don't like. I think you'll be surprised at how the outcome weaves together. Let your faith be a launching pad for the life you desire. To your faith, add prayer and positive confessions. When negative situations or instances arise in your life, don't identify with those problems, identify with the solution. The Bible says, as a man thinks in his heart (or mind), so is he. You have to think that you can make it before you make it. Think it, speak it, see it! When we don't have faith to see the positive, that's when we get stuck. It's not that we don't have the ability to rise above certain situations; it's that we lack the faith to get past them.

The Process

While faith is important to your life's success story, I'd be remiss if I also didn't take the time to remind you about the process. The process is hinged on two other important factors: time and preparation. All throughout my life, in one way or another, my notable moments of progress were all dependent on the time being right and the degree that I had prepared for certain opportunities. The best example I can use is regarding our family business. The success of our

Reflections to the Reader

childcare didn't start with a three-level property renovation and hundreds of enrolled children. It began in the basement of my apartment where I didn't even have money for a down payment upon moving in. We only evolved to the success of the three-level property after I prepared for that responsibility. Like any other profession, I had a lot to learn about industry guidelines, licensing, laws, and business in general. Some knowledge required me going back to school and getting certifications and training. Other knowledge, I had to learn experientially. This learning didn't happen overnight but rather was a process over time. I had to handle customer service for four children before we were ready to handle it for hundreds. I had to be able to organize financial numbers for myself before we were able to cut checks for a multi-person staff. In fact, my faith wasn't even ready for the center-based location during my early years of starting out. But after I had prepared myself with education, licenses, and experience, I was ready for the opportunity whenever it arose.

An important note about time: sometimes, the timing for the opportunity isn't necessarily when we want. This can be frustrating, but trust that when the time is right, you will know.

Right before I moved my business into my first center-based location, where I shared the property with the social worker landlord, I prayed and asked God if the time was right for me to purchase a building of my own. I clearly sensed that the answer was no. Timing is very significant in this instance because all the while as I continued to prepare myself, what I didn't know was that a man would be buying the three-level commercial property and turning it into a home. The fact that he did that enabled my purchase price to be significantly less and also, some of the renovations that he made to the property were perfect for the vision that I had. But when the time was right, I discovered the property, and the process had prepared me for the opportunity! I hope that you are able to look over your life with a critical and patient eye. While you dare to dream big, I hope that in the meantime—during the process—that you can stay optimistic and focused about where you are now, simply preparing you for where you want to be. In difficulty and challenges, your problem-solving skills are being sharpened. When resources are lacking, your perseverance is being developed. When you have to endure things alone, your personal resolve is being strengthened. It's *all* part of the process. Track your successes up until now, no matter how small they seem and celebrate them. If I waited until we moved into our center-based location to celebrate our success, I would have missed the beauty of the process. More than that, I would have likely been discouraged. Every milestone during the process not only prepared me for the right timing of the opportunity, but they also gave me hope! Find hope in your life's story, no matter what chapter you might be on!

Leaving a Legacy

One of the prevailing themes of importance in my life is legacy. Legacy is simply the lasting contribution that you cultivate to pass on to those after you—particularly your family. It's funny that legacy can be passed on both purposefully (planned by the generation passing it on) or by happenstance (adopted by the generation receiving it). When I look back on my childhood even, my parents passed on to me legacy principles on purpose, and there were, of course, a few that I took upon myself to mimic. Together, my mom and dad passed on the value of education.

Perhaps, if they hadn't, I would've succumbed to the statistical consequences of dropping out of high school after becoming pregnant at 15. Lord knows that even after having Tyronica, I had great opportunities to disregard going back to school entirely or at least put it off. Her care was high maintenance as a preemie, not to mention having to work to have money of my own for a household of my own, and of course, dealing with her father was a full-time job of stress management in and of itself. But all the while, in the back of my mind was this incessant reminder that I *had* to finish. I valued my education on my own, but I'd be lying if I said most of the pressure was from the value—or legacy—that my parents emphasized about education. I'm grateful that they did. How ironic that they had an emphasis on education, and I went on to have a career in education? Separately, two other principles of legacy that my mom and dad passed on to me were family time and entrepreneurship, respectively. I can remember before my mom died, my dad would always emphasize our family eating a daily meal together. It would be either breakfast or dinner but usually breakfast as my father worked at night. And it couldn't be skipped either. Didn't matter if one of my siblings wanted to leave early for an extracurricular practice or some other plan for an excuse—we *had* to be at that table. I don't remember the tradition remaining after my mom passed, but the short time that I do recall it being a thing, impacted me enough to want to do a version with my family.

As my children grew up, I too would emphasize regular face time as a family. When they were younger, it was hard to have family meals together all of the time with their father being in the military, but they still had them with me. As they got older, regular family meals were a bit challenging with bouts of my being in school, Kevin being on active duty, and the kids having their respective extracurricular school schedules. But, I did adopt the concept in the form of family meetings. On Sundays after church—since everyone in my household was obligated to go by my decree (which also is a part of legacy passed on by my parents)—we would get together at my house and I would make the time to catch up with my kids, asking about their coming week, seeing what field trips, projects, recitals, or games, they had, and even intentionally checking in to see if they needed mentoring or guidance about anything in particular. From my mother, I grabbed ahold of the importance of making your own money with your own business. Though she didn't get the opportunity to formally pass the concept of entrepreneurship on to me, I like to think that I got that inclination from watching her work all those years back in our family's restaurant. I started the childcare as a means to an end. The odd jobs that I held prior weren't meeting the needs of my family. I needed stability for my children after a divorce, where my spouse was the primary breadwinner. Well, there was no way I wasn't going to make sure their needs were met, so I had to figure it out. I needed to provide for my children and began thinking about ways I could do that. I sat down and wrote down a list of things that I was good at, as well as a list of things that I enjoyed.

After completing the list, I noticed a reoccurring theme of enjoying working with families. While Tyrone Jr. was gone to basic training and AIT, I worked and volunteered for a home facility for disabled children and adults, In Germany, I worked at my children's elementary school, and I had always volunteered at church. Even as a kid, when I lived with Aunt Athalean, I would teach Sunday School to children at church. And speaking of children, I also noticed that having my own, prematurely, had versed me in a variety of technical knowledge, such as how to use breathing treatments, CPR, and plain old patience and compassion. That's how I became an entrepreneur; I noticed where my passion and experience overlapped. It's the same for you. If you can look over your life and see themes and experiences, whether good or bad, that stir your heart, then in one way or another, your purpose is somewhere intertwined, and the possibility of entrepreneurship probably isn't too far behind that

When it comes to legacy, what are you leaving behind? Are you leaving a legacy to be proud of that's full of intention and selflessness to consider the generations to follow? Or, a legacy of regret and excuses, not taking into consideration that the decisions you make today will affect not only your future but the future of others. That nugget is similar to the words my father said to me after I told him that I was pregnant. It stuck with me ever since. I encourage you to consider that deeply. It's never too late to work on legacy, so I hope you will. I hope you plan traditions and values to pass on to your children and children's children. I hope you walk in your purpose so strongly that you make an impact on the lives around you, whether it's through your personality or running a corporation. Every moment that you have breath in your body is a moment to establish and develop a legacy. The generations behind you are depending on you.

All Things Work Together for Your Good

One of my favorite Bible verses is found in the book of Romans, chapter 8, verse 28. It says that all things work together for the good for those who are in Christ. It doesn't say that everything is good or that everything is necessarily easy, or even right. It reminds us that no matter what trials we encounter in life, that one way or another, God is able to ultimately turn things around. That was a promise of terrific hope for me considering all the things I experienced throughout my life. It's also a promise of hope for you!

My greatest purpose for writing this book was to illustrate the ups and downs of my life so that you could properly see the ups and downs in yours. I'm not sure of all the things that have tried to come against your greatness, but I am sure that no matter what those things might be, that they are not the end of your story. Rather, they are an important part of your journey towards greatness. Concerning the timeline of your life, this perspective is important to adopt about every situation. Everything you've experienced, rather good or bad, has been an opportunity for learning or wisdom. This means that even your instances of hurt and failure are still valuable. They make you stronger, and they are fuel to get you to your destiny. There's a very important principle to note in Romans 8:28. It says that all things work together for the good of those who love God. What does loving God entail? It's including Him in your life on purpose. It's praying and seeking Him for answers, comfort in your soul, and a relationship. You were created for a real and loving relationship with God the Father through Christ Jesus. I'm not sure where your heart stands at present with God, but I would encourage you to make the decision to dedicate your life to Him immediately and totally. A relationship with God is the true difference maker between merely having a life full of broken pieces and a life where the pieces fit together for purpose and success, no matter how complicated or painful they might be.

Your life is about figuring out what God predestined you to become so that you can tap fully into that potential. You get insights about your destiny based on the story of your life. From losing my mother, teenage motherhood, an abusive relationship, and more, I was able to see that part of my destiny was to help enrich the lives of families, even in becoming an entrepreneur.

My business serves families and establishes a legacy for my very own family. I offer loving support and wisdom to others who may experience situations similar to my own. The things that I thought would break me, destroy my will, help me strengthen the lives of others. I'm able to see that now. What if I adopted the mindset that I was a victim, unable to get past my mother's death, or too discouraged by becoming pregnant at 15 that I just accepted the status quo of shame and let it be an excuse for my shortcomings in life? My whole destiny would be wasted, and the lives I was meant to impact through childcare, speaking, and even publishing this book would never be touched. So, you see, we must take hold of our destiny and take it seriously. We do this by refusing to let any one part of our life's story be the final part. We keep going, we press on, and we have the faith to see the bigger picture of how every situation in our life is working together for our good. That's what I did. I dared to dream about living my best life regardless of all that I had been through. That is my prayer for you, my friend: that you too, no matter what, would always dare to dream.

ABOUT THE AUTHOR

With more than 20 years' experience in Early Childhood Education and Family Support, LaFarris L. Risby, CFLE is a woman with renowned credentials and a tangible success story. LaFarris is an author, speaker, business strategist, consultant, and executive coach. She is the founder of Loving Arms™ Childcare and Preschool, the largest African American owned childcare business in her community. She holds degrees in Early Childhood Education, Human Services and is a Certified Family Life Educator (CFLE). Under the umbrella of LaFarris, Inc., she is passionate about helping women embark upon the paths of entrepreneurship, maintaining proper work and life balance, and creating a legacy.

She has authored two instructional audiobooks, "Quality Childcare on a Shoe-String Budget" and "11 Essential Keys to Quality Care and Profitability," and has published a variety of articles relative to her expertise.

Among her outstanding achievements, LaFarris is an alumnus of Goldman Sachs's 10,000 Small Businesses Program and has also been a featured host of its affiliated Small Business Fridays Podcast. She has been featured in publications like the Atlanta Journal, Atlanta Tribune, Kansas City Globe, Daily Union Newspaper, Supplierty News, Patch Media, and Today's Purposed Woman Magazine. She has been a keynote speaker for a variety of conferences and seminars including Coca-Cola's Global Supplier Diversity Curriculum, Dare

2 Dream, Unleash Your Gift to Speak, Kansas Association for the Education of Young Children, LuckiFit Home Brands Summit, and Sisterpreneur.

Still, what's most captivating about LaFarris is the story behind her zeal and commitment for early childhood education and family well-being. Some of LaFarris' most life shaping experiences include the grief of losing her mother at six years old, becoming a teenage mother at 15, giving birth to a premature child, being married to her womanizing and abusive high school sweetheart, and even homelessness. However, LaFarris believed that she could overcome life's obstacles through faith, and her dreams that once seemed impossible, became possible.

LaFarris is a loving wife, mother, and grandmother who is purposefully committed to living a life of legacy that will impact generations to come. Inspired by her late father's notable quote, "the decisions you make today will ultimately affect your tomorrow," LaFarris's goal is to underline the importance of personal responsibility, rich relationships, and legacy in order to create a life of greatness.

Stay Connected with LaFarris:

LinkedIn: LaFarris L.Risby, CFLE
Facebook: LaFarris L. Risby, CFLE
Instagram: @LaFarrisRisby
Twitter: @LaFarrisRisby

For speaking engagements and other information:
Email info@lafarrisrisby.com
or
Call 224-267-LIFE.

www.ingramcontent.com/pod-product-compliance
Lightning Source LLC
Chambersburg PA
CBHW021053080526
44587CB00010B/237